THE WALRUS WAS RINGO

101 Beatles Myths Debunked

BY ALAN CLAYSON AND SPENCER LEIGH

THE WALRUS WAS RINGO
101 Beatles Myths Debunked

BY ALAN CLAYSON AND SPENCER LEIGH

A CHROME DREAMS PUBLICATION

FIRST EDITION 2003

Published By CHROME DREAMS

PO BOX 230
NEW MALDEN
SURREY
KT3 6YY
UK
www.chromedreams.co.uk

ISBN 1 84240 205 6

EDITORIAL DIRECTOR   Rob Johnstone

EDITOR   Rob Johnstone

SUB EDITOR   Tim Footman

DESIGN   Sylvia Grzeszczuk

THE WALRUS WAS RINGO

101 BEATLES MYTHS DEBUNKED
BY ALAN CLAYSON AND SPENCER LEIGH

Prologue: *Ask Me Why*

Billy Shepherd's *The True Story Of The Beatles* was in preparation in 1963. It was the first of many books about John Lennon, Paul McCartney, George Harrison and Ringo Starr; many more than anyone could then have conceived. These have ranged from cornucopias of basic data - such as Mark Lewisohn's *25 Years In The Life: A Chronology 1962-87* (Sidgwick & Jackson, 1987) - to the likes of *Every Sound There Is: The Beatles'* Revolver *And The Transformation Of Rock And Roll* (Ashgate, 2002), a series of meticulous and scholarly essays that cut, dry and dissect every bar of an album released when The Beatles had the means to turn their every whim into audible reality. Titles like 'A Flood Of Flat-Sevenths', 'Premature turns: thematic disruption in the American version' and 'Re-arranging base and superstructure in the rock ballad' drip from the pens of college academics across the globe, telegraphing that you might need to have a dictionary of musicological terms close to hand and undergo a crash course in sight-reading.

Such merchandise provides further printed evidence that, just as the Bible can be manipulated to prove or disprove any religious or moral theory, so the millions of words chronicling and analysing their every act can warp the saga of The Beatles to any purpose. And we, of course, are adding to those millions. As sources of 'new and rediscovered facts' continue to dry up, increasingly desperate efforts to find a fresh perspective on the group have resulted in authors taking liberties with the tired old tale and squeezing paragraphs from, say, an idle afternoon when George Harrison and Klaus Voorman painted a friend's 1966 Citroen 2CV. This, incidentally, was deemed worthy of a half-page of speculation in one Beatle fanzine in which no detail is without value, nothing too insignificant to be totally intriguing.

Likewise, the most flippant remarks have been treated as gospel. After the final concert at San Francisco's Candlestick Park on 29 August 1966, George Harrison's was the most quoted comment by the entourage after the flight back to England: "Well, that's it. I'm not a Beatle anymore." Was this the most profound elegy on the group's downing tools as a working band as George fastened a thoughtful seatbelt - or was it just something he muttered sarcastically as he dozed off somewhere between the time zones over the Atlantic? We don't know because we weren't there. Nor were you - and even if you were, as George himself pontificated in the *International Times* in September 1969, "People can only see each other from their own state of consciousness, and the press's state of consciousness is virtually nil, so they never get the true essence of anything they write about." Sticking with George, during The Beatles' only Australasian tour, was he "outgoing and friendly" as singer Johnny Devlin found him or "deeply introspective and hard to know", the view of radio presenter Bob Rogers?

Regardless of such areas of subjectivity, the main events of almost every day in the lives of the quartet since 1962 has been accounted for in some publication or other, exemplified by the seven hundred pages of Keith Badman's day-by-day diary, *The Beatles After The Break-Up* (Omnibus, 1999).

Yet even the wisest of us can make mistakes - even The Beatles themselves. When Starr narrated a twenty-six part US radio series entitled *Ringo's Yellow Submarine: A Voyage Through Beatles Magic*, he peppered it with tiny factual slip-ups - such as mentioning that 'I'm Down' was the opening number at 1965's celebrated Shea Stadium performance when it was actually the finale. 2000's *Anthology* – "the

Beatles story told for the first time in their own words and pictures" is equally freighted with fallible reminiscences.

The intention of this book is to fine-tune facts, correct errors and shatter myths that have survived the decades since Billy Shepherd's tome. Some of the conclusions are divergent or qualified, but all are the outcome of studying our transcribed interviews with key *dramatis personae* and, especially, wading through oceans of archive material - some of it quite obscure - because, in the context of this discussion, verbatim accounts recreate more of a feeling of being there. This is illustrated in *Anthology*. Unlike the taped reminiscences of Paul, George and Ringo, John's were derived necessarily from media archives and are, therefore, unaffected by turn-of-the-century hindsight.

The written word remains. Yet, whether it's hinged on unassailable fact or the most educated guesses, this is unlikely to be the last word on the aspects covered. After all, The Beatles - for what they were and for what consumers think they have become - are a commodity that can be recycled indefinitely for as long as their influence is acknowledged by every pop artist that matters, and their lyrics are still quoted like proverbs.

1. John Lennon was a working class hero.

"A working class hero is something to be," intoned John Lennon on his 1970 album, *John Lennon / Plastic Ono Band*. It was never one of his hits, but the song was arguably, the most defiant statement that he ever wrote.

Most listeners presumed he was singing about himself. But although John Lennon was a hero, he was not working class.

Though it has become less marked in recent years, at one time everyone in the UK knew what class they belonged to. There was the upper class (for many years, the ruling class, and represented in Liverpool by the Earl of Derby, who nowadays presides over Knowsley Safari Park); the middle class (itself divided into lower and upper components); and the working class. Liverpool's working class men, especially the dockers, were seen as militants with strong union backing. The British Prime Minister in 1970, Edward Heath, tried to be at one with the working classes by pointing out that his father had been a grocer, but he remained part of the establishment, a Tory grandee.

John Lennon's father, Alfred, had come from a poor, working-class environment, but his mother, Julia, and her sister, Mimi, were a step up the social scale. Their father had a decent job with the Glasgow and Liverpool Salvage Company and the family did not approve of Julia marrying Alfred Lennon. Mimi married a dairy farmer, George Smith, and they lived as a middle-class couple at 251 Menlove Avenue in the suburb of Woolton (not far, incidentally, from Brian Epstein's wealthy family). Julia, who wanted to live with another man, placed John with them. Though John was raised there, he was resentful that his mother had rejected him.

In December 2000, an English Heritage plaque was attached to Mendips, where John Lennon lived from 1945 to 1963. Yes, the house even had a name. When the media and invited guests arrived, how many of them thought, 'How could this man call himself working class?'

Like Bob Dylan, John Lennon was rewriting his history. There were no blue suburban skies in his version of the past and, as he confessed in 'I'll Cry Instead', "I've got a chip on my shoulder that's bigger than my feet." Aunt Mimi - not Auntie Mimi, another give-away - told the *Daily Express*: "I get terribly annoyed when he is billed as a street-corner boy. He had a very comfortable home in a good area." Quite right, and the distortion was all John's doing. John wanted to be working class because he associated it with the struggle for human rights and recognition.

Not that the Liverpudlian playwright Alan Bleasdale would agree with this: "There's no surprise that John Lennon wrote 'Working Class Hero'. I heard Paul say that John wasn't working class or a hero. I disagree with that. Although he lived in Menlove Avenue with Aunt Mimi, John was still one of us."

By way of contrast, Julie Burchill wrote in *The Guardian* in 2000: "Working class hero? My arse. The Marianne Faithfull cover version was more heartfelt! Lennon was about as working class as a Wilmslow dentist."

Being interviewed by Tariq Ali for the revolutionary magazine *Red Mole* in August 1971, John Lennon said, "I've always been politically minded, you know, and against the status quo. It's pretty basic when you're brought up like I was to hate and fear the police as a natural enemy and to despise the army as something that takes everybody away and leaves them dead somewhere." Who exactly brought him up to feel this way was not mentioned. It certainly wasn't Aunt Mimi.

He said, in the same interview, of 'Working Class Hero', "It's a song for the revolution. It's for people like me who are working class, who are supposed to be processed into the middle class. It's my experience and I hope it's a warning to people."

To be fair, John Lennon's best friend, Pete Shotton, confirms that John had read The Communist Manifesto in his youth and, indeed, Karl Marx is the only political figure on the cover of *Sgt. Pepper's Lonely Hearts Club Band*. This prompts the question, who is a working class hero? In Marxist terminology, the heroes of the revolution are the tractor-drivers. Many working-class heroes like Joe Hill have been incarcerated or killed for their actions, which prompted the folk song, 'I Dreamed I Saw Joe Hill Last Night'. Possibly John Lennon considered Fidel Castro, who stood up to America, and Chairman Mao, as working class heroes, but it is clear from 'Revolution' that John had mixed feelings about Mao. And also about America - wherever John was, he was a malcontent.

Many real-life working class heroes emerged during the 1960s. Fashion designers, sportsmen and pop stars often had working class origins. They may have lost their social class when they became celebrities, but footballers remain working class heroes. They do a physical job, they play in stadiums in working class areas, and they take orders from their managers. In that sense, footballers, much more than pop stars, are working class heroes.

The late Eric Heffer, a Liverpool Labour MP for many years, wrote in his autobiography, *Never A Yes Man* (Verso 1991): "The Liverpool beat scene was fundamentally working class; Bob Wooler, the disc jockey at the Cavern was a former railway clerk. Working people appeared to be coming into their own at last. It was their youth who were writing, playing and recording the music you could hear in every club and pub."

People were talking about class in the 1960s and effectively, if you weren't working class, you kept quiet about it. The Kinks mocked the upper classes in 'Sunny Afternoon' but they had only affection for the lower orders in songs like 'Autumn Almanac'. Even 'My Old Man's A Dustman' celebrates the working class. John would never have claimed that "A middle-class hero is something to be".

The Beatles themselves played on the image of being working class heroes - the cover of the *Twist And Shout* EP was shot on urban wasteground - but they were far more than that: they were heroes for the whole world, irrespective of class. John regarded himself as a hero - he even told fellow Apple workers that he was Jesus Christ returned. He was given to such remarks as "Genius is pain" (1970), but the line, "A working class hero is something to be" could be ironic. Perhaps John is really saying, "I should not be a working class hero". Any revolution would come from the working classes and having heroes, especially superstars, is a distraction. Britain's working class are not planning radical, anarchic changes: instead, they are, in Lennon's words, "fucking peasants".

Lennon believes that new gods have arisen to obscure the lack of control we have over our own lives. The media (TV and newspapers), the pursuit of sex (the permissive 60s), religion (in his case, the Maharishi) and the taking of drugs blunt the appetite for social change. As he told one interviewer, "The workers are dreaming someone else's dream."

One final point: despite his identification with the working man, John Lennon barely did a day's labouring in his life. He was briefly employed by Scaris and Brick waterworks in Liverpool in 1959, but he was totally unsuited to the job, and they dismissed him.

2. Aunt Mimi opposed John's musical ambitions.

Rock'n'roll was seen as the music of rebellion and by and large, parents wanted their children to study and get a steady job, not be distracted with this new, delinquent music. For the performers themselves, it wouldn't look good if their elders liked what they were doing. But many of the most famous artists - Elvis Presley, Buddy Holly, Ricky Nelson, The Everly Brothers –were encouraged by their parents. Tommy Sands, who recorded 'Teenage Crush', said: "My parents really supported me. I can't think of anyone who had parents who didn't support what we were doing." There are few examples of parental disapproval in rock'n'roll and even then, it is not for the obvious reasons. Neil Sedaka's mother wanted her son to be a concert pianist. "I'd studied at the Juilliard School of Music," he recalled, "and so the fact that I liked rock'n'roll was shocking to her. She changed her mind when she got her mink stole.'

In the Beatle world, Paul McCartney's father had played in a dance band so there was no trouble there. George Harrison's parents indulged him and the fledgling Beatles were allowed to rehearse at his house. Pete Best was actively encouraged by his mother, Mona, who even started the Casbah club for her sons. Ringo Starr had been a sickly child and although his mother didn't want him to give up his apprenticeship, she was glad that he had something that made him so happy. However, she must have been worried about the unhealthy conditions in many of the clubs, especially the dank and smoky Cavern. Ringo played in the group fronted by Rory Storm, whose parents even renamed their house Hurricanesville.

John was raised by his Aunt Mimi and Uncle George, although George died in 1953. It was a strict regime but a loving one. Mimi hated anything "common" and John was raised with immaculate manners and appearance. As a child, he had an enviable collection of Dinky toys and if you look at pictures of him as an adolescent, you will find that he is well dressed. Mimi worked as a buyer for Lewis's stores and so was able to get him good quality clothes.

His mother, Julia, had given him an old Spanish guitar when he was young and he badgered Mimi to get him a new instrument. She recalled: "It cost me £14. That was a lot of money in those days. I begrudged paying it on a guitar but I thought that if it keeps him quiet, there's no harm done. He would stand in the front of his bedroom mirror pretending to be that man Elvis Presley."

Julia taught him and fellow Quarry Man Eric Griffiths banjo chords, which they transferred to the guitar. Aunt Mimi didn't mind John playing music although she often made him practise in the porch as she didn't like loud music in the house. She tried to dissuade John from having George Harrison in the group as she disliked George's Teddy Boy clothes and his marked Scouse accent.

Mimi always regarded John as creative but he had been a disappointing pupil and she worked hard to get him into the Liverpool College of Art. She was again disappointed when he was showing more interest in playing with the Beatles in Hamburg and at the Cavern. Famously, she told him "the guitar's all right as a hobby John, but you'll never make a living out of it."

In his biography of the Beatles, *Shout!*, Philip Norman describes how Mimi surprised John by turning up unexpectedly at the Cavern in January 1961 when he was supposed to be studying at the art college. She was justifiably annoyed but it doesn't quite ring true as John had already been to Hamburg. We prefer the recollections of the Cavern DJ, Bob Wooler, "John Lennon announced one Cavern lunchtime that everyone must behave, which was rich coming from him. Aunt Mimi was coming with a friend and she wanted to see him play. He wouldn't have allowed her to go to a venue in the evening but lunchtime was different. Also, they would perform some quieter or gentler numbers at lunchtime, like 'Over The Rainbow' or 'Falling In Love Again'. I met her there, and there was no swearing while she was around, but I don't know what she thought of the place."

Mimi thought that rock'n'roll was uncouth and working class, but she had mixed thoughts about John's success in the Liverpool clubs, delighted that he was, at last, doing something with his life. And he respected her opinion. Even though John was 21, Mimi met Brian Epstein before he signed the Beatles, and she became very proud of him. Bob Wooler saw Mimi's influence as a good one. "John, surprisingly, was quite dutiful. He might be the first to arrive at the Cavern. Maybe Mimi was the one behind him, telling him to get out of the house."

3. The Beatles emerged seamlessly out of the Quarry Men.

John, Paul, George and Ringo came together in August 1962 and the world would never be the same again. Most people casually assume that the change from the Quarry Men to the Beatles was straightforward and fairly seamless, when it was anything but. There were 15 changes of line-up from the start of the Quarry Men to the Fab Four. Here are the guys who got lost along the way.

Pete Shotton (washboard) was John Lennon's best friend and a founder member of the Quarry Men in March 1957. Ignoring the Teddy Boy drummer who once forced himself on the group for a couple of numbers, Shotton was the least musical person to be on stage with a Beatle. Despite their friendship, Lennon realised he was holding the group back and, following a gig at a party in Rosebery Street, he smashed Shotton's washboard over his head. "It didn't hurt," says Shotton, "and we fell about laughing. John wanted to develop the group into a serious band and that couldn't, by definition, include me." Shotton retained his friendship with Lennon throughout the 1960s and he claims that he contributed more to 'Eleanor Rigby' than Lennon did (that is, a couple of words as opposed to nothing.) Shotton is one of the many people associated with the Beatles who became a millionaire in his own right, in his case from the restaurant chain, Fatty Arbuckle's. He became part of the reformed Quarry Men in 1997 and with his mischievous personality, it was easy to see why he was John's best friend. The highpoint of his musical career was his first ever vocal, an impassioned 'Imagine', performed in St Peter's Church Hall in Woolton. Following the sale of Fatty Arbuckle's in 2001, Shotton left England to become a tax exile in Dublin.

Eric Griffiths (guitar), like John and Pete, went to Quarry Bank and was a founder member of the Quarry Men. He and John had lessons from John's mother, Julia, but she could only teach them banjo chords. He was a founder member of the Quarry Men and he stayed until early 1958 when George Harrison joined: "George was a good guitarist, better than me, and shortly after that I left the group. Paul and John asked me to go onto the bass but that meant buying a bass guitar and amplifier, which I wasn't prepared to do. I was sorry to go and I never played a guitar again. I joined the Merchant Navy and my life went in a different direction." By 1997, Eric had a chain of dry cleaners in Edinburgh but he rejoined the Quarry Men when they reformed.

Rob Cowley, who lived next door to Eric Griffiths in Halewood Drive, Woolton in the 1950s, told the authors in 2002, "My dad used to hammer on the wall to tell them to keep the noise down when they were practising. He called John Lennon 'a right stroppy bugger'."

Colin Hanton travelled on the same bus as Eric Griffiths. Eric knew he had a drum kit and invited him to join the Quarry Men in March 1957. He stayed long enough to play on their recording of 'That'll Be The Day' and 'In Spite Of All The Danger' in the summer of 1958. In 1994, he told one of the authors (SL) that he had a contract from Apple, as the tracks would be appearing on the *Anthology* CD. "I've been offered £2,000," he said. "Ask for more," he was told, and we hope he did, as the album had worldwide sales of 13 million. Colin, whose original drums are in *The Beatles Story* at the Albert Dock in Liverpool, says, "I was living on borrowed time as John and Paul were running the group. I got fed up in the end. I had carted my drums around on a bus for two years as none of us had cars. There were a lot of talent contests where we came second: we were always the bridesmaid and I'd had enough." Colin became a furniture restorer and didn't play the drums again until he rejoined the Quarry Men in 1997.

John and Eric had learnt banjo chords and so theoretically there could have been three banjo players in the group. **Rod Davis** (banjo) says: "I had bought the banjo from my uncle and if he'd sold me his guitar, I might have been a decent enough guitarist to keep Paul McCartney out of the band. I might not, but that was the big limitation. McCartney could play the guitar like a guitar, and we couldn't, and let's face it, a banjo doesn't look good in a rock group. I only met Paul on one other occasion after the Woolton fete and it was at Auntie Mimi's a week or two later.

He dropped in to hear us practising. From my point of view, I was the person he was replacing. It's like Pete Best - you're the guy who doesn't know. Some things had gone on that I wasn't aware of." Davis became the head boy at Quarry Bank and went to Cambridge University. In 1961, he made a record for Decca as part of the Trad Grads, meaning that he got on record before the Beatles. "I bumped into John in Liverpool," he recalls, "and I told him that I now played mandolin, fiddle, banjo, guitar, concertina and melodeon. He said, 'You don't play the drums, do you? We need a drummer to take back to Hamburg.' That was my second bad career move. My sister remembers my mother saying, 'He's not going to Hamburg with that Lennon. He's taking his degree.' That's the way she always spoke of him - she never called him anything but 'that Lennon'." Rod became a teacher and translator, and, in his spare time, a champion windsurfer. He has maintained his interest in music, usually playing in bluegrass or folk groups. He is the one who organises the bookings for the Quarry Men today: he shares the lead vocals with Len Garry, he has recorded with Tony Sheridan and he is the best musician in the group.

Ivan Vaughan introduced Paul to the Quarry Men on 6 July 1957, and for a brief time he played tea-chest bass with the group. Ivan became a teacher and then a university lecturer. He retained his friendship with the Beatles, his wife, Jan, helping Paul with the French section of 'Michelle'. When the Beatles set up Apple, they had plans for an Apple School, fronted by Ivan and Jan, but nothing came of it beyond the inspection of a few properties and the attempted establishment of a steering committee. In his thirties, Ivan developed Parkinson's Disease. Because it was so rare for a young person to succumb to this illness, he became the subject of a BBC documentary, *Ivan*, produced by Jonathan Miller in 1984. He wrote about his illness in *Ivan: Living With Parkinson's Disease* (Macmillan, 1986) and he used his body in experiments to see how he behaved on and off drugs. Ivan died in 1994, an event that inspired Paul McCartney to write some poetry.

Bill Smith (tea-chest bass) played a few gigs with the Quarry Men but it didn't last: "I pinched a tea chest from the woodwork room and that became the bass.   never had a proper instrument and I wouldn't have wanted to practice anyway. I did play the jew's harp later on and I still play it now and again." Bill joined Cunard and went to sea, later emigrating to South Africa. When he returned to Liverpool in 2002, he joined the Quarry Men for a short set at *The Beatles Story*. The solitary string of his tea-chest bass broke during the first number and so we are unable to comment on the quality of his current technique.

The role of tea-chest bass player in the Quarry Men seemed to change from gig to gig. **Nigel Whalley** had a couple of attempts but decided to become the Quarry Men's manager (!) instead and even had business cards printed to that effect. Whalley arranged their first appearance at the Cavern, but Paul McCartney didn't think that a manager should take a part of the fee and Whalley's association with the Quarry Men ended. In July 1958 he witnessed the death of John's mother in a road accident. He later became a golf professional in Kent.

Len Garry (tea-chest bass) was at the Liverpool Institute with Ivan Vaughan and Paul McCartney. He met John Lennon in 1955 and he was invited to become the regular tea chest player in the band. John also said that he could do some backing vocals but as John would have the one and only mike, he would not be heard. In August 1958 Len contracted tuberculosis and was in hospital for several months.   He studied architecture for a few years and then worked for Birkenhead Council. He was married in 1965. He and his wife became devout members of The People's Church, which emphasises the wickedness of pop music, and Len had to burn all his memorabilia from the Quarry Men days. He returned to the devil's work in 1997 when he became the lead singer and guitarist with the reformed Quarry Men. He is actually a talented singer and he could have been successful if he'd joined a Mersey group in the 1960s.

John Duff Lowe (piano) and Paul McCartney had auditioned for the choir at Liverpool Cathedral on the same day, with the Duff one being accepted. He joined The Quarry Men in February 1958 but his bookings were conditional on there being a piano at the relevant venue. He played on 'That'll Be The Day and 'In Spite Of All The Danger' at Percy Phillips' studio and the solitary acetate copy of that recording ended up in his possession. He sold this on to Paul McCartney in 1981. Working as a stockbroker in Bristol he had no interest in returning to music until the 1990s. Then he worked with Rod Davis and the latter-day Four Pennies. Together they made an album as the Quarry Men, *Open For Engagements*, in 1994. But he has been excluded from the Quarry Men's reunion gigs, one reason being that he was not with the group for the famous photograph at St Peter's Church.

The bookings for the Quarry Men were thin and so, in January 1959, George Harrison decided he had had enough and joined the Les Stewart Quartet. They were booked to open the Casbah in August 1959, but an argument split the group. George Harrison got hold of his mates John and Paul and with **Ken Brown** (guitar, vocal) from the Quartet, *they* opened the Casbah instead. This line up did six further bookings at the Casbah until another disagreement led to Ken Brown leaving. Brown then formed the Black Jacks with Pete Best. Les Stewart himself (guitar, vocal) later played in Lee Castle and the Barons and the Kansas City Five. He had minor chart success in the UK as part of The Long And The Short ('The Letter', 'Choc Ice') in 1964. Bob McKinley, the lead singer of this Liverpool and Wigan amalgam became one of Britain's leading country-rock performers, and he says, "Les was a fine guitarist and a good singer and songwriter too. He deserved to have more success." Les became a draughtsman and emigrated to South Africa.

In 1960 when the Beatles were offered a residency in Hamburg, George Harrison asked his schoolfriend, **Arthur Kelly**, to buy a bass guitar and join them. He decided to stick at his job as a junior clerk with Cunard, but he later became an actor playing Monkey Gibbons in *Coronation Street* and Detective Sergeant Chegwyn in *The Chinese Detective*. Very aptly, he also played Bert in a touring production of Willy Russell's *John, Paul, George, Ringo…And Bert*.

Legend has it that John Lennon's friend from the College of Art, **Stuart Sutcliffe** won a prize in the John Moores art exhibition and was encouraged to purchase a bass guitar with the winnings. This is not true however as Sutcliffe's hire purchase agreement for the instrument with *Frank Hessy's* has come to light. He was buying the guitar in monthly instalments (and so this book really dispels 102 Beatle myths). Stu had some lessons from Dave May of the Silhouettes and although he was not particularly proficient, he did not perform with his back to the audience as is often stated (103?). Once he got to Hamburg and befriended Astrid Kirchherr and Klaus Voormann, he realised he wanted to continue with his studies. He died from a brain haemorrhage in April 1962. Most art critics agree that his work shows immense promise.

The Silver Beetles (John, Paul, George and Stu) impressed the impresario Larry Parnes enough to get the job of backing the Liverpool singer, Johnny Gentle on a short Scottish tour. They didn't have a drummer so they asked a local jazz musician, **Tommy Moore**, to join them. He was 26 while the rest of the Beatles were teenagers and, not being too bright, he was regularly mocked by John and Paul. Gentle, who was driving the van, had an accident in which Moore was concussed. He left the group when they returned to Liverpool, his girlfriend telling them that he had a steady job driving a forklift truck at Garston Bottle Works. Moore spoke at an early Beatles Convention, describing Lennon as "big-headed and aggressive". He died of a stroke in 1981.

No longer with Tommy Moore and having a few bookings at The Grosvenor Ballroom, Liscard, in July 1960, the Beatles asked a social club drummer and picture framer, **Norman Chapman**, to join them. Their gig of 6 August 1960 was cancelled following complaints of rowdy behaviour. 'I remember us trying to hide on stage for fear of getting a missile in the bonce,' says Norman today, 'but we kept going.' Norman was one of the last young men to be conscripted into the army before National Service was abolished, ending his short tenure in the Beatles drum seat. "I remember keeping time on a bar with two pennies while two lads were playing guitars, and Ringo said to me, 'You keep time pretty good, who have you been playing with?'" Later, Norman worked with a beat group, the In Crowd, in social clubs on Merseyside.

Pete Best (drums) joined the Beatles for their first trip to Hamburg in August 1960 and was sacked two years later. Why it took the Beatles 500 gigs to find out that he wasn't up to the job is anyone's guess.

Chas Newby was a member of Pete Best's band, the Blackjacks. When the Beatles returned from Hamburg in December 1960, they were without a bass player, Stu Sutcliffe having stayed behind with Astrid. Chas, who was studying chemistry at university, was asked to step in on bass and although he only made four appearances with the Beatles, they were significant ones. One of them was that famous night at Litherland Town Hall on 27 December 1960. He turned down the offer to join the Beatles full time and later worked in industrial management in Birmingham.

The reformed Quarry Men have been gigging on and off since 1997. Rod Davis, Len Garry, Eric Griffiths and Colin Hanton put on an entertaining show, but none of the *legendary* Quarrymen have ever shown up.

4. The Cavern was opened as a venue for the many emerging Liverpool beat groups.

Mathew Street is just off Liverpool's city centre, but no shopper would have gone there in the 1950s. The narrow street was little more than two rows of seven-storey warehouses, and lorry-loads of fruit and vegetables were unloaded there throughout the day. 10 Mathew Street was typical: the basement had been an air-raid shelter during the war and was later used for storing wines and spirits and later as an egg-packing station. In 1956 the upstairs building was used to store electrical goods, but the basement was vacant.

A young Liverpool jazz promoter, Alan Sytner, had recently returned from Paris and was impressed by the jazz clubs and bohemian lifestyle he had witnessed there, particularly liking an underground club called Le Caveau. "An estate agent, Glyn Evans, told me he knew of an old cellar which was full of arches and derelict," he recalls. "I got the keys and went down a rickety ladder with a flashlight. Glyn Evans didn't realise that he was showing me a replica of Le Caveau and that is where the name came from. Mathew Street looked like a little narrow street in the Latin Quarter in Paris, so I felt I was bringing the Left Bank to Liverpool.'

The first job was to clear out the site and for this he recruited many volunteers. Alan Sytner: "The place had been reinforced to make an air-raid shelter and the brick reinforcements had to be removed with sledgehammers as we couldn't get a pneumatic drill in. Well, we didn't even know where to get one. We did it by hand and we were left with a lot of rubble. That was the ideal foundation for the stage, which was made of wood and just went over the bricks. It did a great job of balancing the acoustics, and the acoustics in the Cavern were terrific, absolutely brilliant."

Missing the Christmas and New Year trade, the Cavern opened on 16 January 1957. The opening bill featured The Merseysippi Jazz Band,

The Wall City Jazzmen, the Ralph Watmough Jazz Band and The Coney Island Skiffle Group. The guest of honour was to be the 21-year-old drummer, the Earl Of Wharncliffe, who in the event didn't turn up. The journalist Bob Azurdia was there: "The queue stretched all the way down Mathew Street and into Whitechapel. Prior to the Cavern, the Temple was the only evening venue for jazz in the city and it opened only on Sunday nights. Life was very different in those days. The only other places you could go to were a cinema, a palais for strict-tempo dancing or a coffee bar. Young people tended not to go to pubs, which in any case closed at ten p.m. without any drinking-up time. The Cavern was therefore very welcome."

The doorway was lit by a single bulb. Eighteen stone steps led down to the cellar which was divided by archways into three long, dimly-lit barrel vaults, each a hundred feet long and ten feet wide. The walls were painted plainly with emulsion and there were no curtains or decorations. The entrance to the first vault was used to collect admission money and there was also a cloakroom. The second and largest area contained the stage and a few rows of wooden chairs. All the lighting (there were no coloured filters or bulbs) was concentrated on the stage. There was only dancing - the Cavern stomp - when there was room to move. It was an ideal arrangement out front, but the lavatories were appalling, the bandroom tiny and the air-conditioning non-existent. Within minutes of opening, the Cavern could contain hundreds of sweaty bodies, and condensation would cover the walls and drip off the ceilings. And most people smoked in those days.

Intriguingly, Alan Sytner decided against applying for a liquor licence for the Cavern. "I wasn't anti-booze but my heart wasn't in it and I didn't think that I could meet the requirements for a liquor licence. I was going to get a lot of young people in the place and so it wasn't a good idea to have booze there. They could always get a pass-out and go to the White Star or the Grapes, where incidentally they might find me."

Many Beatle books have them entertaining up to 1,100 fans at the Cavern but that is an impossibility. Alan Sytner: "The maximum ticket sale that we had was 652, and that was on the opening night when we turned more away than we let in. Only a third of the people got in. We had mounted police to control the queue which stretched for half a mile, but, unlike today, there was no trouble when they told people to go home. We got very close to 652 on several other occasions, but it got very heavy when it got to 600. It is also good to say 'Sorry, we're full' when you're in the entertainment business. We didn't get to 600 that often, but when we did, we would say, 'That's enough.'"

John Lawrence of The Merseysippi Jazz Band: "I can't remember what triggered the Cavern's instant success as I can't remember Alan doing a lot of advertising about the Cavern. I thought that we were taking a bit of a chance by moving from a moderately comfortable pub to a damp cellar, but it was the best thing that ever happened to us. They came flooding in every time we played there. The stage was just about big enough for an eight-piece band, but the piano was hanging over the edge. Acoustically it was very good as there were three long tunnels - the outside tunnels were full of benches and chairs and the centre tunnel with the stage at the end was acoustically just right. It was a long room with hard surfaces, brick and a stone floor, which is always good. If you play in a room full of curtains and thick carpets, you can blow your teeth out trying to make the sound right."

In March 1957 a public health inspector blew up some football bladders at the Cavern to obtain air samples. Outside it was 52 degrees Fahrenheit and inside 82, a remarkable difference when there was no heating in the club. However, the inspector lacked the powers now available to an environmental health officer and could only recommend that the owner should improve his facilities. Sytner didn't have the finances to do that.

The Merseysippi Jazz Band played the Cavern five times during the opening month and it quickly established itself as the hippest place on Merseyside, not that there was much competition. Alan Sytner: "There were very marked demographics according to the night of the week and what was being put on. On Thursdays I put on modern jazz to please myself and again I got a very hip, very cool audience - crew-cuts, button-down collars and little skinny ties. They thought they were massively superior and cleverer than everybody else. These were people who had their own cars and so we could stay open a little later. Sunday was the Merseys' night and they attracted a very middle class audience with lots of people from the Wirral and Crosby. These people didn't cause any trouble at all, obviously, and as they formed the majority, nobody else did either. Friday night was completely different. We used to get kids from the top end of London Road. There were quite a few gangs and they used to love making trouble, similar to football hooligans today and the same sort of people. If I'd had any sense, I would have closed on Fridays. On Saturdays you got a cross-section. If there was a band with a strong appeal, you would get a nice audience. If it was a so-so band, you would just get whoever was out on Saturday night and going to the Cavern for want of anywhere else to go."

The gospel singer Sister Rosetta Tharpe was backed by The Merseysippi Jazz Band in Manchester and then by The Wall City Jazzmen at the Cavern. She voiced her doubts about appearing at the Cavern by saying, "You might wonder what a woman of God like me is doing in a place like this. Well, our Lord Jesus went down into the highways and the byways and if it's good enough for Him, it's good enough for me." Being unlicensed, the Cavern was not wayward enough for Tharpe's husband, who was known as Lazy Daddy. Jazz critic Steve Voce: 'The licensing laws baffled all Americans except Lazy Daddy, who had a complete working knowledge of opening hours within 20 minutes of stepping off the boat.'

The Cavern was going so well that it had a membership of 25,000 by 1959. The First Springtime Jazz Festival, which included Humphrey Lyttelton, was a great success. Professional musicians working at the Grafton or Reece's would come to the Cavern to jam when they had finished. Alan Sytner had introduced lunchtime sessions (a brilliant innovation) and bingo afternoons (not so clever) to bring in more revenue. The club was thriving and both of Alan's parents helped with the administration. The

Cavern also mounted successful events on board the Royal Iris and the Royal Daffodil, thus emulating the riverboats in New Orleans. The boats would take audiences up and down the Mersey - a genuine case of the music going round and round.

But two things pushed the Cavern off course. One was Alan Sytner's lavish playboy lifestyle and the other was that beat music was threatening jazz's popularity, and Alan had no interest in the new sounds. Ray McFall, who worked for Sytner's accountants, bought the lease: "I took the Cavern over as a jazz club in the later stages of Alan Sytner's ownership. The club's fortunes were going down and it was obvious that there was a tremendous interest for beat music. Skiffle had come and gone and I felt that I had to introduce beat music steadily, which worked very well. It took two or three years for jazz to be phased out but some bands like Acker Bilk's retained their popularity. He opened the club for me and maintained regular appearances throughout."

Ray McFall booked The Swinging Blue Jeans for a weekly guest night, a skilful move as they had a foot in both camps. Ralph Ellis: "We had a jazz flavour but we had a front lineup of three guitars rather than sax, trombone and trumpet. We had a trad jazz feel but with a Merseybeat sound about it. In the end the people wanted rock'n'roll. Bob Wooler has never got over the fact that we changed to rock'n'roll as he thought we had a unique sound, but we wanted to make records that would sell."

Don Lydiatt of The Merseysippi Jazz Band: 'The change happened very quickly. One January we were booked to top the bill at a festival at Bury Golf Club in July. Come July the whole thing had overturned, the audience only wanted to see the beat groups and we were met by hordes of screaming kids. Later on, we found out that the groups were as astounded as we were. They hardly had to sing as the fans screamed solidly and they certainly didn't want us on stage.'

"I remember The Beatles doing the interval for us at the Cavern," recalls jazz legend Kenny Ball, "and I had never seen guys in all-leather suits before. It can't have been much fun for them as it was very damp down there. The fellers liked us and the girls liked them and I thought there must be something wrong with us."

Another icon of the trad revival, Chris Barber remembers: "We never played the Cavern but we did concerts every six months in Liverpool, usually at the Phil. We did meet The Beatles a couple of times and bought them drinks and were friendly. The Beatles were quite surprised because I don't think they'd met any jazz musicians who'd been friendly before. It didn't stop John making his famous pronouncement that he didn't like jazz."

George Melly, singer, writer and raconteur: "We used to play the Bodega in Manchester on Saturday and the Cavern on Sunday. It was before The Beatles were well known, but gradually the Liverpool sound became popular, in Liverpool first of all, and The Beatles used to play in our interval. We ran over to the Grapes and Lennon always resented British jazz very much. He used to say that these old men had got in his way and he would have been more successful earlier. My father much preferred it when we moved from the Cavern to Mardi Gras as it was a much more commodious place."

Although The Beatles found success at the Cavern in Ray McFall's tenure, Alan Sytner is sure of his place in history: "Without me no Cavern, without me no Beatles, without me none of the bloody things really. If there had not been a Cavern, none of this would have happened. The talent came out at the Cavern, there was nowhere else and there wouldn't have been anywhere else because the Cavern created a precedent. People opened the Mardi Gras and the Iron Door and all the others, but they didn't think of it for themselves: they looked at the Cavern and created an alternative. None of the owners had any interest in music or knew anything about music. They thought it was a good business and jumped on the bandwagon. I don't think any of this would have happened without me. Obviously, Lennon and McCartney were geniuses, but would they have flourished without the Cavern? If they had been playing in church halls in Maghull, would anyone have taken any notice?"

5. *John Lennon came up with the name, The Beatles.*

In the first issue of the *Mersey Beat* newspaper in July 1961, John Lennon wrote: "Many people ask what are Beatles? Why Beatles? Ugh, Beatles, how did the name arrive? So we will tell you. It came in a vision - a man appeared on a flaming pie and said unto them, 'From this day on you are Beatles with an A.' Thank you, Mister Man, they said, thanking him." Well, the man on the flaming pie, in all probability, wasn't John Lennon, but his close friend, Stu Sutcliffe.

Considering that John Lennon was the most rebellious boy in Quarry Bank school, it is ironic that his group was called The Quarry Men and that the name lasted from March 1957 to October 1959. Then The Quarry Men became Johnny and the Moondogs for an audition for the *Carroll Levis TV Star Search* show at the Liverpool Empire, effectively because the template for the names of popular groups at the time was "Someone and the Somethings". John may have liked his name being to the fore, but it didn't last long.

In January 1960, John, Paul and George added Stu Sutcliffe to the line-up and it was Stu who suggested Beatals (sic) as it was similar to Buddy Holly's group, the Crickets, who were among their main inspirations. In a letter written at the beginning of 1960, Sutcliffe, signing himself Stu Sutcliffe (manager), wrote to a club looking for work calling the group, "The ~~Quar~~ Beatals" and this is the moment that the group's name changed. Writing to Butlin's Holiday Camp in Pwllheli, also early in 1960, Paul McCartney asked about employment, saying, "I should like to apply for an engagement at your holiday camp. The group is known as The Beatals and is led by John Lennon."

Albert Goldman, in *The Lives Of John Lennon*, claims that the name came from Lee Marvin's rival gang in Marlon Brando's motorcycle film, *The Wild One*. But as the 1954 film was banned in the UK until 1967, it is unlikely that they would know much about it, and so this must be put down to coincidence. George Harrison did subsequently attribute the name to the film, but even if they knew of its existence it would have been highly unlikely that they'd even know, let alone pick up on, the name of the film's rival gang. Paul McCartney's authorised biography, *Many Years From Now*, says that John and Stu confronted him with the new name, so we know it definitely wasn't Paul or George.

To add to the confusion, the beat poet Royston Ellis came to Liverpool in 1960 and was backed by the group, then called Johnny and the Moondogs, for a reading at the Jacaranda coffee bar . Lennon told him that they were going to be The Beetles and, according to Royston's website, 'it was Ellis who suggested spelling it with an 'a'.' The text continues, 'The Beatles went on to have a Number 1 hit with the song Lennon and McCartney wrote about Ellis, 'Paperback Writer'.' Yes, well…

In May 1960 they became The Silver Beetles and then The Silver Beatles with their friend, Brian Casser, of Cass and the Cassanovas, thinking of *Treasure Island*, suggesting Long John and the Silver Beatles. Pete Best joined the group in August 1960 for their first appearances in Hamburg and they shortened their name to The Beatles, the name shown on their contract with the Indra Club. They had also given up the idea of having pseudonyms so Paul Ramon, Carl Harrison and Stuart de Stael were consigned to the dustbin. With two exceptions: Paul used "Paul Ramon" when he recorded 'My Dark Hour' with Steve Miller in 1969; and later the New York punk band, The Ramones, took their name from Paul's pseudonym.

6. 'Love Me Do' was the first record ever released to feature a Beatle lyric.

The London beat group impresario Larry Parnes had struck up a friendship with the owner of the Jacaranda coffee bar, Allan Williams, when they jointly promoted a show at the Liverpool Stadium on 3 May 1960 featuring Gene Vincent. He was impressed with the local talent on the show and he later auditioned Liverpool groups as backing bands for some of his acts, most notably Billy Fury. Fury attended the auditions just one week later on 10 May at the Wyvern Social Club in Seel Street. Fury was not impressed enough to take any of them on, but Parnes asked Cass and the Cassanovas to work with Duffy Power and The Silver Beetles to back Johnny Gentle on short tours in Scotland.

Duffy Power recalls: "Cass and the Cassanovas were wicked boys. They used to do the first set and one night they did my whole act for a laugh. I didn't know whether to phone Larry or not. I went on and did the songs again, and I went down all right anyway."

Considering that some other good Liverpool beat groups had turned up for the audition, including Gerry and the Pacemakers, it is surprising that Parnes should have prefer the ramshackle Beatles. He recognised the limitations of their bass player, Stuart Sutcliffe, and they hadn't even a drummer, using Johnny Hutchinson from the Cassanovas for the day. However, unlike other groups with their day jobs, The Beatles were available and Parnes needed a group urgently to back Johnny Gentle for seven dates in Scotland starting on 20 May.

Johnny Gentle (Liverpool-born John Askew) was a ballad singer who wrote his own songs. He had had near misses with 'Wendy' and 'Milk From The Coconut', and had performed on the tragic final night of Eddie Cochran's tour only a month earlier. With a brief rehearsal, Johnny Gentle and The Silver Beetles took the stage at the Town Hall in Marshill, Alloa in the south of Scotland and then headed for the Highlands. Gentle says: "We did a quick rehearsal of well-known songs and we went on stage together. It worked well as the chemistry was right between us. They did their own spot as well and I told Larry Parnes that they were better than me."

These were low-key affairs and according to Gentle's memoir, *Johnny Gentle And The Beatles* (Merseyrock, 1998), everything went very well. Johnny Gentle told Larry Parnes how good they were. But could this be revisionism? - surely if they were that good, Larry Parnes would have used them again - and he never did.

Larry Parnes had the opportunity to sign The Beatles but he didn't take it, although, in his defence, they hadn't yet been to Hamburg and he normally preferred to sign solo acts.

Johnny Gentle and The Beatles got on well and when Gentle returned home for a weekend in July, he found out where The Beatles were playing and joined them on stage at the Grosvenor Ballroom in Liscard.

But by far the most interesting revelation from the Scottish tour comes from Johnny Gentle: "I can remember playing John Lennon a song I was working on, 'I've Just Fallen For Someone'. I couldn't work out a middle eight and John came up with something that seemed to fit. (Sings) 'We know that we'll get by / Just wait and see / Just like the sun tells us / The best things in life are free.' It flowed well but I thought he was out of order because I'd been writing songs for a year. I recorded it for Parlophone under the name of Darren Young but there was no question of him getting a songwriting credit as we all helped each other in those days. It's one of his first recorded compositions, if not the very first." You're right, Johnny, it's the very first, and it's a good pop record, arranged by John Barry in the Adam Faith style [the song was later recorded by Faith and released as track two, side one, of his eponymous 1961 album].

The wording of the middle eight indicates that John had heard the Barrett Strong record 'Money (That's What I Want)', which had been released in the UK in March 1960.

'I've Just Fallen For Someone' by Darren Young was released in July 1962 on Parlophone R 4919, and is currently available on *John Barry; The Hits and The Misses* (Play It Again Play007). A few weeks later, 'Love Me Do' was released on Parlophone R 4949.

7. Allan Williams was
'The Man Who Gave The Beatles Away'.

Then as now, Liverpool is full of colourful characters, but for 40 years Allan Williams has stood alone. He is regarded in the same light as Arthur Daley in *Minder* or Delboy in *Only Fools And Horses* and though this may seem unfair, the image is of his own making as, even now, the entrepreneur can be found in Liverpool pubs, dreaming up schemes to make him millions. Somehow they never come off. His scheme to turn Spain into another Blackpool by manufacturing rock for tourists fell foul of the authorities, and he was seen on street corners muttering, "Psst, want to buy a stick of rock?" Some old black leather trousers, allegedly worn by Paul McCartney, appeared in a Sotheby's catalogue with a certificate of authenticity from Allan Williams. McCartney said that they were too small for him anyway, but the retort was that the second owner, Faron of Faron's Flamingos, was six inches shorter than Macca and had cut them to size.

In September 1958, Allan Williams, a one-time plumber, opened the Jacaranda coffee bar in Slater Street in Liverpool's city centre. The Beatles helped him decorate the small basement and he invited acoustic groups to play there. The club also featured Lord Woodbine's steel band, who later found some work in Hamburg, playing at the Kaiserkeller for Bruno Koschmider. Apparently intrigued by this, Allan Williams took some tapes of The Beatles and other groups to Hamburg in order to secure work for them, although this story is hard to credit.

Williams met Larry Parnes when the Gene Vincent and Eddie Cochran tour came to Liverpool, and he arranged for Liverpool groups to support Gene Vincent at a concert at the Liverpool Stadium in May 1960. The auditions for groups to back Larry Parnes' artists took place later in May, and Derry and the Seniors were annoyed with Allan when some promised work did not materialise. Howie Casey, the group's burly sax player, threatened Williams and as a result he took them to London's 2 I's coffee bar, where Tommy Steele, Terry Dene and Wee Willie Harris had been discovered. As luck would have it, Bruno Koschmider was in the 2 I's looking for groups for the Kaiserkeller. Thus, Derry and the Seniors became the first Liverpool group to play Hamburg.

As the Seniors were successful in Germany, Allan Williams was asked to supply further groups. But Howie Casey wrote to Williams telling him not to mess up the scene by sending over "a bum group like The Beatles". Williams secured some local bookings for the band and he took an agency percentage of 10 per cent, but not a management fee. Norman Whalley for The Quarry Men and Stu Sutcliffe for The Beatles had claimed to manage John Lennon and his friends before him.

Once in Hamburg, The Beatles arranged a return visit to the Top Ten club for proprieter Peter Eckhorn but there was a dispute with Williams over the agency fee. Letters were exchanged, which clearly show that he was acting as their agent and not their manager. (Indeed, an Allan Williams visiting card for The Beatles, auctioned in Liverpool in August 2002, did not state he was their manager.) Williams never forgave The Beatles for this betrayal and even though a goldmine was his for the asking, he never cleared the air and assumed their management. They were better off without him - it was Allan Williams who had booked The Beatles to back Janice, a well-endowed stripper from Manchester, in one of his clubs. Not the big-time they wanted. When Brian Epstein was thinking of managing The Beatles, Allan Williams advised him against it.

Allan's memoir, *The Man Who Gave The Beatles Away*, tells a different story, suggesting, despite the evidence, that the Beatles were his to give away to Brian Epstein. When Allan asked Paul McCartney to sign his book, Paul said, "I've got to be careful here. Whatever I write is going to be quoted on the paperback." He wrote, "To Allan, Some parts of this book are partially true, Paul McCartney." A few years later he was less circumspect as he referred to Williams as their manager in the *Anthology* TV series.

Allan Williams owned one of the key Liverpool clubs, the Blue Angel, and he introduced bullfighting (with a bullock, then a goat and then a waiter wearing a costume) into Liverpool clubland. In 1977, it was Allan Williams who planned the release of the tapes of The Beatles in Hamburg: he also thought of cutting up the original tapes and selling them in one-inch strips in key-chain souvenirs. On the videotape of *Imagine...The Sixties*, the Liverpool DJ Billy Butler refers to a club burning down, adding, "And Allan Williams didn't own it."

Allan Williams and the former Cavern DJ Bob Wooler have often appeared at Beatle Conventions, even travelling to New York for one prestigious event. They later stayed in the same hotel as Richard Nixon and several of his aides in Paris, and Allan and Bob had the larger bar bill, paid naturally by the organisers. A rogue to the end.

But Allan Williams, for all his faults, is a loveable rogue. He is also a wonderful raconteur who has kept Merseysiders entertained for 40 years and even today he can always be assured of a drink any time he walks into a city pub.

8. *Paul McCartney's only taste of prison life was after his drugs bust in Tokyo in 1980.*

In 1980 Paul McCartney, about to play dates in Japan, was arrested at Tokyo Airport for possessing marijuana after attempting to carry it through customs. This was a shock to many, as most rock stars would expect their roadies to do the carrying (and carry the can, if caught) and it says something for McCartney that he had the drugs himself. It was a foolhardy move however as he must have known the consequences. The Japanese authorities cancelled the concerts and put him in jail. Paul kept a prison diary, completing 20,000 words, but unlike Lord Archer, he has not published it.

However, that was not the first time Paul had been inside.

In August 1960 The Beatles went to the red light district of Hamburg to play for Bruno Koschmider at his club, The Indra. They were given unappealing, windowless accommodation behind the screen at the Bambi Kino cinema. They performed well but there were complaints about the noise (from the owners of the adjoining sex clubs!) and in October they were moved to Koschmider's other club, the Kaiserkeller, better situated near the top of the Grosse Freiheit. The intention was that they would play at the Kaiserkeller until the end of the year, splitting their shifts with Rory Storm and the Hurricanes (with Ringo on drums). Koschmider was not amused when the club's rickety stage was demolished, actually when Storm was performing. What would they destroy next?

In October 1960, another music club opened on the Reeperbahn. This was the Top Ten and its owner, Peter Eckhorn, intended to steal the Kaiserkeller's audience. As a wise precaution, he employed Koschmider's chief bouncer, Horst Fascher. He booked Tony Sheridan and his group the Jets, who had also been at the Kaiserkeller, and it wasn't long before The Beatles were jamming with them on stage.

Koschmider was furious and it's somewhat surprising that his henchmen didn't beat up The Beatles. Instead, he gave them a month's notice, ending on 30 November, but he also reported George Harrison to the police for being under 18. George was deported on 21 November but the remaining Beatles worked out their notice. They still socialised at the Top Ten and they accepted Eckhorn's offer of accomodation in the attic above his club.

On 29 November, Paul McCartney and Pete Best were at the Bambi Kino after it had closed, to pack their belongings. A fuse had blown so they hung four condoms from nails in the hallway and lit them, also using matches to see what they were doing. They were only in the cinema for a few minutes and the condoms were smouldering when they left. Little damage was done but Koschmider, still raging after their defection, decided it was arson and referred the matter to the police. Both Paul McCartney and Pete Best were arrested and thrown into the cells at the police station on the Reeperbahn overnight. After their release they returned to the Top Ten to sleep but a few hours later they were woken by police and told that they were also being deported on the midnight plane the same day. They only had a few minutes to pack their belongings again, but it was enough time to arrange to play the Top Ten the following April, subject to the lifting of the deportation order. Pete even had to leave his drums behind. They were not allowed to contact the British Consul and they arrived in Liverpool on 1 December.

Stu remained in Hamburg with Astrid Kirchherr, so John had to make his way back on his own. John Lennon was such a dreamer and so disorganised that it is surprising to find him travelling from Hamburg to Liverpool alone.

9. John Lennon was born during a Luftwaffe bombing raid.

Perhaps to give it a more rounded texture, many accounts have propagated the dramatic notion that John Lennon's life began and ended with the sound of gunfire. Even Phillip Norman's *Shout! The True Story Of The Beatles*, accepted by most as the standard work on the group, has it that "John Lennon was born during one of the fiercest night raids by Hitler's Luftwaffe on Liverpool". Hunter Davies had written much the same in his official biography over a decade earlier.

The maiming of one of the enemy's most crucial ports was certainly among the German air force's priorities during the Second World War. In 1940, hardly a month would pass without alarm bells, sirens and anti-aircraft guns executing a discordant threnody as the slip-slapping Mersey shone with the brightness of flames. Houses and blocks of flats, shops and cinemas, public buildings and dockyards crumbled in a haze of smoke and powdered plaster, or else were blown more cleanly out of existence by direct hits throughout aerial bombardments that often lasted until the grey of morning.

When the hostile shadows vanished from the sky, the lull allowed human moles to emerge from underground shelters to find broken crockery from their cupboards, burnt mattresses from their beds, and splinters from their furniture scattered across the streets, and the crunch of grit, brick-dust and shards of glass under their feet.

Nevertheless, when John Winston Lennon was prised into the world in central Liverpool's Oxford Street Maternity Hospital on Wednesday, 6 October 1940 at 6.30 p.m., there had been no raids since the previous night. The Liverpool Echo for that week confirms too that neither was a single German aeroplane to fly over the city for the next twenty-four hours.

Indeed, the BBC Home Service weatherman forecast that the evening of Lennon's birth would be dull but mild - which it was. Dull but mild it remained for more or less the next fortnight - though before the baby was brought home to the suburban calm of Woolton, the Luftwaffe returned to drop further booming tons of death and destruction.

10. There was nothing particularly distinctive about Mersey Beat - it was just beat music played by Liverpool musicians.

The initial impetus of American rock'n'roll had lost its bite by 1960. There are many reasons for this but all the main protagonists had pressed the self-destruct button: Buddy Holly had died, Elvis Presley was in the army, Chuck Berry was in jail, Little Richard was a minister, Carl Perkins had been in a car smash - and although there were excellent, second-generation rock'n'rollers (Freddy Cannon, Brenda Lee, Larry Williams), the trend was for good-looking, clean-cut boys singing romantic ballads. It wasn't all that different from the early 1950s except that the lyrics now had teen appeal and there was a beat to the ballads. Just like 2002, in fact. The UK was dominated by Cliff Richard, Adam Faith and Marty Wilde, and the tendency for wannabe groups was to copy Cliff and the Shads.

Singing the hits of the day, Gerry and the Pacemakers in their neat, monogrammed jackets went to Hamburg and, despite copping a few licks from Tony Sheridan, there was little change when they returned. Rory Storm and the Hurricanes remained essentially a showband and a showcase for Rory's exceptional looks and daredevil escapades. They were hampered from being musically more adventurous because of the limitations of Storm's voice. The Beatles scarcely had an act when they went to Hamburg in 1960, but when they returned, they had been transformed. They were loud and raucous and their leather jackets also came from Hamburg. It was the German photographer, Astrid Kirchherr, who fashioned their look and although she did not take the cover of their *With The Beatles* LP, it could be regarded as the best-known example of her style.

So what was Mersey Beat, or, if you prefer, the Liverpool Sound? Firstly, the music has to be played by an act from the Liverpool area. Secondly, the act should have been playing in local beat clubs such as the Cavern and the Orrell Park Ballroom. This rules out the Hollies, who played the Cavern many times but whose home base was Stockport. Their lead singer, Allan Clarke, has pointed out that Stockport was on the Mersey, but that is pushing the definition.

Already there are complications. Billy J. Kramer with the Dakotas are regarded as a Mersey Beat act band, but although Billy was born in Bootle, the Dakotas came from Manchester. In that case, why are Herman's Hermits not regarded as Mersey Beat? Herman (Peter Noone) was raised in Huyton, Liverpool and the Hermits are from Manchester. Their exclusion is probably because Peter had played Len Fairclough's son in the Salford (Manchester) soap, *Coronation Street*.

At first it was raucous R&B with songs from relatively obscure American artists like 'Money' (Barrett Strong), 'Some Other Guy' (Richie Barrett) and 'Anna (Go To Him)' (Arthur Alexander). Pete Best's pounding drum beat was crucial and could be likened, however unintentionally, to German military drumming. What had come from Hamburg was an ability to lose your inhibitions and do what you liked on stage. Sometimes the Beatles would perform one song for 20 minutes. What impressed the other bands most was their attitude, their swagger, their insouciance - they were cool in a way that Gerry and his monogrammed blazers could only dream of.

If you talk to Hamburg musicians and their contemporaries, they refer to the music as the Hamburg sound and not the Liverpool sound. Kingsize Taylor, who spent more time in Germany than most, says: "People think they are listening to the Liverpool sound, but what they actually hear is the Hamburg sound, because that is where it was created." Whatever, when the music returned to Liverpool, it was to change again, especially under Brian Epstein's tutelage.

The archetypal Mersey Beat group came to be three to five white males in their late teens or early twenties who dressed identically. Three electric guitars and drums was the standard line-up but both Howie Casey and Brian Jones of the Undertakers played sax. Pianos were rare because it was impossible to carry one around the clubs, electric keyboards weren't available, and the pianos at the venues were of indifferent quality - the Cavern's, defying the odds, was okay. Les Maguire and Sam Hardie did the best they could for The Pacemakers and The Dominoes respectively. The rhythm guitarist drove the beat along while the drummer often stomped every beat in the bar simultaneously on kick-bass, snare and hi-hat, a habit often acquired in Hamburg, but instrumental numbers and drum solos were rare. The lead singer was usually supported by two harmony singers and, in many groups - including the Beatles - the lead vocals were shared. Even after the popularity of Mersey Beat, most of the groups from other cities concentrated on one lead singer.

The song itself was either a group original or a cover from an early 60s black American R&B act, in which case the overall sound was smoother than the original. The Animals from Newcastle might add rough edges but the Mersey groups never did. Mostly the bands sang in pseudo-American accents, but their Scouse accents could show through (e.g. the Merseybeats' delightful "wear your hur just for hur" during 'Wishin' And Hopin''). The performance was usually jaunty, the verses and the choruses were melodic, and the subject-matter was usually unconsummated heterosexual love.

Some groups would be Mersey Beat no matter what they did. Gerry and the Pacemakers' 'You'll Never Walk Alone' was a Mersey Beat record, despite the fact that the song came from *Carousel*. The best example of the genre are the two Oriole albums, *This Is Mersey Beat*, recorded in Liverpool at the Rialto Ballroom, though without an audience.

On the other hand, no one calls *Sgt. Pepper* a Mersey Beat LP and the Beatles' previous album *Revolver* probably falls outside the definition too. There was a time limit on Merseybeat; it ends around 1966. None of the other Liverpool musicians followed the Beatles on their passage to India.

11. Sixties pop music developed from white boys discovering the blues.

Not in Liverpool, it didn't.

Many Mersey Beat musicians will tell you about seeing Eddie Cochran, Bill Haley or Buddy Holly in Liverpool, but none of them saw Muddy Waters on Merseyside in 1958. The audience there consisted of jazz and blues fans and the fledging rock'n'rollers didn't attend. This is indicative of Mersey Beat music as a whole as there were no blues bands and few groups included any blues songs in their repertoires. The Roadrunners were the only contemporaries of the Beatles who regularly performed blues tracks, although the Mojos – who didn't start playing until 1964 – also included several such numbers in their set. Although the Liverpool groups covered around 300 American sourced cover versions, the only blues numbers among them were Muddy Waters' 'Got My Mojo Working'- done naturally enough by the Mojos - and Sonny Boy Williamson's 'Good Morning Little Schoolgirl' by Ian and the Zodiacs.

The Rolling Stones and the Yardbirds in London, the Animals in Newcastle, Them in Belfast and numerous other bands in most of the UK's cities concentrated on the blues, so why did the music bypass Liverpool? Probably because it bypassed The Beatles, and other groups followed like sheep. The Beatles preferred the more commercial side of black American music. They liked the pop R&B records by the Drifters and the Shirelles with their songs from young Brill Building writers. Songs like 'Save The Last Dance For Me' and 'Will You Still Love Me Tomorrow' appeared more sophisticated than the blues and so it would appear old hat to be singing the blues. Also, blues was very much a black man's music and they may have felt they could not do it justice. There was a ongoing debate during the 1960s, usually summed up as "Can white men sing the blues?", over the merits of stars like Eric Clapton and Peter Green. The white kids presumably won, as no one asks the question now.

Pete Best has told us that The Beatles occasionally performed the blues in Hamburg, but this was more expediency than anything else: if you have to play for an hour in the wee small hours, it may be easiest to get a blues riff going - and keep it going for ten minutes. Indeed, the Big Three used to write blues on the spot.

But there was also a feeling that the blues was going to die out. There were few new American bluesmen and the existing performers were getting older. As it happened, the blues impressed a whole generation of twenty-something white guitarists in the mid-60s and their playing alerted numerous fans to the original sources. But George Harrison's style owed much more to the rockabilly picking of Carl Perkins.

Today there is a healthy blues scene in Liverpool with Robert Cray, Guy Davis, Keb' Mo' and Eric Bibb all performing in the city recently. In 2002 B.B. King played to 4,000 fans at the Summer Pops in Liverpool. The blues has many more fans now in Liverpool than it ever had in the 60s.

12. The Merseyside groups got their songs from the 'Cunard Yanks', Liverpool sailors who brought back the records from New York.

The origins of the Cunard Yanks lie in the 1930s. The sailors on the cruise ships from Liverpool to New York would bring home dance band and jazz records from America. There were gramophone societies in Liverpool where such records would be regularly played. Both during the war and afterwards, the American forces stationed at Burtonwood brought over records that found their way into the local population.

In the mid-1950s, most of the significant American rock'n'roll records were issued in the UK, but jazz, blues and country music fans were poorly served and they would look to either the Cunard Yanks or to individuals, like Harold Culling, who specialised in importing records. John McNally of The Searchers remembers his brother bringing home country records from his travels in America - not, you note, rock'n'roll.

The first British rock'n'roll singers relied heavily on cover versions - Cliff Richard, Billy Fury, Adam Faith and Marty Wilde recorded scores of them, and they weren't averse to covering Elvis and being compared, usually unfavourably, to him. Some reasonable rock'n'roll writers emerged in the UK - Ian Samwell, Jerry Lordan, Johnny Worth, Lionel Bart (for a time) and Billy Fury himself - but, by and large, their songs supplemented the cover versions. Quite often the Brits covered obscure American records - the originals of 'Don't Bug Me Baby' (Milton Allen / Cliff Richard), 'Wondrous Place' (Jimmy Jones / Billy Fury), 'Ah, Poor Little Baby' (Crash Craddock / Adam Faith) and 'Love Bug Crawl' (Jimmy Edwards / Marty Wilde) are as obscure as anything found by the Mersey Beat groups. The British rock'n'roll artists were not, on the whole, seeking out these obscure records - rather they were relying on London music publishers to push decent songs their way. Amazingly, Cliff Richard recorded the first version of 'I Gotta Know', later recorded by Elvis Presley.

The Mersey Beat groups needed large repertoires, especially if they were performing for several hours a night in Hamburg. As they did not have recording contracts at first, their songs came from records, usually American ones. They did not, however, come from the Cunard Yanks. We cannot find a single example of a song that was performed by a Liverpool group at the time, being released in America but not in the UK.

Brian Epstein insisted that NEMS was very well stocked and he would order at least one copy of every single released in the UK. The Beatles and other groups would be able to hear these songs in the listening booths at NEMS and might have scribbled down the lyrics. They would often be covering songs that they didn't even possess, and this explains why the performances are sometimes so wayward. The best-ever example comes from Cavern regulars, Herman's Hermits, tackling 'Walkin' With My Angel' - listen to the middle eight carefully and you will realise that Peter Noone is slurring the lyrics because he is clueless about the words on the Bobby Vee original. The Big Three didn't sing the correct words on 'Some Other Guy' and Derry Wilkie has the sun coming up in the evening during 'Hallelujah I Love Her So'.

On the whole, the Liverpool groups seemed to like to cover fairly obscure tracks which had not made the UK charts, and to a large extent, in this, they were following The Beatles' lead. Arthur Alexander's repertoire is a good example here with 'Anna (Go To Him)', 'A Shot Of Rhythm And Blues', 'Soldier Of Love' and 'You Better Move On' all covered by The Beatles. He never had a UK hit but the songs *were* all released here. Similarly, The Shirelles' 'Boys', 'Baby It's You', 'Everybody Loves A Lover' and 'It's Love That Really Counts' were all covered and even though none had originally been hits in Britain they were all released as singles here. ('Boys' was the B-side to their only UK top twenty hit 'Will You Love Me Tomorrow'). Chan Romero's 'Hippy Hippy Shake' only sold a few hundred copies in the UK when released on the EMI imprint Columbia label in 1959 (*Record Collector* magazine currently rates an original copy in mint condition to be worth £60 – almost double that of an original red label 'Love Me Do') but Bob Wooler had one and played it relentlessly at the Cavern, leading to a 1963 Top 10 single for The Swingin' Blue Jeans.

Yet the myth of the Cunard Yanks persists. Liverpool playwright Alan Bleasdale voiced this belief in a recent BBC radio documentary. And a T.V. documentary, *Who Put The Beat In MerseyBeat?*, screened by Granada TV in 1995, went to great lengths to emphasise the importance of black culture in Liverpool. It was espousing a fashionable view but there were few black musicians amongst the beat groups, and rock n' roll and R&B were not being performed in the black clubs around Toxteth. The black musicians looked down on rock n' roll and favoured jazz

One of the authors [SL] has personal experience which further debunks this myth. He bought many US R&B records, usually from NEMS, yet he never knew a sailor.

It's a good, romantic story that's persisted for more than forty years but it remains untrue.

13. Bob Dylan introduced the Beatles to drugs.

Up until the 1960s, there was very little trade in illegal drugs in the UK and addicts were few and far between. The activity was largely confined to poets and jazz musicians and took place mostly in London. Adrian Barber of Cass and the Cassanovas and The Big Three had experience of certain drugs in London, but found none in Liverpool. Even when the Liverpool beat scene was under way, very few people were involved. When the London blues singer Alexis Korner collapsed at the Cavern before making a live album in 1964, his band said he needed drugs and the attempts of the organisers to find something in Liverpool shows how alien they were to the drug world.

Talking of his childhood to Hunter Davies in 1968, John Lennon said, "I would find myself seeing these hallucinatory images of my face changing, and the eyes would get bigger and the room would vanish", which suggests that he could put himself into a trance at will

When the beat poet Royston Ellis came to Liverpool in 1960, he befriended the would-be Beatles and showed them how to extract and swallow the benzedrine strips from Vick inhalers. This information comes from an interview with Ellis for the 1964 book, *Generation X* (Tandem 1964), but he does not risk the allegation that The Beatles practised this. When writing *Backbeat*, one of the authors [AC] obtained confirmation from Pauline Sutcliffe that they did try it, but this, the equivalent to glue-sniffing, would appear to be their solitary experiment in getting high before they went to Hamburg in August 1960.

In Hamburg, the Beatles were contracted to play for several hours, night after night and they were soon dog-tired. They quickly learnt that they needed stimulants and they took the slimming pills Preludin or Captigun to achieve this. Taken on their own these would suppress the appetite, but taken with beer, they would release enormous reserves of energy for 12 hours or more. Adrenalin would pour into the system, confidence would increase and you would talk and talk. You lost your inhibitions, though John Lennon didn't have many to lose.

The Liverpool bands came back to Liverpool with these pep pills. Bob Wooler recalled: "I left the table at the Black Rose club one afternoon and when I got back, there were two pills floating in my drink. I said, 'What's that?' and Lennon said, 'Oh, give it here' and knocked it back. It was two Preludin tablets and they had brought them back from Germany. Preludin was a slimming tablet really, an amphetamine that suppressed the appetite and you stayed up all night. You became very active, and I did experiment with them. They came in metal tubes and I used to say to them, 'Anyone travelling by tube tonight?'"

Wooler also recalls a stronger drug: "There was a rare instance of cocaine when Davy Jones, a little coloured rock'n'roll singer who'd been with the Beatles in Hamburg, appeared at the Cavern. He was a Little Richard / Derry Wilkie type, very outgoing and bouncy. His big record was an oldie, 'Amapola', and its lyric about the 'pretty little poppy' must have appealed to him. Alan Ross, who was a local compère, brought Davy down to the Cavern, and that was when I had cocaine for the first and only time in my life. I told Davy Jones about my sinuses, and he said, 'This'll clear it.' Alan Ross gave me a smile of approval, I tried it…and nearly hit the roof. There was laughter galore, and I rushed out into Mathew Street, trying to breathe the effects out. I remember Pat Delaney on the door saying, 'What's wrong, Robert?' and I said, 'Nothing, I'm just a bit giddy.' The Beatles welcomed Davy Jones with open arms, so I'm sure the drug-taking didn't stop with me. That is the common factor with the Beatles - whatever was going, they wanted to be part of it."

The first time that John Lennon smoked a reefer was at a basement flat in Bayswater. The actress and Hill's Angel, Cherri Gilham, was there and she remembers John Lennon puking in the bath when it didn't agree with him. Then The Beatles tried marijuana as a group at a party at Brian Epstein's flat in Knightsbridge late in 1963.

It wasn't until early the following year that they met Bob Dylan in a hotel in New York. He suggested that they should smoke some pot. They said that they weren't used to it. Dylan was surprised: "What about your song? The one about getting high?" Dylan had misheard "I can't hide, I can't hide, I can't hide" as "I get high, I get high, I get high." The party got under way and The Beatles got high with a little help from their friend, as Paul McCartney describes in *Many Years From Now*. They became regular users, making most of their second film, *Help!*, under its influence. They needed to - it was such a nonsensical script.

Also in 1964, Timothy Leary's supplier, Michael Hollingshead, brought the first samples of LSD to the UK. He gave some to Victor Lownes who ran the Playboy Club. The girl who supervised the bunnies at the club was dating a dentist, who had George Harrison as a patient. The dentist asked Lownes for some hits for The Beatles. At a dinner party, John, Cynthia, George and Patti were given spiked coffee. The dentist told them not to leave his flat and John assumed an orgy was about to take place. They insisted on leaving, and the dentist followed George who was driving them in his Aston-Martin. A chase ensued with George pulling up at the Pickwick Club. John experienced some strange effects and the girls wanted to sleep. They left again for George's house where John had 'the horrors'. He had thought he could counter the effects by taking speed and he had dreams of a submarine floating over walls – an image that came in useful later.

In 1965 Lennon dropped acid again, this time with Peter Fonda at Mulholland Drive in Los Angeles. Fonda kept saying, "I know what it's like to be dead", which found its way into the song, 'She Said She Said'. Lennon was still having bad experiences but then he learnt how to control it by reading one of Timothy Leary's books. Some of Leary's words were used in his psychedelic prayer, 'Tomorrow Never Knows', and also in 'I'm Only Sleeping', an evocation of his lifestyle when he wasn't touring.

14. The Beatles made their debut at the Cavern on a Swinging Blue Jeans guest night on 21st March 1961.

The Cavern had opened as a jazz venue in January 1957. Rock'n'roll was forbidden but skiffle was tolerated as the owner Alan Sytner recalls: "There were hundreds of skiffle and blues groups in the country, the Lonnie Donegan factor was mega, so on Wednesdays I put on a competition for local talent. It encouraged kids who were learning to play, and I would have a couple of more accomplished groups who could play. These kids did the Lonnie Donegan, Dickie Bishop and Johnny Duncan repertoires and they were all pretty awful. Talent night was no talent as far as I was concerned but I wasn't being altruistic as skiffle was very commercial."

The Quarry Men played the Cavern when it was a jazz venue on Wednesday, 7 August, 1957. It was a skiffle session featuring Ron McKay's Skiffle Group, The Dark Town Skiffle Group, The Deltones Skiffle Group and The Demon Five. John Lennon was the lead singer with The Quarry Men but although Paul had joined the group, he was away at scout camp. Their drummer was Colin Hanton: "We did some skiffle numbers to start off with but we also did rock'n'roll. John was passed a note and he said to the audience, 'We've had a request.' He opened it up and it was a note from Alan Sytner saying, 'Cut out the bloody rock'n'roll.'"

The next time, billed as the Quarry Men Skiffle Group, they played at the Cavern on 24 January 1958 alongside The Merseysippi Jazz Band. Both John and Paul were in the line-up. Jazz critic Steve Voce: "We disliked skiffle with almost the same contempt that we disliked rock'n'roll. I didn't like Lonnie Donegan in the least, but he saw an opening and seized it. The only reason that skiffle was tolerated at the Cavern was because it made some money for some jazz musicians whom we were sympathetic to. The genuine skiffle music - Big Bill Broonzy, Blind Lemon Jefferson, the people from the '20s - was marvellous, but the later thing was a fraud."

Alan Sytner: "Skiffle was a breeding ground for musicians - one or two of them became jazz musicians, but more ended up doing rock. Lennon and McCartney were there, I know that because I had a girlfriend at the art college who was in the same class as John, and she persuaded me to let them play and they were diabolical. I knew John Lennon quite well as we lived in the same area: he lived 400 yards up the road from me. They were 16 and arrogant and they hadn't got a clue, but that was John Lennon, and no doubt Paul McCartney caught it from him. John Lennon was considered a huge personality at the art college by all the kids and Ann told me that he would like to play. They'd only been playing for a short while so you wouldn't expect them to be any good but they became world class, the best. At the time, they couldn't play to save their lives and all I can remember is their cheek and their chat."

With the Cavern under new ownership, The Beatles played a lunchtime session there on 9 February, 1961. Their appearance had not been advertised and they received £5. They were immediately successful and further dates followed on 21 and 28 February, and 6, 8, 10, 13, 14, 15, 16 and 20 March. On Tuesday, 21 March, 1961 they supported the Swinging Blue Jeans on their guest night along with the Remo Four and Dale Roberts and the Jaywalkers. It marked the first *evening* appearance of John, Paul and George as The Beatles at the Cavern, but most Beatle books list this as their first Cavern appearance as The Beatles. The club's DJ, Bob Wooler, recalled: "The Blue Jeans played a mixture of pop and traditional jazz tunes then, and they were very popular. Indeed, I was most impressed with the Swinging Blue Jeans as a jazz band. They had an upright, string bass and they played at a lower volume than they did later. There was none of the stridency of 'Good Golly Miss Molly' when they performed 'Down By The Riverside'. Ray McFall allowed them to choose whomever they wanted for their Tuesday guest nights and they invited Dale Roberts and the Jaywalkers, The Remo Four and The Four Jays - groups that wouldn't clash or be more popular than themselves. One night Ray McFall put The Beatles on with them, a good move for the Cavern, but The Beatles' fans swamped The Blue Jeans' fans. The Blue Jeans were not happy and there were altercations between their leader, Ray Ennis and Ray McFall at the top of the steps to the Cavern. Ray Ennis said, 'We're not having them on with us again.' Ray McFall liked The Beatles and he was also thinking of his receipts, so shortly afterwards the Blue Jeans went elsewhere."

Wooler continued: "There was a short period at the Cavern where beat groups would be billed alongside jazz bands. It was a strange combination and it wasn't clear for whom Ray McFall was catering. Ray would book the jazz bands, who would say it was no use to be on such a bill. The jazz element became disenchanted with the Cavern and so the club turned completely to rock. Some of the jazzmen now say, 'Oh, I knew right away that The Beatles were going to be stars.' Absolute rubbish. I have heard the country singer Hank Walters talking on BBC Radio Merseyside about how he enjoying playing alongside The Beatles - more rubbish. His attitude was, 'Do we have to suffer this lot?' Fair-weather friends, or what?"

Three members of the Merseysippi Jazz Band were asked what they remembered about The Beatles. Don Lydiatt: "Very little - about as much as they remember about us, I should think. The pseudo-skiffle cum beat groups came on in the interval and we beat it out to the Beaconsfield for a drink. They were just another young group coming up."

Ken Baldwin: "I wasn't really aware of local beat music until they started these shows at the New Brighton Tower and they must have put on half a dozen groups at a time. I can't really criticise the groups because they were pinching American songs just like us, but at the time we never bothered listening to them. It was electric noise and we were very much against that. We were so anti-beat music that we never stopped to speak to them and ask them how they were doing."

John Lawrence: "I remember with some embarrassment that when we came off stage to go to the pub and they came on stage, we never spoke to each other. We had a barely-concealed contempt for each other. We were older than they were and later on John Lennon described us as the old buggers who didn't want them on stage, which was correct. We lived in different worlds." In 2003, some 40 years on, those old buggers still have a weekly residency in Liverpool, with four original members in their line-up.

15. Mass unemployment was the underlying factor for the large number of beat groups in Liverpool.

Liverpool is depicted in the media as a city of unemployment and union strife. The Communist newspaper, *Daily Worker*, wrote a much-quoted editorial in 1963 in which it stated that Mersey Beat had been born out of unemployment. The thinking was that all these lads were on the dole, bored out of their skulls with nothing to do, and so they turned to music.

A plausible theory - but far from the truth. There was plenty of work around Liverpool in the early 60s, so much that you could give two fingers to your boss on the Friday and walk into a new job on the Monday. The vast majority of musicians around Liverpool had day jobs and it was a major issue for them as to whether to go professional. One reason that The Beatles got so many bookings including numerous lunchtime sessions at the Cavern was because they didn't have day jobs. John Lennon was at the Liverpool College of Art, Paul McCartney was in the sixth form and Pete Best didn't otherwise work. George Harrison was a trainee electrician at Blackler's Department Store in the city centre, but he gave it up to go to Scotland on the Johnny Gentle tour. In 1960 Ringo Starr gave up his apprenticeship at Henry Hunt's climbing frames to play a summer season at Butlin's, Pwllheli, as part of Rory Storm and the Hurricanes. None of the jazz bands had been professional and so The Beatles and The Hurricanes were Liverpool's first fully professional groups.

Gerry Marsden worked at British Railways, but he and the Pacemakers gave up their day jobs to do lunchtime sessions at the Cavern. Otherwise, the groups kept their jobs until the last minute. The Coasters wanted to stay at work and Brian Epstein had to find another group to back Billy J. Kramer.

Dave Lovelady of The Fourmost says: "We were the second group that Brian Epstein asked to go professional but we turned him down because we were students. Brian O'Hara was studying accountancy, Billy Hatton was with the Atomic Energy Authority and Mike Millward was with a solicitor. We turned Brian Epstein down three times. Six months later he asked us again. By this time Gerry and Billy had had Number 1s. We realised that this wasn't a flash in the pan, so we agreed. If we'd said yes immediately, we would have been second in line and maybe we would have been given the songs that Gerry got."

Les Braid of The Swinging Blue Jeans recalls: "We were working six nights a week. We were resident in the Cavern, and in the Downbeat, and in the Tower Ballroom in New Brighton. I worked for the Corporation and I had to be at work at a quarter to eight in the morning. Very often I never got home until half past one. We did this for two and a half years before we went professional and I was so tired during the day that I don't know how I managed to get through the work. One day I was sent to the Town Hall to do a job on the door of the main ballroom. I was half asleep as usual. The door was catching on the carpet, and so I had to kneel down to repair the broken hinge. I thought, 'This carpet feels nice and comfortable,' and I fell asleep on the floor. When I woke up I carried on with the job and went home."

Ironically, the rise in Liverpool music in the 1980s *was* born out of unemployment. People used their time on the dole to practice their music and it was even possible to get a government grant in some circumstances.

By this time, Pete Best was working for the Government employment scheme, Restart. When a person who had lost his job came to the Restart offices, he would be told, "Pete Best will see you." "Whatever they'd been through," said Pete, "They knew I'd been through it as well."

16. There was no such person as Raymond Jones, the lad who came into NEMS and asked Brian Epstein for 'My Bonnie'.

While The Beatles had been in Hamburg, they had recorded a single with vocalist Tony Sheridan. It was a rock n' roll version of the standard 'My Bonnie' and was released by the German label, Polydor, credited to Tony Sheridan and the Beat Brothers. Pete Best remembers: "We gave a copy of 'My Bonnie' to Bob Wooler and asked him to play it, either at the Aintree Institute or Litherland Town Hall. It sounded good to hear our record coming out of the speakers alongside the American stuff." Local fans who heard the record also wanted to own it. A key factor in The Beatles' story is that an 18-year-old lad called Raymond Jones went into NEMS in Whitechapel in October 1961 and asked for 'My Bonnie', which would have needed to of been imported. But there are conflicting stories about whether this actually happened.

Alistair Taylor worked for Brian Epstein at NEMS as his personal assistant. In 1997 Raymond Jones was listed as one of the guests at the Penny Lane Beatles Festival. When he was introduced to speak, Taylor stood up and said "I am Raymond Jones". He has repeated this on several occasions since, notably on the Brian Epstein *Arena* special. According to Taylor, people were asking for 'My Bonnie' but Brian wouldn't order it until he had a definite order in the stock-book. Taylor said, "It was me. I ordered The Beatles' record for Brian".

Alistair Taylor wrote his autobiography (*Yesterday - The Beatles Remembered*, Sidgwick And Jackson) in 1988, but he doesn't identify himself as Raymond Jones in that.

Sam Leach, the Liverpool impresario and associate of Brian Epstein, claims in his book *The Rocking City* that he was the one who told Brian about The Beatles, but Brian didn't want to acknowledge his presence. Sam says: "If I was the reason Brian went to see the lads for the first time, he would never have admitted it. He would invent a fictitious character instead and my own opinion is that Raymond Jones was a figment of Brian's imagination."

Well, Raymond Jones does exist. He owned a printing company in Burscough, which is now run by his son and daughter, as he has now retired and lives in a farmhouse in Spain. One of the authors (SL) spoke to him in recent years and learnt that he was a shy person who has never been interested in Beatles Conventions and he is disgusted that people are claiming to be him. He says: "I never wanted to do anything to make money out of The Beatles because they have given me so much pleasure. I saw them every dinner time at the Cavern and they were fantastic. I had never heard anything like them. Everybody had been listening to Lonnie Donegan and Cliff Richard and they were so different. A friend of mine, Ron Billingsley, had a motorbike and we would follow them all over the place - Hambleton Hall, Aintree Institute and Knotty Ash Village Hall."

How did he come to be talking to Brian Epstein? "I used to go to NEMS every Saturday and I would be buying records by Carl Perkins and Fats Domino because I heard The Beatles playing their songs. My sister's ex-husband, Kenny Johnson, who played with Mark Peters and the Cyclones, told me that The Beatles had made a record and so I went to NEMS to get it. Brian Epstein said to me, 'Who are they?' and I said, 'They are the most fantastic group you will ever hear.' No one will take away from me that it was me who spoke to Brian Epstein and then he went to the Cavern to see them for himself. I didn't make them famous, but Brian Epstein made them famous and things might have been different without me."

Brian Epstein knew The Beatles' name through the banner headlines in *Mersey Beat*, but he had not shown any interest in them before Jones's intervention. Although Raymond Jones was heterosexual, no doubt Eppy was entranced that such a good-looking boy should be following the Beatles and he determined to find out about them for himself.

By the way, this Raymond Jones should not be confused with another Raymond Jones, a Manchester lad who played with The Dakotas.

17. Because his word was his bond, Brian Epstein never signed his management contract with the Beatles.

Late in 1961 Brian Epstein met The Beatles at his NEMS office in Whitechapel to discuss management and the need for a contract. The Beatles had not been taking his offer of management too seriously as three of them were late, Paul McCartney by a full half-hour as he was taking a bath. George Harrison remarked that Paul would be "late but very clean". Brian stressed the need for something official and John said, "Give us something to sign, Eppy, and we'll sign it."

Brian Epstein asked his neighbour, the solicitor Rex Makin, to draw up an unbreakable contract for himself with The Beatles, but Makin said that this was impossible and he didn't draft anything for him. Makin tried to talk Brian out of it but Brian went to another solicitor, David Harris, who drew up the necessary paperwork.

On 24 January 1962 Epstein met The Beatles - John, Paul, George and Pete - at the Casbah Coffee Club to have it signed. Epstein's personal assistant, Alistair Taylor, witnessed the signatures of all four Beatles. According to Taylor's book, *A Secret History*, Epstein told Taylor to witness his signature and he would sign it later.

The contract ran from 1 February 1962 for five years and it gave Epstein 10% on income under £1,500 per annum for each Beatle and if it exceeded that, he received 15%. Either side could get out of the contract by giving three months' notice, so it was not unbreakable.

The contract itself has never been published, except for the closing signatures. There is a space where Epstein's signature should be and although it has been witnessed by Alistair Taylor, it was not signed by Brian Epstein. Epstein realised that he could use this to his advantage, reprinting it in his autobiography *A Cellarful Of Noise* and giving conflicting reasons for it not being signed. Firstly, The Beatles would not be bound to him if they lost confidence in him (but didn't he want an unbreakable contract?), and secondly, his word alone was sufficient. In which case, why weren't The Beatles' words alone sufficient? The 'Man who gave The Beatles away', Allan Williams, had warned Epstein about their unreliability and he believes that Epstein didn't sign the contract so that he could walk away from them if he wished to later on.

However, as Rex Makin now astutely points out, we have only seen one copy of the contract, presumably Brian's (as it was reproduced in his book) and the Beatles would have had their own copies, which Brian would have undoubtedly signed. It would not have made a difference to him if his own copy didn't have his own signature on it.

On 1 October 1962, just prior to the release of 'Love Me Do', another management contract, which would cover the next five years, was signed by Epstein and The Beatles. Maybe it was to clarify matters with the new line-up of John, Paul, George and Ringo, but it also increased his earnings to 25%. This was high, but a long way from Colonel Parker's 50% from Elvis Presley's earnings.

18. Pete Best was sacked because he was too good looking.

The sacking of Pete Best is a mystery worthy of Agatha Christie and we have never been given the full story. Pete Best has written his autobiography (three times!) but a person who is being sacked never knows what is being said behind his back. Brian Epstein put a Blairite spin on the issue, and the other Beatles, probably because they were ashamed of what they had done (or at least the way they had done it), have only made a few, conflicting comments.

The comparison with Agatha Christie is apt because in *Murder On The Orient Express*, the passengers on the train, for a variety of different motives, take their turns at stabbing the victim, most of them not knowing that he was already dead. Similarly, no single issue seems to have sealed Pete's fate. Instead, there was a combination of factors, some of which weighed heavier with the different individuals than others. So what did John, Paul, George Harrison, Brian Epstein and George Martin dislike about Pete, and why?

Whether The Beatles like it or not, most people think that Pete Best was sacked from The Beatles because he was too good-looking. There's no question of that - look at any picture of the early Beatles and you are drawn to Pete's face. But let's look at the evidence.

Pete had plenty of girlfriends, but the others also did well and indeed John had just married Cynthia. It might have annoyed The Beatles that the girls cried out for Pete at their shows, but they could surely see that would only benefit the group as a whole. Brian Epstein would have been pleased by the reaction and although Pete knocked back his sexual overtures, it would not have bothered him as he was knocked back with some regularity. If sexual rejection disqualified a performer from a business relationship, Brian would never have taken on Billy J. Kramer, or possibly even John Lennon.

Another criticism is that he didn't fit in with The Beatles. Sure, he was quiet, but so was George and in any event, you can't have four garrulous members in one group. If quietness were a crime, the Rolling Stones would have sacked Charlie Watts. Les Chadwick, like George Harrison, was quiet and studious about his music and an unlikely companion for Gerry Marsden, yet he fitted perfectly into Gerry and the Pacemakers. John, Paul and George had been with Pete for two years, including several months in Hamburg, and Pete had no inkling that anything was wrong. He didn't have a Beatles haircut, because he had curly hair and Astrid Kirchherr couldn't do anything with it, but this was hardly his fault.

A more damning reason is the quality of his drumming. Pete was a good rock'n'roll drummer and was excellent on their 1961 single with Tony Sheridan, 'My Bonnie', but he lacked versatility and was known to play the same pattern, either slow or fast depending on the speed of the song. John Lennon may not have wanted to stray from rock'n'roll, but Paul McCartney was constantly trying show songs and standards and may have noticed his limitations. Furthermore, the drums and bass are closely wedded as the foundation of a band's sound and so he would have been acutely aware of what Pete was doing.

Bob Wooler, the DJ at the Cavern, recalls: "The Beatles used to play the Cavern at lunchtimes and sometimes they would stay behind and rehearse, and just myself and the cleaners would hear them. One day I came back from the Grapes about ten past three and The Beatles were rehearsing. Paul was showing Pete Best how he wanted the drums to be played for a certain tune and I thought, 'That's pushing it a bit.' At times Pete would be like a zombie on the drums: it was as though he was saying, 'Do I have to do this?' and that went against him with Paul McCartney, who was all for communication. Pete had no show about him - he always looked bored - but he certainly came alive for photo sessions as he was very photogenic." When Clive Gregson caught The Pete Best Band in Nashville, Pete was looking at his watch – one can only imagine how behaviour like that would have gone down with the ultimate showman, Paul McCartney.

The Beatles' first session for EMI is on the first *Anthology* set. They play 'Love Me Do' and Pete Best was having a bad day as it sounds like he is playing bin-lids, especially in the instrumental break. If this is all George Martin heard, then no wonder he thought he couldn't be on the single. He was quite happy to use a session drummer, but the fact that Pete Best might be getting in the way of John and Paul and success may have sealed his fate with them.

Accustomed to on-stage inconsistencies of tempo caused by the mood of the hour, drummers were the most prone to substitution in the studio. "The reasons were purely financial," elucidated Clem Cattini of the Tornados and a regular session drummer, "You were expected to complete four tracks in three hours. An inexperienced group might need a week to do two titles, not because they were incapable but because sessions are quite different to being on the road. You can't get away with so much. You need more discipline." Having someone ghost Pete Best's drumming might compound the doubts, justified and otherwise, that the others had about him.

Ringo Starr was one of George Harrison's best friends and naturally George would have been delighted to have his mate in the band. At the time, it was not known that Ringo would be that much better as he only played in a band that was regarded as a musical joke, Rory Storm and the Hurricanes.

Before Brian Epstein, Pete Best's mother, Mona, had handled The Beatles' bookings. She wanted Brian to do his best for the group and, in particular, for Pete. She was constantly calling him and asking him about what he had in mind. Mrs. Best was a formidable opponent and maybe Brian had had enough of it. Mrs. Best, for the best of intentions, might have sealed her son's fate.

The West End play about The Beatles in Hamburg, *Presence* by David Harrower (2001), suggested that Pete actually wanted to leave as he was fed up playing in Hamburg:

Pete: I'm leaving in the morning.

Paul: And what about the rest of us?

Pete: You can do what you want.

Paul: No, you don't understand. We can't do without a drummer. If you go, we can't play. Then they really will sack us.

Pete: I don't care.

Paul: That's your problem, Pete. You should care about us.

Pete: Fuck off.

Paul: What will you tell them back home? Back on your own?

Pete: It didn't work out.

Paul: 'Cause I'll them them you up and left us. Deserted us. Ruined our chances just as we're getting going. That you can't be trusted one fucking inch. And you don't want that, do you, Pete? Everyone back home knowing that. No one will have you, will they? No one will want you. So I'd unpack the bag if I was you. It's only six weeks more. And as soon as we're on British soil, we'll kick you out.

It may be fiction, but it does have a ring of truth about it.

Bob Wooler also said: "It was very wrong of The Beatles to suggest on the *Anthology* video that Pete Best was unreliable - well, they didn't suggest it, they stated it and it is largely untrue to say that. The most unreliable Beatle was Paul McCartney, who had the worst punctuality record, although he was not consistently late for engagements. I would say to Paul at the Aintree Institute, 'You've missed the middle spot and you'll have to go on last', which is going home time. He'd say, 'Sorry, I was busy writing a song.' That didn't impress me at the time as I had a show to put on." Also, on the *Anthology* video, George said it was karma that Ringo was meant to be with The Beatles. This may be so but it was hardly a thought he would have had in 1962.

The Beatles had sacked people before - John smashed a washboard over Pete Shotton's head to dismiss him from the Quarry Men - so why did they ask Brian to do it? Probably because they were ashamed of what they were doing. Perhaps John was distracted as he was marrying Cynthia, and Paul, who wanted to be rid of Pete, seized the moment. Even though The Beatles would still come across Pete at subsequent shows, they didn't speak to him and even now, they haven't made contact.

There are other, even more complicating factors. When The Beatles returned from Hamburg in June 1962, Neil Aspinall left his job as a trainee accountant and became their full-time roadie. He was very friendly with Pete Best and had lodgings in Hayman's Green with the Best family. He made Mona Best pregnant and she gave birth to a son, Roag, on 21 July 1962. When Pete was sacked from The Beatles, he told Neil he would have to leave the house if he was to continue with The Beatles. Neil was effectively being deprived of seeing his son. This is a situation worthy of *The Jerry Springer Show*. Apart from the situation with the band, if your best friend was having it off with your mother, surely he wouldn't be your best friend anymore?

Bill Harry, the editor of *Mersey Beat*, must have known of the tensions caused by Pete Best's sacking, but he was so taken with Brian Epstein that he accepted Eppy's press release and on 23 August 1962, his readers were told, "Pete Best left the group by mutual agreement. There were no arguments or difficulties, and this has been an entirely amicable decision." So much for investigative reporting.

19. Pete Best played a fairly insignificant role in the history of the Beatles.

Although Ringo is The Beatles' key drummer, we have calculated that John, Paul and George were more often on stage with Pete Best than with Ringo Starr.

The statistics for The Beatles' live shows for their time with Pete Best as their drummer are as follows:

Year	Appearances excluding Hamburg	Nights in Hamburg
1960	4	106
1961	247	98
1962	181	48
Totals	432	252

The statistics for The Beatles' live shows for their time with Ringo Starr as their drummer are as follows:

Year	Appearances excluding Hamburg	Nights in Hamburg
1962	101	27
1963	246	0
1964	118	0
1965	45	0

1966	21	0
1967	1	0
1968	0	0
1969	1	0
Totals	533	27

The totals have been taken by adding the daily gig listings in Mark Lewisohn's book, *The Beatles - Live!*, but some adjustments need to be made:

- The first of the *Anthology* TV programmes in 1996 suggested that Pete Best was unreliable, but there is no evidence to support this. Pete Best told me, "I only missed two gigs with them - one was when I had to go to court and the other was when I had flu. I missed the afternoon session at the Cavern, but I pulled myself out of my sickbed to turn up for the evening one, but to my knowledge they were the only two I missed." Ringo had sat in with The Beatles before he joined them and so these two performances could be allocated to him.

- Ringo Starr missed five shows in June 1964 when he had tonsillitis. Jimmy Nicol stood in as drummer. There is no evidence that Starr missed any other gigs.

- The Beatles spent 279 nights in Hamburg but did they play every one of those nights? The club-owners were hard taskmasters but did they work them that hard? In most instances, the clubs were shut on Mondays, thereby reducing the number of nights they played in Hamburg.

Drummer	Appearances excluding Hamburg	Nights in Hamburg	Total
Pete Best	430	216	646
Ringo Starr	530	23	553

On the face of it, therefore, our premise is true - Pete Best did play more gigs than Ringo Starr with The Beatles. But it's not that straightforward.

Many of The Beatles' appearances from 1963 to 1966 were as part of a touring package with two (and occasionally three) shows a night. Ringo's appearances could be increased by 233 as they would be playing to separate audiences, thus giving him a tally of 786 as opposed to 646.

However, this is an unfair bias towards Ringo, as The Beatles would be playing for four or five hours a night in Hamburg and there would be a different audience by the end of the evening (the under-21s had to leave at 10pm by law), so maybe the Hamburg figures should be doubled too, putting Pete back on top with 862 to 809. In addition, there would be other gigs in Hamburg when they sat in with Tony Sheridan.

Ringo Starr might object to the calculations on the grounds that this takes no account of the size of the audience. Unquestionably, the Ringo Starr version of The Beatles played to more people. Even a month in the Star-Club wouldn't top one 'sold out' night at the Shea Stadium.

Pete might respond that he played more hours on stage with The Beatles. Given the length of the Hamburg nights and the shortness of The Beatles' sets on concert appearances, this is unquestionably true. In the Pete Best period, it is reasonable to assume 90 minutes for a UK gig and 4 hours in Hamburg. With Ringo, it is an hour outside of Hamburg and 2 hours in Hamburg (as by then they were minor celebrities):

Drummer	Hours on stage excluding Hamburg	Hours on stage in Hamburg	Total
Pete Best	645	864	1,509
Ringo Starr	530	46	576

Pete Best, therefore, wins hands down for hours on stage.

Pete might also add that he played a bigger repertoire with The Beatles. This would be difficult to establish, but The Beatles had a repertoire of around 150 songs in the Pete Best days. Ringo joined when they were becoming a recording act and promoting their own songs. There are around 50 new songs that Ringo performed on stage with The Beatles. If he did not perform at least 100 of the old songs, then Pete would win. Given that The Beatles did shorter sets with Ringo and were obliged to do certain songs, it is more likely that The Beatles had a larger stage repertoire with Pete Best.

There are enough possible questions here that they could fill a book of their own. Did, for example, Ringo Starr spend more time on stage with Rory Storm and the Hurricanes than he did with The Beatles? In the end though Ringo is sure to have the last laugh. He had rather more recording sessions than Pete. And possibly earned more money...

20. George Martin chose 'Love Me Do' for The Beatles first single as John and Paul hadn't written anything better.

Before recording for Parlophone, John and Paul had around 100 original songs and considering the potential of several of them, it is surprising that they didn't play them for George Martin in 1962. We know that he considered 'Love Me Do' to be mediocre and yet they had far better compositions to hand. Mitch Murray: "I blush to say this, but George Martin liked 'How Do You Do It' and told them, 'When you can write songs as good as this, we'll record them.' I cringe just thinking of it now." Still, George Martin's comment might have been the impetus for 'Please Please Me'.

Everyone knows that John and Paul had a stockpile of songs at that time, but most people assume that there was nothing much of significance there. Paul McCartney made light of them on his *Unplugged* appearance in 1991 by performing, very much with tongue in cheek, the first song he ever wrote, 'I Lost My Little Girl'. However, The Beatles had written many fine songs before their Parlophone single in October 1962, and they could have told Martin that they had something to offer. For example…

HELLO LITTLE GIRL (Lennon)
John Lennon told *Playboy*, "That was me. That was my first song. I was fascinated by an old song called 'Scatterbrain' and my mother used to sing that one." The Beatles included the song in their audition for Decca Records.

Mitch Murray, writer of 'How Do You Do It', Gerry and the Pacemakers' first record and a No 1, says: "John Lennon had written 'Hello Little Girl' and given it to Gerry and the Pacemakers. He threatened to thump me if I got Gerry's follow-up. I did get it, that was 'I Like It', and I figured it was worth a thump." 'Hello Little Girl' was given to the Fourmost and was a Top 10 hit in 1963.

ONE AFTER 909 (Lennon)
John Lennon wrote this when he was 17. The Beatles did record it for the *Please Please Me* album but it wasn't released. It finally appeared in a new version on 1970's *Let It Be*.

I CALL YOUR NAME (Lennon)
John Lennon told *Playboy*, "That was my song. The first part had been written before Hamburg even. It was one of my first attempts at writing a song." The first recording was by Billy J. Kramer with The Dakotas on the B-side of his 1963 Number 1, 'Bad To Me'.

I SAW HER STANDING THERE (Mostly McCartney)
Paul McCartney wrote this song in 1961 and would have been a stronger choice for the first single: "Originally the first two lines were 'She was just seventeen, Never been a beauty queen'. When I played it through the next day to John, I realised that it was a useless rhyme and so did John. John came up with 'You know what I mean', which was much better."

WHEN I'M 64 (McCartney)
Paul McCartney: "I wrote that tune when I was about fifteen."
It's not clear when Paul added the lyric but, of course, it formed part of *Sgt. Pepper's Lonely Hearts Club Band*.

I'LL FOLLOW THE SUN (McCartney)
John Lennon: "That's Paul, written almost before The Beatles, I think."
Paul McCartney: "I remember writing that in our front living room at Forthlin Road on my own."
The song appeared on the 1964 LP, *Beatles For Sale*.

LOVE OF THE LOVED (McCartney)
John Lennon: "Paul's, written when he was a teenager."
The Beatles performed this at their Decca audition and it was a Top 30 hit for Cilla Black in 1963.

LIKE DREAMERS DO (McCartney)
John Lennon: "Paul's, another one he'd written as a teenager."
Also performed at the Decca audition, the song was passed to the Applejacks as their follow-up to 'Tell Me When' and it made the Top 20 in 1964.

A WORLD WITHOUT LOVE (McCartney)
John Lennon: "McCartney, and resurrected from his past. That has the line, 'Please lock me away', which we always used to crack up at." The song became a Number 1 for Peter and Gordon in 1964 and has been revived by the Mavericks. The songwriter Doc Pomus said it was his favourite Beatles' composition.

TIP OF MY TONGUE (McCartney)
John Lennon: "That's another piece of Paul's garbage, not my garbage." Tommy Quickly's first record.

YOU'LL BE MINE (Lennon - McCartney)
An affectionate parody of the Ink Spots, attributed to both writers on *Anthology 1* as distinct from 'Cayenne', which is solely credited to McCartney.

WHAT GOES ON (Lennon - McCartney - Starr)
John Lennon: "That was an early Lennon, written when we were the Quarry Men. And resurrected with a middle eight thrown in, probably with Paul's help, to give Ringo a song." Ringo is quoted in *Many Years From Now* as saying his contribution was "about five words". The song is on the 1965 LP, *Rubber Soul*.

LOVE ME DO (Lennon - McCartney)
Oddly enough, John and Paul differed over the composition of this one.
Paul McCartney: "'Love Me Do' was completely co-written. It might have been my original idea, but some of them really were 50-50 and I think that one was."
John Lennon: "Paul wrote the main structure of this when he was 16 or even earlier. I think I had something to do with the middle eight." In any event, his harmonica makes, and probably saves, the record.

P.S. I LOVE YOU (McCartney)
John Lennon: "That's Paul song. He was trying to write a 'Soldier Boy' like the Shirelles. I might have contributed something. I can't remember anything in particular."

PLEASE PLEASE ME (Lennon)
'Bing Helps Beatles Shock!'
JL: "That's my song completely. It was my attempt at writing a Roy Orbison song, would you believe? Also, I was intrigued by the Bing Crosby song, 'Please lend your little ears to my pleas', the double use of the word 'please'."

ASK ME WHY (Lennon - McCartney)
"This song was written in 1962 with John as the major contributor," says Ian MacDonald. "Though awkward, its lyric shows personal traces suggesting that Lennon might have had his wife Cynthia in mind."

So The Beatles had enough songs to make an excellent first album of original material. As well as the above, they also had 'I Lost My Little Girl' (McCartney's first composition and used on *Unplugged* in 1991), 'Cayenne' (a McCartney instrumental), 'Winston's Walk' (a Lennon instrumental), 'Cry For A Shadow' (a Lennon - Harrison instrumental, aping the Shadows), 'Suicide' (a McCartney composition that he later sent to Frank Sinatra, who thought, incorrectly, that he was taking the mick), 'Catswalk' (a McCartney instrumental, recorded in 1967 as 'Cat Call' by The Chris Barber Band) and 'In Spite Of All The Danger' (which they had recorded privately in Liverpool).

It is interesting to speculate why they agreed to a Lennon - McCartney arrangement in 1962 as many of their existing songs had been written separately. They possibly saw their future as writing together as a team, like Gerry Goffin and Carole King. However, there hadn't been a major songwriting team in British music since Gilbert and Sullivan. And where did this leave George Harrison? He had written with both of them individually and his material ('Cry For A Shadow' and 'In Spite Of All The Danger') is nothing to be ashamed of.

21. Ringo Starr did not play on 'Love Me Do'.

The Beatles passed their audition for the Parlophone label, but George Martin had decided that Pete Best wasn't up to it. In many of the Beatle books, it is said that he hired a session drummer for their first commercial session on the evening of Tuesday 4 September 1962. He didn't. John, Paul, George and Ringo recorded an original song, 'Love Me Do', and a new song that Martin wanted them to do, 'How Do You Do It'.

But Martin wasn't happy with the results. The Beatles sounded bored (which they were) on 'How Do You Do It' and the producer felt that the drum sound wasn't right on 'Love Me Do'. This may be as much Martin's fault as Ringo's as Martin wasn't used to recording rock'n'roll. He asked the group to return for a second session on the morning of Tuesday, 11 September.

Ringo was dismayed when he found Andy White ready to play drums on the session. The 32-year-old White was a regular session man at Abbey Road, and married to the chartmaker Lynn Cornell, formerly with the Liverpool vocal group, The Vernons Girls. He picked up £5.15.0d (£5.75) for the session. Ringo must have thought his days were numbered, as he struck a tambourine on 'Love Me Do' and played maracas on another original, 'P.S. I Love You'. At the end of the session, they played George Martin a new composition, 'Please Please Me'. He told them to work on it, suggesting they up the tempo.

A single of 'Love Me Do', backed with 'P.S. I Love You', was released on 5 October on the red Parlophone label (45-R 4949) and the first take, with Ringo on drums was used. A mint copy of that single is worth around £35 today. (But who knows when Eppy's 10,000 copies will come on to the market?) Early in 1963, the single was repressed on a black label using the Andy White version. Oddly, a mint copy of that is worth around £75, as there are fewer of them. The *Please Please Me* album also used White's version. There is one simple way of telling one version from the other - listen for the tambourine. If it's there, White's on drums. White's version was reissued as a single in 1982, reaching Number 4.

Andy White continued his career as a session drummer, played for the BBC Radio Orchestra in Glasgow, and worked for Marlene Dietrich from 1964 to 1975. He moved to New Jersey, remarried, and, among other things, became the drum sergeant for the New York Police Band Drummers.

On his 1998 album, *Vertical Man*, Ringo Starr revived 'Love Me Do', joking, "I think I've got the hang of it now."

22. Brian Epstein bought 10,000 copies of 'Love Me Do' to make it a hit.

When the Decca auditions were taking place, Brian Epstein did offer to buy 5,000 copies if they released a single by The Beatles. As many singles would only sell a couple of thousand copies, it is all the more surprising that Decca turned The Beatles down. Presumably they didn't believe him.

'Love Me Do' was released on 5 October 1962. It did not make the charts immediately. Then the positions were:

	NME Top 30	Melody Maker Top 50	Record Mirror Top 50	Disc Top 30
13 October	-	-	49	-
20 October	-	-	46	-
27 October	27	48	41	-
3 November	-	40	32	28
10 November	-	30	37	27
17 November	-	28	29	27
24 November	-	26	23	27
1 December	-	26	21	24
8 December	-	24	26	26
15 December	-	24	19	-
22 December	-	22	22	-
29 December	no chart	no chart	17	-
5 January	-	21	-	-
12 January	-	21	-	-

19 January	-	26	-	-
26 January	-	34	-	-
2 February	-	37	-	-
9 February	-	41	-	-
16 February	-	43	-	-

The single, not unexpectedly, was Number 1 on NEMS's own chart, which was reproduced in the *Liverpool Echo*.

The four national charts show considerably different positions, although bigger variations have been seen with other records. All the charts were based on samples from retailers throughout the UK and hence, trying to manipulate the chart for one paper might make no difference on another.

Albert Goldman says in *The Lives Of John Lennon*: "After its release on 4 October, Brian tried to boost the record by placing a huge order for NEMS but the 10-inch 78 peaked at a disappointing 17." He makes two mistakes in one sentence. 'Love Me Do' was a 45rpm, as 78s were long gone by 1962, and it was released on 5 October. Goldman might even be in error on a third point - Brian Epstein might not have placed an unexpectedly large order. His assertion would imply that the purchases were made just before Christmas 1962.

Peter Brown, who worked for Brian at NEMS, wrote, "Putting a record out on the market without any support is akin to not feeding a new-born child. Brian organised a fierce assault to nourish his baby. He unblinkingly ordered 10,000 copies of 'Love Me Do' for NEMS, a magic number that he thought would automatically land a place on the British charts."

Philip Norman reveals in *Shout! - The True Story Of The Beatles*: "After his experience with Decca, Brian was taking no chances. He himself had ordered 10,000 copies of 'Love Me Do' from Parlophone. He had been told that was the quantity you had to sell to get a Top 20 hit. Though the Liverpool fans had loyally bought 'Love Me Do' and though *Mersey Beat's* Top 20 immediately made it Number 1 most of the 10,000 copies remained in unopened cartons in the back room of the Whitechapel NEMS shop. "Brian took me and showed me them," Joe Flannery says. "He even made up a little song about all the copies he hadn't been able to sell. 'Here we go, gathering dust in May,' he'd sing. A few days later in London, Flannery bumped into Paul McCartney. Paul said he was hungry, he'd only had a cake to eat all day. I was amazed, I said, 'Paul, how?' Paul said, 'Someone had to pay for those 10,000 records Brian bought.'"

Les Ackerley, who owned the Iron Door club and managed the Searchers, also confirms the story of Eppy ordering 10,000 copies of 'Love Me Do', although, he adds, "that does not mean he paid for them". But surely EMI would have not given him 10,000 copies on a sale or return basis. Ackerley also says that Eppy asked him if he wanted to buy some at a cut rate.

It is intriguing that 10,000 is always the figure that is mentioned. It does seem to give some credence to the claim. But what if Brian had done that? What effect would it have had? It would have cost him about £2,000 and he would have lost most of it. He would normally sell around 1,000 copies of a big single so he could not hope to shift 10,000 in any reasonable time.

Such a purchase would have had no bearing on the chart placings. It would have weighted the return for the various NEMS stores on Merseyside, which were made on a ratings basis (that is, the Top 10 records in that store) and not on actual records sold. A high position would have been noticed by the chart compilers. They would have questioned the return and probably invalidated it from the published chart. So, if Brian was hoping to manipulate the charts, he was being naïve. On the other hand, 'Love Me Do' did make the Top 50 in 'Record Retailer', the industry's own paper, on the first week of release, the same chart as used in Record Mirror.

Bob Wooler: "Brian Kelly told me that Epstein had bought 'Love Me Do' into the charts. He was biting and nasty about it but then he wasn't a very affable person. He said that Eppy had bought 10,000 records and he added, 'They're upstairs in NEMS in those vacant offices.' I said, 'Really? Next time I go there, I must do a bit of spying.' I didn't see them but that doesn't mean he didn't do that. If you study the charts, that single yo-yoed, 17 from nowhere and then it disappeared quickly. It was a bewildering movement, which gives support to Kelly's theory. We know that there was jiggery-pokery with the charts around that time as it all came out later, and BE could have been part of it. Over the years, I have been an innocent saying, 'Oh no, that can't be right', but Epstein may have been manipulating things."

If Brian didn't buy those 10,000 records, it makes Joe Flannery, who saw them, a liar, or does it? Supposing Eppy wanted to deceive people. He could easily put some boxes of 'Love Me Do' on top of his other stock and pretend that they were all 'Love Me Do'. But Flannery's story is a little far-fetched. It is hardly likely that Paul McCartney would be deprived of food for such a crackpot scheme and surely The Beatles would have talked about it in interviews later on.

Brian's brother, Clive Epstein said: "My father was very involved in the business then and neither he nor myself at any time were going to risk these thousands of records which have been suggested as part of the stock or part of the hype. Invoices and statements went through the office and every cheque was either signed by my father or myself. Something like that would obviously have been noticed."

What is certain is that Brian Epstein sent his family and friends to record shops throughout the city to see if 'Love Me Do' was in stock. He asked his mother to help create a demand for the record. On holiday in Majorca, she sent a request to the BBC Light Programme's Housewives' Choice, asking them to play 'Love Me Do' and signing herself 'Alice'.

Eppy was a smooth operator and his hype was common knowledge on Merseyside. In the 1963 BBC-TV documentary, *The Mersey Sound*, John Lennon even refers to the rumour and says it is untrue.

23. The Beatles never gave permission for their performance at the Star-Club on New Year's Eve to be recorded.

The Beatles, newly signed to Parlophone and with a hit record in 'Love Me Do', returned to the Star-Club in Hamburg over the last two weeks of December 1962. Adrian Barber had left The Big Three to become the club's stage manager and the other groups on the bill were Kingsize Taylor and the Dominoes and Cliff Bennett and the Rebel Rousers.

Adrian Barber was a sound technician who had constructed the 'coffin' amplifiers used by several Liverpool groups and it may seem surprising that he hadn't been able to record The Beatles direct from the microphones to a tape machine backstage. He says: "I hadn't been there long enough. First of all, you get the sound system beat and then you put in the recording equipment. I made the recording because I wanted to see what the tape recorder picked up in the room. I wanted to know what it sounded like from the front while I was working at the back. Kingsize Taylor had the tape machine, but it may have been part of the Star-Club's equipment."

Kingsize Taylor recalls: "Adrian Barber made the recording. He set up one microphone but it was my machine and my tapes. Nobody ever objected to the fact that we were recording them and I could never understand why The Beatles later objected. The tapes are unique and there is nothing detrimental on them. Although the quality of the original tapes was not brilliant, they had atmosphere. It was exactly what you would have heard if you sat in the club that night, simple as that."

The tapes reveal what The Beatles sounded like in Hamburg although the performances of the various songs are shorter than expected - all the books refer to the groups in Hamburg performing extended versions of their favourite songs to pan out their hours on stage, but there is none of that here. Paul adds Marlene Dietrich's 'Falling In Love Again' to the repertoire and two of the Star-Club's staff, Horst and Fred Fascher, also take vocals. Some of the applause is surprisingly lukewarm but the rave-ups like 'Long Tall Sally' and 'Twist And Shout' are well received.

The legal arguments over the ownership of the tapes have been long and complex, often concentrating on a passing, taped remark of John Lennon's where he asks Taylor if the machine is on. The question is always asked, did John Lennon give permission for the performance to be recorded? The answer must be yes, he did, and there is no reason why he shouldn't. He did not, however, give permission for the recordings to be released, but, in the climate of 1962, who would have done that? There would have been no reason for him to think that the tapes would ever be commercially available or, indeed, that anyone else would want them.

The performances were recorded after The Beatles signed with EMI, so EMI claimed that no one else could release them. The tapes first appeared in 1977 on Lingasong's double-album, *The Beatles Live! At The Star-Club In Hamburg, Germany, 1962*. Whether or not that album was a bootleg is open to question, but the tapes have been bootlegged extensively ever since. The Beatles blocked a remastered and supposedly legitimate CD release in 1998. George Harrison told the High Court in London that he would never permit such 'crummy' recordings to appear under The Beatles' name, but far poorer tapes by The Quarry Men had been included on *Anthology 1*. He said: "Even if John had given Taylor his permission to tape The Beatles' performance, that does not make it legal for the tape to be turned into an album. One drunken person recording another bunch of drunks does not constitute a business deal. I could go out tonight and tape Mick Jagger, but it doesn't mean I could go and sell it. The bottom line is that John didn't give permission and even if he had, he couldn't have given it for us all. We were a democratic band."

As a result of George Harrison's testimony, the courts found in The Beatles' favour and the CD reissue was withdrawn. However, if you listen to the tapes, The Beatles do not sound like four drunks - they are playing well and Paul McCartney engages in happy repartee with the audience. Even if John was drunk, he was still regarded as the leader of The Beatles and furthermore, the other three presumably heard him asking Taylor if the tape was on. Harrison is wrong in what he says about Mick Jagger - he has to have Jagger's permission before he records him - why else would bootleggers be thrown out of concert halls?

Despite George's comments, we feel that in time these tapes are certain to become part of the official Beatles' canon and, given another ten years, we can see a special CD package commemorating their time at the Star-Club - especially as by then the 50 year copyright protection will have expired and they will enter the public domain, meaning that anyone can release them, at least within the E.E.C [presuming this hasn't been changed in the meantime].

24. Mersey Beat acts dominated the charts between 1963 and 1965.

In 1963 George Martin, Brian Epstein's acts and Liverpool musicians started a remarkable occupation of the Number 1 spot on the UK charts:

Gerry and the Pacemakers - *How Do You Do It* (3 weeks)
The Beatles - *From Me To You* (7 weeks)
Gerry and the Pacemakers - *I Like It* (4 weeks)
Frank Ifield - *Confessin'* (2 weeks)
Elvis Presley - *(You're The) Devil In Disguise* (1 week)
The Searchers - *Sweets For My Sweet* (2 weeks)
Billy J. Kramer with The Dakotas - *Bad To Me* (3 weeks)
The Beatles - *She Loves You* (6 weeks)
Brian Poole and the Tremeloes - *Do You Love Me* (3 weeks)
Gerry and the Pacemakers - *You'll Never Walk Alone* (4 weeks)
The Beatles - *I Want To Hold Your Hand* (5 weeks)

34 of those weeks belonged to Liverpool groups, 32 weeks were Brian Epstein's acts and produced by George Martin. On such statistics, it has been assumed that Mersey Beat acts dominated the charts but this is not the case. Just look at their Top 20 tally for the key years 1963 to 1965 inclusive:

The Beatles - 11
The Searchers - 10
Gerry and the Pacemakers - 7
Billy J. Kramer - 6
Cilla Black - 5
The Fourmost - 3
The Merseybeats - 3
The Swinging Blue Jeans - 3
The Mojos - 1

That is a total of 49 Top 20 hits over 36 months. The chart for 16 November 1963 had Gerry, The Beatles and The Searchers in the Top 3 positions, but the only other Liverpool act on hand was Billy J. Kramer at Number 8. Cliff Richard, Adam Faith and Mark Wynter are still around. There's a London beat group and a Manchester one, but the rest is a mixture with several American stars, a couple of Phil Spector hits, some world music and the start of the Greenwich Village folk scene.

The top selling record in 1965 was a Liverpool act, but it was Ken Dodd reviving a singalong ballad, 'Tears'. When he was Number 1, the only other Merseyside record in the Top 20 was 'Help!' and his challenger for the Number 1 slot was Andy Williams with 'Almost There'.

It can be argued that the groups from outside Liverpool might not have made the charts without the impetus of The Beatles and certainly some established acts such as Adam Faith with 'The First Time' and Eden Kane with Liverpool's TT's on 'Boys Cry' switched to the new sounds. There were also novelty hits like the Barron Knights with 'Call Up The Groups', a send-up of Mersey Beat hits, and Dora Bryan with 'All I Want For Christmas Is A Beatle'.

One of the Beatles' biggest influences, the late Lonnie Donegan, liked to joke that his last week in the top 30 coincided with the chart entry of 'Love Me Do'. That is true, but with the right record he could have returned. The Liverpool sound was hugely influential but there was plenty of room in the charts for other things.

25. John Lennon was a pacifist.

'War Is Over (if you want it)' declared John and Yoko. They gave any number of interviews to that effect and participated in anti-war demonstrations. But that does not mean that John Lennon was all peace and light. In the late 1960s, Lennon is alleged to have funded the IRA - the evidence is not clear - and in 1975, while separated from Yoko, John ran amok in LA, getting into several brawls. The most notorious was in the company of his drinking buddy Harry Nilsson, disrupting a night-club performance by The Smothers Brothers.

John also showed no inkling of his pacifist leanings while in Liverpool. He never, for example, participated in Ban The Bomb demonstrations, a pastime of many art school students at the time. Although he did not like fighting anyone his equal, he enjoyed bullying. Ritchie Galvin of Earl Preston and the TTs recalled: "There was a floating beat night on the Royal Iris with Earl Preston and the TT's and the Beatles. We shared the captain's cabin as our dressing room and John was helping himself to the whisky in the captain's rack. Girls were coming in for autographs and you know what ship doors are like. One girl had her hand on the jamb and John just kicked the door on her hand and laughed. No-one else laughed and the girl's hand was dripping with blood. To be honest, I never liked him much."

However, the best example of John Lennon's bully boy tactics was at Paul McCartney's twenty-first birthday party at his Auntie Gin's house, 147 Dinas Lane, Huyton, on 18 June 1963. Many of his fellow NEMS artists including Billy J Kramer, The Dakotas and The Fourmost had been invited as well as their new friends, The Shadows, and some old ones including Bob Wooler. To accommodate the numbers, a marquee was erected in the back garden.

At the end of April 1963, John Lennon had taken a short holiday in Spain with Brian Epstein. They had returned early in May and The Beatles had then undertaken three weeks of touring around the UK. In-between some recording sessions for the BBC in London, they returned to Liverpool for Paul's party. John Lennon went with his wife Cynthia and such was the rivalry between the two chief Beatles that he probably resented Paul being the centre of attention.

At one stage, Bob, John and Brian Epstein found themselves going through the back door into the garden. The Beatles books vary in their accounts of what happened next. Albert Goldman says that Lennon launched a murderous attack on Wooler. Beryl Adams, who worked for Brian Epstein and later married Bob Wooler, says that Bob often made witty remarks, which could, on occasion, be taken the wrong way. The odds are that he made a remark such as "How's the honeymoon, John?". Certainly, John hit Bob more than once, but they were separated before it got too serious.

Although he should have been ejected from the party, John went into the marquee where he grabbed a girl who was with Billy J Kramer. Billy Hatton of The Fourmost leapt from the bandstand and grabbed Lennon. Billy says: "There is a technique where you can get your hand down somebody's collar if they are wearing a tie, fingers down, and you twist, and it is like a tourniquet and they can't breathe, and I had him like that. I had my fist drawn back and I was going to plant him one. He was being a right bastard and he deserved a smacking, but someone shouted, 'Billy, if you hit him, The Fourmost are finished.' He was right, we hadn't even made a record then, and it would have been *Bass Player In No-Mark Group Beats Up John Lennon*."

While this was going on, Billy J Kramer had been shouting, "Lay off, John" and pulling Rose, his companion, away from him. Lennon snarled, "You're nothing, Kramer, we're the top."

Brian Epstein took Bob Wooler to hospital and then to Beryl's flat: "I wasn't at the party, but I saw him afterwards. He had marks on his face, his head and his hands. He had a black eye too, but it did look worse than it was.". Wooler's friend, Allan Williams, came round the next morning and arranged an article with Bill Marshall for the *Daily Mirror*. It may well have been the first Beatles story that appeared as a news item in a national daily paper. Brian Epstein cannot have been pleased with the national publicity but the feature does have an element of spin-doctoring about it, as though Brian Epstein has told John Lennon to be contrite.

"Guitarist John Lennon, 22 year old leader of The Beatles pop group, said last night, 'Why did I have to go and punch my best friend? I was so high I didn't realise what I was doing.' Then he sent off a telegram apologising to 29 year old Liverpool rock show compère and disc jockey Bob Wooler. Wooler said, 'I don't know why he did it. I have been a friend of The Beatles for a long time. I have often compèred shows where they have appeared. I am terribly upset about this, physically as well as mentally.' John Lennon says, 'Bob is the last person in the world I would want to have a fight with. I can only hope he realises that I was too far gone to know what I was doing.'"

The telegram read, "Really sorry Bob. Terribly worried to realise what I had done. What more can I say?" Does that sound like John Lennon? Epstein also apologised for John to Billy J Kramer, but Kramer said "I refuse to accept a second-hand apology." A few days later, Lennon did apologise to him in person.

On the day that Bob received the telegram, he took the stage at the Cavern. Billy Kinsley of the Merseybeats: "We were topping the bill that night and Bob was wearing dark glasses. He took them off to reveal his black eye and he said to the audience, 'I got this at Lennon's Supermarket.'" (Lennon's Supermarkets were widespread in Liverpool at the time, the Morrisons of their day.)

One reason for John's apology could be that Brian Epstein feared a lawsuit, which Lennon would be bound to lose. Both parties agreed on an out-of-court settlement of £200. Beryl says, "He could have got more but he didn't want any fuss made of it."

Bob Wooler did not see The Beatles again until 3 August on what was to be their last appearance at the Cavern: "I had been wondering what was going to happen when we met again. It was an awkward situation and he looked sheepishly at me. He didn't put his arms around me and say sorry. I knew then that the telegram had been sent by Brian Epstein." The fact that John showed no remorse surely indicates that it was more than a one-off drunken incident that he regretted.

On the whole, Brian Epstein was lucky with John Lennon as there could have been worse incidents. The photographer Dezo Hoffman remarked that Lennon "was like a dog with rabies. You never knew when he would jump and bite."

Perhaps the fight did some good, because according to a 1972 quote, John became committed to peace after the fight. "That really is nonsense," said Bob Wooler, "Didn't he go berserk with Nilsson in the 70s and there were fisticuffs then? I would hate to think that I was the catalyst for 'Imagine' because I detest the song."

26. The 50-50 split in songwriting between John and Paul was fair.

Cole Porter, wanting to irritate Rodgers and Hammerstein, said, 'How can it take two men to write one song?' But many of the best songs of the century have been written by more than one person - usually two people, one writing the words and the other the music. In most of the relationships, the role was clearly defined, we know W.S. Gilbert, Tim Rice and Bernie Taupin wrote the words and that Sir Arthur Sullivan, Andrew Lloyd Webber and Elton John supplied the music. On the whole, Mick Jagger wrote the lyrics and Keith Richards the music.

With some relationships, the roles are less clearcut, and the most famous example of a songwriting partnership, that of John Lennon and Paul McCartney, is also one of the most unusual. This is because each one wrote words and music. Quite often, they would work separately, and so each have their names on songs that they did not contribute to - for example, 'Yesterday' in the case of Lennon and 'I Am The Walrus' with McCartney.

At first John and Paul were both writing both separately and together. Their 1958 acetate, 'In Spite Of All The Danger', had credits for McCartney and Harrison on the label, and 1961's 'Cry For A Shadow' was attributed to Lennon and Harrison. In 1961 Tony Sheridan and The Beatles individually wrote their CVs, which are reproduced in Bear Family's *Beatles Bop - Hamburg Days* CD booklet. Paul says that he has written around 70 songs with John Lennon, while John states, "Written a couple of songs with Paul." We don't know how jokingly these were completed, but on the face of it, they are pretty revealing.

Shortly after this, John and Paul agreed that they would write under a 'Lennon - McCartney' credit irrespective of who wrote the song, and our guess would be that John was pushing for this. In recent years, Paul McCartney has suggested that the credits be changed on some of the Lennon - McCartney songs, but to what? It is hard to determine what the credits should be, but McCartney certainly isn't happy that his most famous composition, 'Yesterday', also credits John Lennon. What's more, John's name comes first. McCartney approached Yoko Ono just before the *One* compilation was released asking her if his name could come first on this one track; she refused. However, when Paul put a live album out in 2002, under his own name, he did change the order of credit on certain Beatle songs including 'Yesterday'. Yoko was clearly not amused.

As it happens, the first single, 'Love Me Do', had the credit '(McCartney - Lennon)': who persuaded Paul that '(Lennon - McCartney)' looked or sounded better and why did he agree? Was he even consulted? Did he like Lennon's name being on the single when he had contributed very little to the writing of the songs?

In 1963/4, John and Paul did write as much together as apart, but it gradually shifted to a point where they wrote separately and let the other comment on what they had written and sometimes improve it. More often that not, as the years went by, John or Paul was inviting the other to improve a song that wasn't too strong in the first place.

These are the key songs that are true joint compositions:

FROM ME TO YOU (1963)
John Lennon: "We were writing it in a car and I know the first line was mine. After that we took it from there. It was far bluesier than that when we wrote it. You could rearrange it pretty funky."

SHE LOVES YOU (1963)
John Lennon: "It was written together and I don't know how. I remember it was Paul's idea. Instead of singing 'I love you' again, we'd have a third party. That kind of little detail is in his work now where he will write a story about someone and I'm more inclined to write about myself."

Author Dave Marsh: "Listen to 'She Loves You' and you'll discover a very dangerous message. She loves you and if you're too big a fool to respect that, I'm going to go after her. That's what the song is really about. It's John Lennon at his slyest."

I WANT TO HOLD YOUR HAND (1963)
John Lennon: "We wrote a lot of stuff together, one on one, eyeball to eyeball, like in 'I Want To Hold Your Hand', I remember when we got the chord that made the song."
Paul McCartney: "'Eyeball to eyeball' is a very good description. 'I Want To Hold Your Hand' was very co-written."

IF I FELL (1964)
Paul McCartney: "We wrote 'If I Fell' together but with the emphasis on John because he sang it."
John Lennon: "That's my first attempt at a ballad proper."

BABY'S IN BLACK (1964)
John Lennon: "Together, in the same room."

WE CAN WORK IT OUT (1965)
Playwright Willy Russell: "I particularly like 'We Can Work It Out' because it combines absolute Lennon with absolute McCartney. McCartney wrote the verses and Lennon added the middle sequence which gives the song its toughness. Paul McCartney's melodic gift with John Lennon's rough edge was an unbeatable combination."

The songwriter, Bill Martin ('Puppet On A String', 'Congratulations'), bought John Lennon's house in Weybridge and later asked John which songs had been written there. John sent him a list that included 'We Can Work It Out - middle eight only'. Bill Martin still has the letter.

WITH A LITTLE HELP FROM MY FRIENDS (1967)
There's an excellent section in Hunter Davies' biography of The Beatles where he observes Lennon and McCartney writing the song.

A DAY IN THE LIFE (1967)
An unusual collaboration quite late in the day.

The idea and the first verse came from John, and they worked on the rest of the lyric together. The middle section about being on the bus comes from an earlier song of Paul's, and Paul perfected the avant-garde ending.

BABY, YOU'RE A RICH MAN (1967)
John Lennon: "That's a combination of two separate pieces, Paul's and mine, put together and forced into one song."

FREE AS A BIRD (Lennon - McCartney - Harrison - Starr) (1995)
John's 1977 demo was augmented by the other Beatles, who also added a new section. John Lennon of course could not give his consent for this collaboration.

In terms of quantity, Lennon and McCartney's output cannot be compared to Irving Berlin or many Broadway composers, but they were performing most of the time and were recording artists throughout their time together. As a measure, Bob Dylan's output in the 1960s comes to around 200 songs and his lyrics are often substantially longer.

Still, The Beatles' output is far more impressive than contemporary bands such as their acolytes, Oasis. The much vaunted view that Oasis copy The Beatles style is partly true: they copy a certain type of Beatles song, usually John's, and fashioned around 'Dear Prudence', Don't Let Me Down' and a few others. If they had cribbed a few of Paul's ideas, they might have made the whole world sing.

Unlike Oasis, The Beatles did not have long periods away from the recording studio. This can partly be explained by Brian Epstein's strong management, but after Epstein's death, you can see the surge in Paul's creativity as he attempted to hold the band together.

The songs can be summarised as follows:

	Liverpool Years	Moptop Years	Experimental Years	Final Years	Total
	Up to 1963	1963-1965	1966-1968	1969-1970	
Lennon-McCartney	5	25	12	2	44
Lennon	4	28	24	12	68
McCartney	7	24	30	14	75
Total	**16**	**77**	**66**	**28**	**187**

This table shows that, in terms of productivity, McCartney is about 10% ahead: on these totals, for a typical album, you might have five McCartney, four Lennon and three joint compositions. Possibly some solo compositions are true joint compositions where John or Paul should be sharing the credit with their dealers.

Many people believe that The Beatles were all McCartney or all Lennon, usually according to their preferences. There's a myth that McCartney couldn't write good lyrics or that Lennon good music, but they could both write excellent words and music. Typically, some of Lennon's comments show him contributing to the myth by downgrading Paul's lyrical abilities.

It was a partnership of equals, but in terms of quantity, McCartney has the upper hand, probably because he worked longer hours. Rather than 50-50, a fairer split would have been 55% to Paul McCartney and 45% to John Lennon. So technically, several of John Lennon's and now Yoko Ono's millions equitably belong to Paul McCartney. If John Lennon's work with The Beatles is worth £100 million, then perhaps £5 million of that should be Paul's, and it all stems back to an adolescent agreement.

27. John and Paul wrote for other artists as a serious side project.

Generally speaking, John Lennon was very dismissive of much of their work, particularly songs they wrote for other artists, whereas Paul McCartney, ever the diplomat, hardly ever says that anything is substandard. We wonder whether John really thought this or whether he was only showing off for journalists. These are the songs they actually gave to others: Paul had originally intended 'Let It Be' for Aretha Franklin but he kept it for The Beatles, although Aretha later recorded it.

I'LL BE ON MY WAY (McCartney) (1963) (First recording by Billy J Kramer with The Dakotas)
John Lennon: "That's Paul's through and through. Doesn't it sound like him? Paul on the voids of driving through the country."

BAD TO ME (Lennon) (1963) (First recording by Billy J Kramer with The Dakotas)
John Lennon: "I wrote that for Billy J Kramer. That was a commissioned song and I remember playing it to Brian Epstein when we were on holiday in Torremolinos."
Although attributed to Lennon, "The birds in the sky will be sad and lonely" sounds more like Paul. It resembles a Tin Pan Alley song, and it's apt that Mitch Murray said, "I thought 'Bad To Me' was better than a lot of the songs they were writing for themselves."

I'M IN LOVE (Lennon) (1963) (First recording by The Fourmost)
John Lennon: "That sounds like me, but I don't remember anything about writing it."
Dave Lovelady of The Fourmost: 'We needed another song for a recording session in London the following day. John Lennon came 'round and sang the song into Brian O'Hara's ropey old tape recorder. John had just finished a gig, was really tired and his voice was croaky. We learnt the song in the coach going down to London.'

HELLO LITTLE GIRL (Lennon) (1963) (First recorded by Fourmost)
The Beatles recorded this at their Decca audition but passed it to Gerry and the Pacemakers, who did a demo which, in turn, was passed to the Fourmost. Top 20 in 1963.

I'LL KEEP YOU SATISFIED (McCartney) (1963) (First recording by Billy J Kramer with The Dakotas)
Very underrated McCartney song. It could have been a huge hit for Billy J Kramer if he hadn't blown it with a disastrous live appearance on *Sunday Night At The London Palladium*.

I WANNA BE YOUR MAN (Lennon - McCartney) (1963) (First recording by the Rolling Stones)
The Rolling Stones were having trouble at a recording session. John and Paul were around and said that they would write them a song. They completed it in about 20 minutes, although the lyric is so weak that you wonder what kept them. Nevertheless, it was a hit for the Stones, largely saved by Brian Jones' guitar solo. The ease at which Lennon and McCartney wrote the song inspired Jagger and Richards to start writing themselves.

TIP OF MY TONGUE (McCartney) (1963)(First recorded by Tommy Quickly)
Light-hearted pop ballad given to Tommy Quickly for his first single.

LOVE OF THE LOVED (McCartney) (1963) (First recorded by Cilla Black)
John Lennon told the Liverpool singer, Beryl Marsden, that he and Paul had a song for her, 'Love Of The Loved', but it went to Cilla for her first single and made the UK Top 40.

A WORLD WITHOUT LOVE (McCartney) (1964) (First recording by Peter and Gordon)

A pre-Parlophone song that they didn't record themselves. Ideal for Peter and Gordon.

ONE AND ONE IS TWO (McCartney) (1964) (First recorded by Mike Shannon and The Strangers)
Originally intended for Billy J Kramer and prompting John's remark, "Billy J's finished when he gets this."
John Lennon: "One of Paul's bad attempts at writing a song."
No, John, Paul's worst.

NOBODY I KNOW (McCartney) (1964) (First recorded by Peter and Gordon)
John Lennon: "Paul again. That was his Jane Asher period I believe."

FROM A WINDOW (McCartney) (1964) (First recorded by Billy J Kramer and The Dakotas)
John Lennon: "Paul's, his artsy period with Jane Asher."

IT'S FOR YOU (McCartney) (1964) (First recorded by Cilla Black)
Distinctive jazz-waltz written by McCartney.

LIKE DREAMERS DO (McCartney) (1964) (First recorded by the Applejacks)
Another song from the Decca auditons and one that stayed with Decca as the producer Mike Smith recorded it with the Applejacks and it make the Top 20 in 1964.

I DON'T WANT TO SEE YOU AGAIN (McCartney) (1964) (First recorded by Peter and Gordon)
Not much of a song from Paul McCartney and not a hit for Peter and Gordon.

THAT MEANS A LOT (Lennon - McCartney) (1965) (First recorded by PJ Proby)
John Lennon called this Paul's song, but PJ Proby is convinced it was Lennon's. Should have been a bigger hit for Proby as it is a strong

ballad with a great middle eight – "Love can be suicide". That line is the antithesis of "You can always get a simple thing like love anytime" from 'I'll Keep You Satisfied'.

WOMAN (McCartney) (1966) (First recorded by Peter and Gordon)
Curiously, Paul McCartney, Mike McCartney and then John Lennon have all written songs called 'Woman'. Paul wrote his song for Peter and Gordon and allegedly, he wanted to see whether his songs would sell without 'Lennon - McCartney' on the label. However, Peter and Gordon had released a Lennon - McCartney composition, 'I Don't Want To See You Again' as a single and very few people had bought it. Why, anyway, did Peter and Gordon agree to such nonsense? If the song was a major hit, Paul would say, 'That proves my point' and if it wasn't, it showed that Peter and Gordon hadn't got much standing on their own. 'Woman' reached Number 28 and we don't know whether that proved anything or not.

CAT CALL (McCartney) (1967) (First recorded by the Chris Barber Band)
Waste not, want not. The Beatles performed this instrumental on Merseyside in the early 60s, but Paul polished it up and gave it to Chris Barber in 1967.

STEP INSIDE LOVE (McCartney) (1968) (First recorded by Cilla Black)
Cilla didn't like the way she was to introduce her TV series so Paul said he would write an opening number. It was demoed in a noticeably lower key by Cilla, accompanied by Paul on acoustic guitar.

THINGUMYBOB (McCartney) (1968) (First recorded by The Black Dyke Mills Band)
Paul writing for a brass band on an early Apple single.

COME AND GET IT (McCartney) (1969) (First recorded by Badfinger)

Paul McCartney: "I did a demo for 'Come And Get It' for Badfinger which took about 20 minutes, it was before a Beatles session." Later used in *The Magic Christian*.

PENINA (McCartney) (1969) (First recorded by Carlos Mendes)
Paul McCartney, holidaying in Portugal in 1969, gave this ballad to a local performer, Carlos Mendes. Not much of a song: sounds like Steve Coogan as Tony Ferrino.

The fact that John and Paul wrote 15 hit songs for other artists suggests that they took this seriously, but they only gave away a total of 22 songs. Despite the preponderance of hit records, very few of them are classic Lennon and McCartney compositions and the indication is that they kept the best songs for themselves.

28. The Beatles were international globetrotters.

Before 1963, The Beatles had only appeared in the United Kingdom (England, Scotland, Wales) and West Germany (Hamburg). Contrary to public belief, they did not then become international globe-trotters. They only went to Northern Ireland twice. In November 1963 they made their first appearance in Dublin, and never returned to the Republic again. Was it because Dublin was the only suitable location in Ireland and they couldn't be bothered to go over for a few dates? (The Irish Beatles fans are now amongst the most enthusiastic, even holding conventions there. This seems very generous when The Beatles all but ignored their country.)

Outside the UK and Ireland, The Beatles appeared in the following countries:

OCTOBER 1963 – Sweden.

JANUARY 1964 – France, including 20 nights at the Olympia Theatre, Paris.

FEBRUARY 1964 - First shows outside Europe: USA – Washington DC and Carnegie Hall, New York.

JUNE 1964 - Their one globe-trotting month: bookings in Denmark (2 shows in Copenhagen), the Netherlands (2 in Blokker), Hong Kong (2 in Kowloon), Australia (20 shows) and New Zealand (11 shows).

JULY 1964 - Sweden (4 shows in Stockholm).

AUGUST / SEPTEMBER 1964 - First American tour (dates in the US and Canada).

JUNE / JULY 1965 - short European tour (France, Italy, Spain).

AUGUST 1965 - Second American tour (dates in the US and Canada).

JUNE 1966 - West Germany, Japan (five shows in Japan) and the Philippines (2 shows).

AUGUST 1966 - Third American tour.

The Beatles were clearly jaded by their final tour as their repertoire relied on old favourites rather than rehearsing anything new. By Elvis Presley's standards, such touring is highly commendable, but The Beatles rarely went abroad for more than a month and there were many countries that they did not visit. South Africa is an understandable omission, mainly because Paul McCartney refused, and appearing in China or Russia would have been an impossibility then, but why not Argentina, Austria, Belgium, Brazil, Cyprus, Israel, Mexico, Nigeria, Norway, Portugal and Switzerland?

We invited The Beatles' press officer, Tony Barrow, to comment on these findings. He says: "The tours were determined jointly by NEMS and EMI. EMI recommended their key markets abroad. Consolidating and increasing album sales was always a priority, hence the strong emphasis on the US. Australia was a place for special attention because of its ties with the UK and the fact that Australians spoke English. Language problems were important to Brian and the boys. Even in Sweden, I remember them coming home with complaints that crew and stage hands and local entourage didn't always understand what they wanted. The local market had to be as big as Japan to overcome the cons of foreign language in their view.

"I have no real reason to offer for the lack of attention to Eire and Ulster except shortage of available touring dates after the bigger markets had been catered for and, as time went by, shortage of suitably big venues with good staging facilities.

"The quality of local security arrangements and staging facilities and expertise played a considerable part in persuading Brian Epstein to decide for or against a particular country. I was in on one of his tour planning meetings at EMI but it concerned aspects of the US dates - how well the entourage would be looked after (at venues, hotels and travelling between) and whether the group would be adequately protected during the visit.

"As for the final 1966 dates in Asia, Manila would not have taken place and possibly not Tokyo were it not for pressures from Vic Lewis, now part of NEMS, who persuaded Brian of the great value to all his artists if he (Vic) was allowed to build a better relationship with local promoters out there by giving them The Beatles and then pushing other NEMS acts in their wake.

"I do remember that Brian talked about a visit to Israel for The Beatles and he was keen to get them there. I think this was in early 1966, too late for anything to be firmed up and agreed with The Beatles before Candlestick Park and their retirement from touring."

29. *'Yesterday' is a totally original composition by Paul McCartney.*

Paul McCartney awoke one day with the music for 'Yesterday' in his head. It had come so naturally that he was convinced it was some song he'd remembered. He put a dummy lyric to it about scrambled eggs, and played it to the other Beatles and George Martin, but no-one could identify it. "I thought it can't have come to me in a dream," he said. "It's like handing things in to the police - if no one's claimed it after two weeks, it's yours."

It's never been said before but 'Yesterday' does have a link to a previous song, namely, Nat 'King' Cole's hit, 'Answer Me':

> "You were mine yesterday,
> I believed that love was here to stay"

Both the lyrical content and its execution are close to 'Yesterday' and the melody is not far away. McCartney's song is not a steal, but if someone had pointed out the similarity to him, would we have even heard 'Yesterday'?

Our evidence was presented to the music historian, Dominic Pedler, who says: "The rhythmic phrasing makes for a great comparison. The opening three syllables (of course) and the scanning of all the verse lines (except ironically for the word yesterday in 'Answer Me'), is virtually identical.

"While the pitch of the melody notes are mostly very different, a musicologist would also definitely point to the way the closing verse line 'sweetheart' rises (rather than falls) from 5th to 3rd, an unusual stylistic touch which also appears in 'Yesterday' (again 5th to 3rd)."

Also, if Paul was having trouble with the lyric, why didn't he ask John to help him out? Does this add further weight to the argument that they mostly wrote separately? Maybe Paul thought that this kind of ballad wouldn't appeal to John. Worse, did he think that John's more abrasive writing might wreck the piece?

The lyric is straightforward enough. Through a careless mistake, Paul has lost his girlfriend and he wants to put the clock back. We never find out what happened – "I did something wrong" - but that could be good songwriting. Willie Nelson says, "In a way he told you everything. 'Yesterday, all my troubles seemed so far away, Now it looks as though they're here to stay.' (laughs) Period. End of story."

George Martin realised that the song could have been written at any time during the 20th century and to give it a sense of timelessness, he suggested a string quartet (two violins, cello and viola). 'Yesterday' was included on the *Help!* LP, but not in the film. Because the other Beatles were not featured, it was never intended to release the song as a single in the UK, although it was finally released in 1976 and became a number 8 hit.

Paul offered it to Billy J Kramer, who told Paul that he would prefer "a real headbanger". He now includes the song, with this anecdote, in his cabaret act. Chris Farlowe also turned the song down. 'Yesterday' was a chart hit for Matt Monro, whose version was produced by George Martin, and Marianne Faithfull. Paul's version was a single in the US where it became The Beatles' tenth Number 1. It has since become the world's most recorded song with over 2,500 cover versions. Performers include Frank Sinatra, Elvis Presley, Ray Charles, Otis Redding and Cilla Black. On a TV show at the time, Spike Milligan sang a parody: "Yesterday, Someone came and took the stove away." Well, it sounds better than "Scrambled eggs. Oh my baby, how I love your legs."

30. Brian Epstein was out of his depth and not a good manager.

There has been much criticism of Brian Epstein's ability as a manager but much of it is unfounded. No other act had been as big as The Beatles - they even put Elvis in the shade - and so Brian Epstein was swimming in uncharted waters, with a lot of sharks around.

Above all, he showed himself as a manager that The Beatles could trust. Everyone recalls that he was scrupulously honest. How many other British acts had honest managers? The Animals, The Searchers, The Kinks, The Merseybeats, The Small Faces, The Move and The Rolling Stones (with Allen Klein) all had their problems, and this ate away at their creativity. There were no strange investments in peculiar tax havens (which is what happened with The Animals) and, in more recent times, with Willie Nelson. Just as important, Brian Epstein was a manager that others could trust. Promoters could make deals with him in good faith, knowing that they would be honoured. A good example here is when The Beatles started having hits, they already had contracts to play small venues at £100 a night, and Brian insisted that they played those dates.

The Beatles could rely on Brian Epstein and could get on with the job of being Beatles. But he also had enormous vision. In contrast with Colonel Parker's attitude to Elvis, Epstein appreciated that The Beatles were not a here-today-gone-tomorrow pop group, and he wanted to establish their career as a long-term project. He may have lacked the macho, manic drive of some managers, but that was generally a good thing. In any event, everybody wanted to hire The Beatles.

Johnny Rogan in his study of British Pop Management, *Starmakers And Svengalis*, berates Brian Epstein for being 'provincial' but this was an asset and, in any event, he most definitely was not some coarse northerner. He spoke beautifully and was soon accepted by the movers and shakers in London society. When Brian Epstein was on *Desert Island Discs*, Roy Plomley asked him if he had been born in Liverpool, and he responded, "Oh yes, I'd say it was essential."

Brian Epstein was also a very good judge of staff, bringing several employees to London with him. Was there ever a more dedicated fan club secretary than Freda Kelly? His press officers, Tony Barrow and Derek Taylor, were both, in their very different ways, superb.

Epstein made several excellent decisions, in particular launching them in America at just the right moment, thus allowing them to become the first British act to conquer the States. He could make instant decisions about the people he wanted to deal with and Sid Bernstein was allowed to present The Beatles in concert on the basis of a friendly telephone call. He also befriended the music publisher, Dick James. James may have taken too much of the cake, but he knew how to further The Beatles' music.

When The Beatles were recording 'Till There Was You', Epstein passed some comment about their playing. Lennon retorted, 'We make the records, Brian, and you count the percentages.' Generally, Brian did that very well, but he knew little about marketing rights and his friend, the London solicitor David Jacobs, said that he could handle the arrangements on Brian's behalf. Jacobs asked Nicky Byrne to set up companies to license The Beatles name, using Stramsact in the UK and Seltaeb in the US. Jacobs' judgment was faulty as the return to The Beatles was ridiculously small, maybe as little as 10 per cent of the retail cost. The contracts were badly drawn up – for example, one company might be allowed to manufacture cheap jewellery, and another watches. The first company would sue on the grounds that "jewellery" included watches, a confusion not explained in the contracts.

Although Brian has stated that he didn't want anything tatty, the market, particularly in America, was flooded with tawdry Beatle wigs, Beatle plastic guitars, Beatle lunch-boxes and Beatle stockings. Eppy had no quality control but, then as now, shoddy souvenirs are what a large proportion of the public wants. When The Beatles saw how little they were getting from the marketing, they turned against Brian. Paul accused Eppy, "We should be making millions out of this, it's your fault that the contracts were not signed properly." The Beatles were forgetting that he had helped them make millions in the first place and no act had inspired this quantity of merchandising before.

When Brian Epstein is called a poor manager, it is invariably over these marketing rights. It is easy to say that, with hindsight, something different should have happened, and Epstein himself knew that. He had accepted wrong advice from David Jacobs, but he can hardly be blamed. No one, except possibly Elvis, had achieved this level of fame. Brian had nothing to guide him and any other manager at the time may have done the same. This has become a role model in how to do it, and the marketing revenue is an important slice of a pop star's income.

Many pop managers were gay (Larry Parnes, Simon Napier-Bell, Tam Paton), which can be a good thing as they are likely to have more free time without the responsibility of a family. This worked fine for a few years, but as time went on, Brian couldn't cope with his troubled social life. After his death in 1967, a tough American manager, Allen Klein, told The Beatles he could resolve their financial problems. He negotiated a better deal with Capitol Records but he also presided over the demise of the group.

Right from the start and long before Brian Epstein, The Beatles were unruly and critical of authority. Epstein held them together. That he managed to hold such a wayward spirit as John Lennon in check for five years could be his greatest achievement.

31. There are no photographs of Elvis Presley's meeting with the Beatles.

When The Beatles appeared on *The Ed Sullivan Show* on 9 February 1964, they received a telegram from Elvis Presley (in reality Colonel Parker on Elvis's behalf) congratulating them on their success. Ed Sullivan read out the telegram on air. Shortly after the show, Brian Epstein spoke to Colonel Parker on the phone and they had a couple more conversations. The Beatles were invited to stay with Elvis at Graceland during their first US tour that summer but in the end they didn't play Memphis.

When they toured America in 1965, Elvis Presley was filming in Hollywood and was staying at his home in Bel Air at 565 Perugia Way. Paul McCartney spoke to him on the phone and he invited them over as they would be playing San Diego on 28 August. The Beatles themselves had rented a luxury bungalow at 2850 Benedict Canyon.

There was much debate over the place and time - should it be at Elvis's place or theirs and if so, when? And who should be there? George Harrison was adamant that it should be a private meeting and not a media circus. John Lennon was equally keen that the rooms should not be full of hangers-on. Chris Hutchins of the NME, who knew Colonel Parker well, was told to sort out the details. If he kept it confidential, he would then have the story to himself.

The Beatles, Brian Epstein and their entourage drove over to Perugia Way on 27 August 1965. They had with them their publicist, Tony Barrow, and their road managers, Mal Evans and Neil Aspinall. Elvis, in a red shirt and grey trousers, met them at the door at 11pm and introduced them to the Memphis Mafia and their wives. Elvis had fielded the larger team. Tony Barrow recalled being impressed by Elvis's technology and his obsession with TVs. The sets were on all the time and Elvis would be channel-hopping until he found a picture he liked. There was a jukebox packed with Elvis's records and these were played from time to time. Tony Barrow later remarked that The Beatles would have never had their music in the background if they'd been the hosts.

Elvis drank 7-Up and The Beatles Scotch and coke. The conversation between them was stilted. They talked about touring and flying experiences. Paul asked Elvis how long his movies took. 'Not more than a month if I'm lucky,' replied the King. Things got better when they had a jam session - Presley had guitars to hand - and one of the songs they worked on was Cilla Black's hit, 'You're My World'. Elvis had a new electric bass and he knew the start to 'I Feel Fine'. None of this was taped and indeed, there were no official photographs of the event, which seems to have been pushing exclusivity too far.

Ringo played pool with some of the Memphis Mafia, and Colonel Parker and Brian Epstein played roulette and their conversation, whatever it was, could have been the most meaningful of the evening. Priscilla was floating around, looking like Cleopatra, a walking Elvis trophy. As they left at 2am, Colonel Parker gave each of the guests some Elvis Presley albums. John, impersonating Peter Sellers, said, 'Tanks for de music. Long live ze king.' As they were leaving, a fan who had been waiting outside took some photographs of their goodbyes. He is the only person who has any photographic record of the event. One of these is reproduced in the middle photo section of this book.

As the car pulled away, John Lennon said, "That wasn't Elvis, it was just a feller." Everyone was disappointed except Ringo who enjoyed his game of pool. Tony Barrow described Elvis as "a boring old fart." There had been no drugs. Despite the lack of anything significant, a hit West End and Broadway play could surely be made of this meeting.

In 1967 Elvis sent The Beatles a telegram on the death of Epstein, "Deepest condolences on the loss of a good friend to you and all of us." When Presley returned to performing the following year, the group sent their best wishes. However, Presley soon changed his stance on The Beatles. He believed they were corrupting America and, in a rambling letter to President Richard Nixon, he asked to be enrolled as a Federal agent to combat "the hippie element". Nixon complied with his request.

For a few years, it was dangerous to speak the Beatles' name in his presence. He referred to The Beatles in his recording of the Hoyt Axton song, 'Never Been To Spain' (1972) and he recorded 'Something', 'Get Back', 'Yesterday' and 'Hey Jude'. Both George and Ringo met him separately backstage during the 70s and he approved of George, telling his stepbrother, David Stanley, that he was "a seeker of the truth, like myself". Commenting on Elvis' death in 1977, John Lennon said, "Elvis Presley died while he was in the army."

32. After Help!, The Beatles were determined not to make a third film.

Although it was fiction, The Beatles liked the raw documentary approach to *A Hard Day's Night*, but they felt *Help!* was too contrived. Their boredom, or their poor acting, is evident in several scenes. The film was saved by witty cameos and excellent songs, not least John Lennon's *Help!*, a last minute addition which replaced the original title, *Eight Arms To Hold You*.

The Beatles were obliged to make two other films for United Artists and they eventually resolved the contract by agreeing to a cartoon film, *Yellow Submarine* (in which the Beatles themselves appeared only briefly, at the end) and a film of them making an album, *Let It Be*. However, they nearly did star together in a third scripted movie, *Up Against It*, although given the storyline, the title *Eight Arms To Hold You* might have been equally appropriate.

Leicester-born Joe Orton was a controversial British playwright who was in jail for defacing library books when The Beatles were recording 'Love Me Do'. He wrote *Entertaining Mr. Sloane*, *What The Butler Saw* and *Loot*. His work was full of anarchic humour, like a swinging 60s version of Spike Milligan, and so he seemed the ideal choice to write a film script for The Beatles. Alun Owen had done a marvellous job on *A Hard Day's Night*, but *Help!*, written by Charles Wood and Marc Behm, was juvenile, and The Beatles wanted something more substantial.

The film producer, Walter Shenson, already had a possible script in *Shades Of A Personality* and he asked Orton to improve it. It was about four aspects of one man, one of whom will successfully propose marriage to a girl. It sounds like a nothing of an idea, but Orton wrote in his diary: "Lots of opportunities for sexual ambiguities - a woman's bedroom at night, her husband outside and four men inside. Could be funny. As long as I wasn't expected to write a naturalistic script."

When Shenson and Orton met, Shenson said that his first thought had been to remake *The Three Musketeers* with The Beatles. "That's been done to death," said Orton. "But not with Brigitte Bardot as Lady de Winter," he added. Orton retorted: "She's been done to death as well." "My, you are quick," laughed Shenson.

Orton had a meal with Epstein and McCartney, who complimented him on his West End success with *Loot*. They had a good evening and Orton was commissioned to write a first draft for £5,000. Shenson impressed on him that 'the boys shouldn't do anything in the film which would reflect badly on them.' Orton hadn't the heart to tell him that the boys would be depicted having sexual shenanigans, involved in political intrigue, and committing murder and adultery. The title, *Up Against It*, had a phallic significance and, in terms of writing for The Beatles, Joe oughtn't.

Orton wrote it so fast that he asked his agent, Peggy Ramsay, to hang onto it for three weeks before sending it on. She sent the script to Shenson on 6 March 1967. He heard nothing for a month, when it was returned on 4 April. He recorded in his diary, 'No explanation why. No criticism of the script. And apparently, Brian Epstein had no comment to make, either. Fuck them.' This is standard practice within the film industry because to comment on a rejected script might be to invite a rewrite, which would have to be paid for.

On April 10, the script was bought by another producer, Oscar Lewenstein, for £10,000 and 10 per cent of the production's net profit. The film would be made by Woodfall, whose successes included *A Taste Of Honey* and *Tom Jones*. Lewenstein asked Richard Lester, the director of *A Hard Day's Night* and *Help!*, to make it, but without The Beatles.

A meeting was arranged on 9 August 1967 to discuss the production. A car was to sent to pick Orton up but he was not there. The chauffeur said that there was a body on the floor and the tragic consequences of the 34-year-old Orton's fame were discovered. His partner, Kenneth Halliwell, had felt worthless in the face of Orton's success and he had smashed his head in with a hammer and then taken an overdose. 'A Day In The Life' was played at Orton's funeral.

All attempts at filming Orton's screenplay have failed, despite rewrites from Roger McGough and Charles Wood. The script has been published (Grove Press, 1979) and it is all too clear why it was turned down. It is hopeless.

33. The album cover with the Beatles as butchers cutting up dolls was never released.

Long before *Sgt. Pepper*, The Beatles intended their albums as complete entities, not concepts certainly, but the balance and structure of the LPs had been planned. American albums generally had a shorter playing-time and fewer songs, and so The Beatles' UK albums were butchered and new albums were created from leftovers, singles and UK EPs.

In 1966 US Capitol put together *Yesterday And Today*, 26 minutes of Beatle music, with 'Yesterday' as the key track. The 11 tracks came from a single, the previously released albums, *Help!* and *Rubber Soul*, and the new one, *Revolver*.

The Beatles had been photographed by Robert Whitaker as butchers decapitating dolls. The photograph, the content of which prefigures Alice Cooper, was used on the UK press ads for 'Paperback Writer', and another shot from the session was on the cover of *Disc And Music Echo*. It was mildly sick humour and no one in the UK thought much about it.

The *Yesterday And Today* album did not please The Beatles and they realised that the photograph would be their perfect comment on the LP. 750,000 sleeves were printed but there was an outcry before they reached the shops and Capitol were forced to reconsider. With ridiculous meanness, Capitol decided to paste new sleeves over the old ones and pass the revamped product to the stores. Several thousand were pasted but Capitol realised that they would have to be quicker to meet the demand for the album. They destroyed the remainder and replaced them with new ones. *Yesterday And Today* topped the US album charts for five weeks.

Many fans were able to remove the new cover, and the 'butcher cover' has long been a favourite with collectors. A mono album in good condition cover could fetch £1,000 - and the stereo ones are even rarer. A wave of controversial sleeves followed *Yesterday And Today* including the debut album from Blind Faith, Jimi Hendrix's *Electric Ladyland* and, most infamous of all, John and Yoko's *Two Virgins*. The butcher sleeve has officially been reproduced on the gatefold sleeve for the US Capitol album, *Rarities*, and on the reverse side of the picture sleeve for the 1986 reissue of 'Paperback Writer'.

But for once, we can say that The Rolling Stones were first. In 1965 Andrew Loog Oldham's misguided sleeve note for *The Rolling Stones, Now!,* was criticised in the Commons, which led to a reprint by Decca. The offending passage: "This is THE STONES new disc within. Cast deep in your pockets for loot to buy this disc of groovies and fancy words. If you don't have bread, see that blind man, knock him on the head, steal his wallet and low and behold you have the loot, if you put in the boot, good, another one sold!"

34. John Lennon's statement that The Beatles were more popular than Jesus was simply an unfortunate choice of words.

On 4 March 1966, the London newspaper, *Evening Standard*, published an interview with John Lennon by the journalist Maureen Cleave. John said he was reading about religion and he concluded, "Christianity will go. It will vanish and sink. I needn't argue about that. I'm right and will be proved right. I don't know which will go first - rock'n'roll or Christianity. Jesus was all right, but his disciples were thick and ordinary. It's them twisting it that ruins it for me."

The interview came and went in the U.K., but then it reappeared in the US magazine, *Datebook*, which was published on 29 July. This time John's thoughts made the front page and the headline said that John Lennon had claimed that The Beatles were bigger than Jesus Christ, even though he hadn't actually said that.

The timing, as far as The Beatles were concerned, couldn't have been worse. They were about to embark on a US concert tour and they would have to contend with anti-Beatle demonstrations across the Bible belt. There were public bonfires of their records and posters, and even the Vatican joined in: "Some subjects must not be dealt with profanely, even in the world of beatniks".

Brian Epstein thought of postponing the tour until the furore had died down, but he was assured that all would be well if John apologised once he got to the States. John told him: "Tell them to get stuffed. I've got nothing to apologise for." South Africa banned the radio play of all Beatles records and it was feasible that the hatred could become international. John finally told Brian that he would apologise at their press conference in Chicago. Epstein, meanwhile, had criticised *Datebook* saying that the interview had been quoted out of context. Maureen Cleave ran to his defence, "John was certainly not comparing The Beatles with Christ. He was simply observing that so weak was the state of Christianity that The Beatles were, to many people, better known."

At the press conference, John gave something resembling an apology: "I was just stating it as a fact and it is true more for England than here. I'm not saying that we're better or greater, or comparing us with Jesus Christ as a person or God as a thing or whatever it is. I just said what I said and it was wrong. Or it was taken wrong. And now it's all this." Top marks, John, you made it worse. Then he added: "I will apologise if that will make you happy. I still don't know quite what I've done. I've tried to tell you what I did do, but if you want me to apologise, if that will make you happy, then okay, I'm sorry." Wonderful stuff, and John also criticised America's policy in Vietnam. Fortunately for him, the American public wanted to forgive him and, despite some scary incidents, the tour was very successful.

John Lennon's perception of himself would make an intriguing book. We have already seen the confusion over being a working class hero, and he certainly had a Messianic complex. Brian Epstein's claim that The Beatles would be bigger than Elvis was not enough for him. Perhaps encouraged by the drugs, he began to think he was Christ's equal. When he was at Apple, he told the other Beatles and his associates that he was going to announce that he was Christ returned. They persuaded him to postpone it and the next day he was okay again. 'Imagine' itself sounds like a credo for a new religion and John would only have accepted a religion with himself at the head. John's other preoccupation was Hitler - he impersonated Hitler at the Star-Club and to the crowds from the balcony at the northern premiere of *A Hard Day's Night*

35. The Beatles often wrote about their hometown in their songs.

Despite beliefs to the contrary [see George Melly's quote below] and considering that John Lennon, in particular, wrote numerous songs about his own experiences, it is surprising that there are so few Merseyside references in their songs. Even more surprising, considering their experiences, is the fact that none of The Beatles have written songs around their Hamburg trips.

These are the ones that include Liverpudlian references:

In My Life - John Lennon's original lyric describes the bus ride he had from Menlove Avenue into Liverpool, but he changed it to something less specific and turned it into a brilliant song about nostalgia. It is not known why John changed the lyric. Paul noted the reference to Penny Lane in the draft and used that himself.

Eleanor Rigby - There is an Eleanor Rigby (1895-1939) buried in St. Peter's churchyard in Woolton and possibly Paul noted the name while he was at that memorable garden fête in 1957. Whatever the case, as George Melly has pointed out, 'Eleanor Rigby' has many local connotations: "Liverpool was always in their songs but this was about the kind of old woman that I remembered from my childhood and later, very respectable Liverpool women, living in two-up, two-down streets with the doorsteps meticulously holystoned, and the church the one solid thing in their lives. It was a complete portrait, a thumbnail sketch that was as solid as a Rembrandt drawing."

Yellow Submarine - "In the town where I was born." Well, not really.

Penny Lane - Paul McCartney's look at the suburban shopping street through psychedelic spectacles. The pretty nurse selling poppies on a tray is a childhood acquaintance of John's, Beth Davidson.

Strawberry Fields Forever - John Lennon wrote this while he was making the film, *How I Won The War* and though it has a sense of nostalgia about it, the lyric has little to do with the Salvation Army home, Strawberry Field, that was close to Menlove Avenue and which he used to visit as a child. There was a tree house in John's garden, hence, "No one I think it is in my tree, I mean, it must be high or low".

As 'Eleanor Rigby' may be coincidence and 'Yellow Submarine' hardly counts, we are left with only three Liverpool references in a total of nearly 200 Lennon and McCartney songs for The Beatles.

Their solo work is also scant on local colouring, though the cover of Ringo Starr's album, *Sentimental Journey* (1971), promised much. Ringo Starr stood outside a Liverpool pub, the Empress, in High Park Street in the Dingle, but none of the songs on the album relate to the city.

In 1991 Paul McCartney wrote his *Liverpool Oratorio* with the classical composer Carl Davis. It is partly autobiographical, but does not contain many specific incidents. It doesn't tell us much about Liverpool despite the line, "Being born where you were born carries with it certain responsibilities." McCartney loved the idea of classical voices singing about "sagging off school" and "the perfect place for a kip".

Some other songs that have been written about Liverpool: 'Driving Away From Home' (It's Immaterial); 'Equestrian Statue' (Bonzo Dog Band); 'Ferry Cross The Mersey' (Gerry and the Pacemakers); 'Going Down To Liverpool' (The Bangles singing about UB40s); 'Greenbank Drive' (Christians); 'Heart As Big As Liverpool' (Pete Wylie); 'In My Liverpool Home' (Spinners); 'Kardomah Café' (Cherry Boys); 'The Leaving Of Liverpool' (Spinners); 'Liverpool Girl' (Ian McNabb); 'Liverpool Lou' (Dominic Behan, Scaffold); 'Liverpool Lullaby' (Cilla Black); 'Long Haired Lover From Liverpool' (Little Jimmy Osmond, at a time when coming from Liverpool was very unfashionable); 'Maggie May' (means Maggie will - a song about a Lime Street prostitute which The Beatles recorded, but is associated with The Spinners); 'Mist Over The Mersey'

(Jack Owen); 'Tales Of The Riverbank' (Lightning Seeds); and 'Thank U Very Much' (although Scaffold have never explained what the Aintree Iron was). Frankie Goes To Hollywood's second album was called *Liverpool* although none of the tracks deal with the city.

36. 'Lucy In The Sky With Diamonds' wasn't a reference to LSD.

On release, the critics and public alike appreciated the brilliance of *Sgt. Pepper's Lonely Hearts Club Band*, but many wondered if its unusual songs were the result of taking drugs. The BBC considered that 'A Day In The Life' was peppered with drug references and banned it. Although it was not banned, the Corporation also had its doubts about 'Lucy In The Sky With Diamonds', particularly as the initials of the key words in the title are LSD. John stressed that its inspiration was a painting his four-year-old son, Julian, had done at school of his friend, Lucy O'Donnell, in the sky with stars, which he called diamonds. John and Paul (and indeed nearly everyone connected to the Lennons) had seen the painting and they worked on the song. John said that the imagery was inspired by Lewis Carroll's *Through The Looking Glass*.

The painting may well have existed but the imagery cannot be anything but psychedelic and drug-induced. As the commentator George Melly says: "There was a certain moment in The Beatles' development when they took LSD and it changed their music and their imagery utterly. Now, you can say that LSD was a very bad thing, and certainly it was for some people, there are some who 'blew their minds' who are still casualties today, but treated as a help towards art, in The Beatles' case and in some other cases, it changed their visual approach to life. I only took LSD once, I didn't like it much but I had to admit that you did hallucinate. Here were four creative figures who previously had to rely on the world as seen by everybody else. Okay, a joint blurs things a bit but it doesn't do much. But after LSD, in which the wallpaper fills up with kissing mouths and sofas become hippopotamuses, a stream of consciousness was released which went into the songs."

George Martin says: "The thought that 'Lucy In The Sky With Diamonds' deliberately stood for LSD is rubbish. John Lennon wasn't like that at all and people credit him with too much subtlety. He liked to shock people and if he'd really wanted to write about drugs, he would have done so, straight out. You'd never have been in any doubt as to what he was singing about." We don't agree. John wrote obliquely about one of his affairs in 'Norwegian Wood', which is as cryptic a song as you can find. When John released his harrowing 'Cold Turkey', most listeners took it a powerful and highly anguished rock song and few linked it to heroin withdrawal. Listening to it now, it is easy to make the connection, but John was not stupid. He would have been putting his career on the line to admit to smack addiction in 1969.

This has never been discussed before, but further evidence may have been staring rock journalists in the face. When Chas Chandler discovered Jimi Hendrix, he brought him to London, and both The Beatles and The Stones publicly praised Jimi and his musicians. Hendrix became very friendly with Lennon and McCartney, and Tony Bramwell, who helped to run Brian Epstein's Saville Theatre, criticised Chandler for letting Hendrix, Lennon and McCartney take acid together. "They're pouring it down their throats," he said.

While they were taking acid, is it not possible that they made a pact that both The Beatles and The Jimi Hendrix Experience would make records with the mnemonic LSD in their titles? How else do you explain 'The Stars That Play With Laughing Sam's Dice', the B-side to Hendrix's August 1967 single, 'The Burning Of The Midnight Lamp'? The song, recorded in May 1967, has Jimi as "your friendly neighbourhood experience maker". It ends: 'It's happening, baby, I hope you're enjoying your ride - I am.' Jimi, perhaps knowing Lennon's title, brought the stars into it, and, going one better, another hallucinogenic drug, STP. As Jimi Hendrix said in a radio interview in Frankfurt in 1967, "Drugs, it's a very bad scene, especially when you get caught with it, you know."

37. *'I Am The Walrus' is totally meaningless.*

Rick Wakeman says: "'I Am The Walrus' is absolutely stunning and illustrates the remarkable empathy between George Martin and The Beatles." And so it does. But does it add up to anything? Do the remarkable lyrics have any meaning?

The majority view is that the drugs were working when John recorded 'I Am The Walrus' and although the composition is drug-fuelled, it is also brilliant craftsmanship, written unlike any song he, or perhaps anyone else, had written before. John put a sheet of paper in his typewriter, wrote the first two lines, and added images as they occurred to him. He took his time and the result is an amazing collage that tells us much about John's thoughts, preoccupations and beliefs. John often complained that George Martin spent more time on Paul's songs, but the arrangement here is extraordinary, paying homage to Beethoven and Vaughan Williams and ending with a montage which underlines the apparent randomness of the composition.

The song was prompted by John's love of Procul Harum's summer of love hit, 'A Whiter Shade Of Pale', an elusive song full of rich imagery. John admired the wordplay of Bob Dylan, but also thought that many of his songs were nonsense. "Dylan got away with murder," he said. " I can write this crap too." With the help of his friend Pete Shotton, Lennon revisits schoolboy rhymes with "Yellow matter custard dripping from a dead dog's eye" and "Oompah, oompah, stuck it up your jumper", which add to the richness and humour of the composition.

Including a police siren in the arrangement emphasises that the dominant theme of 'I Am The Walrus' is law and order. John savages law enforcement at demonstrations and picket lines ("pretty little policemen in a row") an image expanded by Randy Newman in 'Jolly Coppers On Parade'.

The persecution and prosecution of drug users is evident in "Man, you should have seen them kicking Edgar Allan Poe", a writer who was also a junkie. Possibly John is saying that creative work is sometimes dismissed, erroneously, for this reason. George Harrison told the writer Barry Miles that "semolina pilchard" was a reference to Sgt. Pilcher, who arrested Mick Jagger and Keith Richards. None of the users heed the warnings on drugs because they are too stoned to notice ("Don't you know the joker laughs at you?"). He scorns eastern religions ("I am he as you are he" is a mantra he presumably took from a book) and he regards Hare Krishna as a waste of time ("Elementary penguin singing Hare Krishna"), telling *Playboy* that the penguin was a reference to Allen Ginsberg.

Sexual imagery is also in 'I Am The Walrus'. "Boy, you been a naughty girl, You let your knickers down" is, if taken literally, a reference to transvestites, but it could be some private reference. The eggman is Eric Burdon, who had a passion for breaking eggs over his girlfriends' bodies, but if you didn't know this, the reference is lost.

Lennon calls himself the walrus, a nod to the children's poetry of Lewis Carroll, although the imagery of 'I Am The Walrus' owes as much to James Joyce as Carroll. Reading Carroll's poem, 'The Walrus And The Carpenter', after releasing the song, Lennon realised that the walrus was the bad guy, and maybe this is why he stated "The walrus was Paul" in 'Glass Onion'.

By including personal references, Lennon ensured that no one could make out the full implications of 'I Am The Walrus', but the recording only a week after Brian Epstein's death is surely significant. The Maharishi had told them to have happy thoughts as Brian had gone to a better place, but does "I'm crying" indicate his true feelings at the loss of his friend and manager?

Whatever John was trying to say, we still believe The Walrus Was Ringo.

38. Paul McCartney wrote 'Hey Jude' for John's son, Julian.

In June 1968, after John Lennon's marriage had broken up, Paul McCartney went to see Cynthia Lennon and her five-year-old son, Julian. Paul was used to driving out to John's house and developing a song along the way. He said: "I was quite matey with Julian. He's a nice kid, Julian. And I was going out in my car, just vaguely singing this song. I started to sing 'Hey Jules, don't make it bad', and then I changed it to 'Hey Jude', you know, the way you do. It was just a name. It was just like 'Hey Luke' or 'Hey Max' or 'Hey Abe' but 'Hey Jude' was better."

Although Julian's name had prompted the song, 'Hey Jude' is not about him. The song has an inspirational lyric but it is non-specific. The journalist Judith Simons of the *Daily Express* thought it was directed to her, and others have thought that the song was about Bob Dylan. When John Lennon heard it, he thought that Paul was blessing his union with Yoko Ono. He told *Playboy*, "I always heard it as a song to me. He's saying, 'Hey Jude' - 'Hey John'. The words 'go out and get her' - subconsciously he was saying, 'Go ahead, leave me.' On a conscious level, he didn't want me to go ahead. The angel in him was saying, 'Bless you'."

The author Barry Miles put the interpretations to Paul when they were writing *Many Years From Now* but McCartney said: "No, the song is about me." Paul didn't expand on this but if you listen to the lyric and think of Paul driving to Cynthia's, you realise that Paul may have been considering a relationship with John's depressed and discarded wife: "Remember to let her into your heart, Then you can start to make it better."

39. The Beatles had no interest in the 'Yellow Submarine' film.

The Beatles had a contract for United Artists for three films and they had made *A Hard Day's Night* (1964) and *Help!* (1965). Then they were either too busy or too uninterested to make a further film. They rejected several scripts. There had been an ABC-TV cartoon series on The Beatles and the producer, Al Brodax, suggested to Brian Epstein that The Beatles could fulfil their contract by making a cartoon film. When approached, The Beatles were unenthusiastic because they disliked the TV cartoon series. They thought they had appeared 'like the bloody Flintstones'. However, they saw the film as a way out of their contract. John Lennon told Ringo Starr: "Get your crayons. We've got a job for you."

The film-makers wanted The Beatles to do their voices for the cartoon characters, but they refused, which demonstrates their lack of enthusiasm. The Beatles agreed to some new songs - 'Hey Bulldog', 'All Together Now', 'Only A Northern Song' and 'It's All Too Much'. Tony Barrow recalls: "It became a running joke at recording sessions among the inner circle of associates surrounding The Beatles. A song not considered up to scratch for The Beatles' next album was praised to the skies by the lads in a sarcastic sort of way and then declared to be ideal for *Yellow Submarine*. 'Do you think it's good enough?' one of The Beatles would ask the others with a grin. 'Nothing's too good for the film and so that's what we'll give them - nothing.'" As it turns out, the four songs are all excellent with John Lennon's 'Hey Bulldog' being a classic rocker in the Larry Williams mode. The song was inspired by meeting the cartoon's screenwriter, Erich Segal, later known for *Love Story*. He was a professor at Yale University, which has a bulldog as its mascot.

Grudgingly, The Beatles were drawn into the film and gradually, they came to realise how good and how innovative it was. By then it was too late to use their own voices, but they didn't like the possibility of the film being highly acclaimed without their input. By way of an endorsement, they were filmed in the flesh for a brief final sequence. It may have been an afterthought, but it rounded the film off perfectly.

40. Albert Goldman was a scumbag who wrote a totally unfair biography of John Lennon.

Writers such as Peter Guralnick, Greil Marcus and Jon Savage write excellent, analytical books about various aspects of rock, but no biographer has had anything like the fame or infamy attaching to Albert Goldman. He has achieved this with just two books, *Elvis* (1981) and *The Lives Of John Lennon* (1988). Although the books were instant bestsellers, die-hard fans didn't buy them and they were quickly remaindered. Libraries don't have them on open shelving because they know that Elvis or Lennon fans will deface them.

Three of Elvis's former friends had documented his increasingly erratic behaviour in the book *Elvis - What Happened?* Many believe that the public humiliation caused by that book brought about Elvis's early demise, although, quite clearly, he had a lot of health problems. Albert Goldman's biography, published four years after Elvis' death, covered the same ground but was much more detailed and much better written (though some quibbled with Goldman's sensationalist style). The research is impressive - Goldman spoke to hundreds of people about Elvis but he was very selective about what he printed. The book is written with no love for Elvis and the overall impression is of an intellectual New Yorker and Professor of English sneering at some hick from the south: "*Jailhouse Rock* has the gall to present Elvis Presley as an obnoxious young punk and a shallow, egotistical Hollywood show-off. Elvis detested the picture and never had a good word for it. It was too close to the truth."

The author, Barry Miles, believes that Goldman has been misunderstood. See him as someone who wants to be a Jewish comedian and you get a different perspective on the books. That may be true, but Goldman may be distorting someone else's life to do it. Nevertheless, the humour in his books has been missed. The sections where Elvis asks his girlfriends if they would like to meet 'little Elvis' or how he would cheat at Scrabble are hilarious. Calling Elvis the Great I-Ham is a brilliant joke.

By 1984 Albert Goldman had moved to John Lennon and because one of the authors [SL] lived on Merseyside, he asked him to conduct the Liverpool interviews on his behalf. As though butter wouldn't melt in his mouth, he wrote: "I had no intention of muckraking Elvis when I undertook - at the urging of a publisher - to research and write his life: but after three years work and six hundred interviews I found that I had no choice but to record a progressively more sordid history. Needless to say, this was a very ungrateful task and if I could have shirked it, I would have done so; for the injury I sustained to my reputation hurt me nearly and the resistance created by this one book, which is totally unlike my other writings, has presented an obstacle in the work on Lennon. Of Lennon I can say that I was always a great fan and - more to the point - I have solid evidence of my attachment not only in my writings but in such deeds as testifying on his behalf in an obscenity trial in New Jersey, interviewing him at great length in 1971 and pronouncing a virtual eulogy upon him on CBS-TV the night after he died. Nor has anything I have learned subsequently about Lennon made me stop sympathising with him. Mine will be a sympathetic but honest account, one that has been exhaustively researched with no regard for anything but the truth."

Hardly sounds like the same man, does it? You might question why Albert Goldman couldn't do his own research but he preferred to organise a team of researchers and he had been so vilified by the Elvis experience that his safety was at risk in public places. In that sense, he came out of the book worse than Elvis. Spencer didn't believe his silver tongue and declined his offer, although he did compile a list for Goldman of records he should hear. The Merseyside research was conducted by the crime writer Ron Ellis. To Goldman's credit, Ellis was paid well for his work and to his detriment, the interviews that Ellis carried out were reworded and quoted out of context in order to emphasis Goldman's theories. Ron Ellis has over 200 lengthy letters from Goldman and he is planning to publish them with his replies. We hope he does, together with his original research, as this would paint an extraordinary picture as to how Goldman worked.

Because of his reputation with *Elvis*, Albert Goldman had to make U-turns to obtain some of his interviews for *The Lives Of John Lennon* and even then, some key people refused to speak to him. In the sources for his book, he lists some interviewees who, in reality, had refused his offer or those of his representatives. One of those who refused was Tony Barrow, The Beatles' press representative from 1962 to 1968. Reviewing the book for *The Stage*, Barrow wrote: "Most of us who were close to Lennon for any length of time and others who knew him best, his two wives, his family and real friends, refused to cooperate with Goldman, either as interviewees or fee-paid researchers."

Taking the previously published allegation from Peter Brown's book that John Lennon and Brian Epstein had a sexual relationship whilst on holiday, Goldman claims that the pair were partners for a long period of time. Barrow comments: "In all the six years I worked and travelled worldwide with The Beatles, it was women I'd watch disappearing into Lennon's hotel bedroom for the night, never men. Having this good reason for rejecting Goldman's flimsy evidence of John's homosexuality, I find that many of the book's other new 'revelations' similarly unrealistic, simply because they don't make sense to someone who spent plenty of time in Lennon's company." Barrow concludes that the book is a novel and not a biography.

The book is full of careless slips: Mathew Street is spelt as Matthew Street throughout; according to Goldman, Fats Waller recorded 'Ain't That A Shame' and Larry Parnes renamed one of his performers, Dickie Field; 'Love Me Do' was released on a 10" 78 rpm disc. This doesn't matter much but it does dent Goldman's reputation for accuracy. Again, Goldman goes for the kill and Lennon is effectively assassinated for the second time. Goldman dwells on his drug habits and the book contains more examples of vomiting than any other book.

Phil Spector, writing in *Rolling Stone,* said that Goldman was a vulture, which explains why he would wait until people were dead to pick their bones. This is unfair, as his demolition of Yoko Ono is at least as harsh as

Lennon's. From Ron Ellis's letters, we know that Goldman was planning to say that the head injury that hastened Stu Sutcliffe's death came from a fight with Lennon, but, strangely, he then dropped it from the text.

For all its faults, Goldman's books are worth reading. He does make us question much of what we have read and even if we dismiss his conclusions, it is intriguing to watch him make his case.

In 1994 Albert Goldman was travelling from Miami to London to take part in a BBC documentary on biographies. Because of the threats against him, he would travel incognito. He collapsed and died in mid-flight, almost as though no country claimed him, and no one at the time knew his true identity. At the time he was working on another biography, Jim Morrison of the Doors. He seemed an odd subject for Goldman as so much of his drug taking and wild lifestyle was public knowledge. Maybe Goldman was going to claim that it was all a sham: Morrison put on his slippers and watched TV in the evening.

41. There are no Beatle tracks left to be released.

The three double-CDs in the *Anthology* series appeared to give an unwritten guarantee that this was the end of the line, there was nothing left to be released, apart, naturally, from all the alternate takes of existing songs.

These are the key 'new' performances by The Beatles that do exist and could be issued:

SOME DAYS (1960) - Quarry Men home recording of a Paul McCartney song. Paul used 'Somedays' as the title for a different song on *Flaming Pie* (1997).

SUMMERTIME (1960) - Nobody's looking hard enough. Somebody must have this Hamburg recording with John, Paul, George, Ringo and Lu Walters from the Hurricanes.

LOVE OF THE LOVED (1962) - From the Decca audition.

CAT WALK (1962) - Practice session at the Cavern. This instrumental was retitled 'Cat Call' and recorded by The Chris Barber Band in 1967.

A PICTURE OF YOU (1962) - Once again George Harrison turns into Joe Brown for a performance on BBC radio programme *Here We Go*. True to the original recording and with Pete Best on drums.

BAD TO ME (1963) - A new song for Billy J Kramer, demo by John and Paul.

ONE AND ONE IS TWO [1963] – Paul McCartney's demo, a song intended for Billy J Kramer, later recorded by Mike Shannon and the Strangers

I'M IN LOVE [1963] - Brian O'Hara of The Fourmost had a demo of this, but no one seems to know what happened to it when he died? There is a subsequent John Lennon recording, circa 1979, that was included in the US radio series, *The Lost Lennon Tapes.*

TIE ME KANGAROO DOWN SPORT (1963) - Rolf Harris has The Beatles as his backing group on a BBC radio show.

CARNIVAL OF LIGHT (1967) - A 14-minute track recorded for a psychedelia festival at the Roundhouse in London's Chalk Farm. Paul McCartney wanted to include it on *Anthology*, but George Harrison thought it was 'too far out' (that is, crap). The track is to be used in 2003 as the soundtrack for a film montage of Linda McCartney's photographs. We can't wait to hear John Lennon saying 'Barcelona' over and over again.

ANYTHING (1967) - Ringo, of all people, leading the experimentation on a 22 piece percussion track featuring drums, tambourine and congas. What did The Beatles intend to do with it?

ETCETERA (1968) - Paul recorded this ballad during *The White Album* and tried to interest Marianne Faithfull in the song, but no one remembers what happened next.

SOUR MILK SEA (1968) - George Harrison demoing a song for Jackie Lomax.

CHILD OF NATURE (1968) - John Lennon song that, with different lyrics, became 'Jealous Guy'.

HEATHER (1968) - Paul and Donovan dedicate a song to Paul's stepdaughter.

COMMONWEALTH (1969) - The Commonwealth leaders are in London and Paul improvises a song about repatriation of immigrants. Politically incorrect if taken straight, but Paul was being satirical.

SAVE THE LAST DANCE FOR ME (1969) - From the *Let It Be* sessions and originally scheduled for the album.

BYE BYE LOVE (1969) - John and Paul having fun.

DIG IT (1969) - Only a small part of this 12 minute performance was used in the *Let It Be* film and album.

ROCK'N'ROLL MEDLEY (1969) - A long medley featuring 'Shake, Rattle And Roll', 'Kansas City', 'Miss Ann', 'Lawdy Miss Clawdy', 'Blue Suede Shoes' and 'You Really Got A Hold On Me'.

SUZY'S PARLOUR (1969) - From the *Let It Be* sessions, this risqué rock'n'roll song from John was based around the name of the model, Suzy Parker.

I LOST MY LITTLE GIRL (1969) - John taking the lead vocal on Paul's first song.

BILLY'S SONGS (1969) - On the day of the *Get Back* session, Billy Preston demoed two blues songs with The Beatles. They also recorded a slower version of 'Love Me Do'.

GOODBYE (1969) - Paul McCartney demo of a song written for Mary Hopkin.

WAKE UP IN THE MORNING [1969] Only recently discovered, this rarely heard Lennon & McCartney song was recorded during the *Get Back* sessions.

MADMAN COMING [1969] Several versions of this Lennon & McCartney composition were recorded during the Get Back sessions including one that ran over 12 minutes.

How could new albums of Beatle product be packaged?

(1) A lot of the above comes from The Beatles' *Let It Be* sessions, the forerunner of reality TV in which The Beatles were filmed making an album for weeks on end - and George left the *Big Brother* house first. No one appreciated the main lesson: no one can benefit from being filmed continuously. Doug Sulphy and Ray Schweighardt's book, *Get It*, chronicles everything that was taped, and although Phil Spector could have been more generous in what he gave us on the LP, there's not much that could reasonably be salvaged. Maybe a double-CD could be compiled of fragments from the *Let It Be* sessions. As we write, there are plans to issue *Let It Be* album with Spector's contribution being eliminated, although Spector can't have taken kindly to this insult.

(2) The Beatles' Christmas singles for their fans deserve an official release and contain much sub-Goonery and entertaining musical snippets including 'Christmas Time (Is Here Again)'.

(3) A CD of The Beatles talking, based on studio conversation, could work well.

(4) The Beatles were defensive about their live recordings but they were a better live band than they thought. There must be several live recordings of The Beatles in concert during the Beatlemania years, and a CD package could incorporate the Star-Club tapes, officially released at last, and *The Beatles Live At Hollywood Bowl*.

42. The Beatles made a record called 'LS Bumble Bee'.

In 1967 Peter Cook and Dudley Moore recorded a psychedelia pastiche for a Decca single, 'L.S.Bumble Bee'. Unusually for them, the comedy content wasn't strong and so the record could be taken straight. And it was. The single didn't sell but a US bootlegger as a joke included it on an early 1970s LP and the myth has grown from there.

There have been similar scams over the years. A particularly good Beatles soundalike, 'Lies' by The Knickerbockers from New Jersey is sometimes paraded as a Beatles outtake. This 1965 single is a track on the illustrious compilation, *Nuggets: Original Artyfacts From The First Psychedelic Era, 1965 - 1968.*

In 1968 Simon Dupree and The Big Sound made a two-part single, 'We Are The Moles', as The Moles, which was released on Parlophone. The group's identity was not revealed at first and many thought it was The Beatles. Another single, 'Have You Heard The Word' by Fut on Beacon, has also appeared on Beatle bootlegs, and the members of Fut have never identified themselves.

In the mid 1970s, there were rumours that The Beates had regrouped under the name of Klaatu. When a DJ in Rhode Island played their tracks, hundreds of listeners were sure it was The Beatles. A newspaper reporter claimed to have seen Klaatu in concert, adding that they were The Beatles. It was said that if 'Sub Rosa Subway', a track on their debut album, *Klaatu* (on Capitol, incidentally, with no picture of the group) was played backwards, you could hear the message, 'It's us, it's The Beatles.' The scam soon came to light but Klaatu continued to record and tour in their own right. Their best known song, 'Calling Occupants Of Interplanetary Craft', was covered by The Carpenters.

In 1971, a British writer, Martin Lewis, wrote an article on The Beatles for *Disc And Music Echo* and, to amuse himself, he referred to the unissued titles, 'Colliding Circles', 'Pink Litmus Paper Shirt', 'Deckchair' and

'Left Is Right (And Right Is Wrong)'. The respected discography, *The Beatles - A Recording History* by Alan J Wiener (McFarland, 1986) refers to 'Pink Litmus Paper Shirt' and 'Colliding Circles' being recorded at the *Revolver* sessions in April 1966. Lewis became the producer on The Rutles movie and by way of a tribute, Neil Innes incorporated the titles of the songs into the lyrics of his song, 'Unfinished Words'. In 1998 Lewis revealed his prank at a Beatlefest in Los Angeles and the story is now part of his one-man show. Many Beatle fans are convinced that Lewis's confession is the hoax and that the songs do exist.

43. John Lennon would have approved of 'Free As A Bird'.

Well, that's what the remaining Beatles told us, but how could they be sure? On the other hand, what else could they say?

In 1977 John Lennon, in the seclusion of his Dakota apartment, was writing a musical, to be called *The Ballad Of John And Yoko*. It was not going to be a nostalgia trip but would show how his existence as a Beatle had wrecked his health. Strictly speaking, it was the drugs that did that, but never mind. The songs included 'Mirror, Mirror On The Wall', 'Emotional Wreck', 'One Of The Boys' and 'Free As A Bird'. The last was a slow, moody piece, perhaps arising from his depression, and strangely for him, the melody was completed but not the lyrics. After Lennon's death, his demo was heard in the US radio series, *The Lost Lennon Tapes*, but none of the other Beatles heard this - which reveals something about their interest in John Lennon's later work.

Around 1993, Yoko Ono gave the remaining Beatles some of John's demos with a view to them recording band versions. There was nothing altruistic about this: The Beatles had already decided on an *Anthology* series and some new recordings would be excellent publicity. The Threetles considered 'Free As A Bird', 'Real Love' and 'Grow Old With Me' as potential songs, but the latter two had been released, albeit on lesser-known projects. Paul said, "The good thing about 'Free As A Bird' for us is that it was unfinished. The middle eight didn't have all the words, so that was like John bringing me a song and saying, 'Do you want to finish it?'" They worked on the song, and the version on *Anthology* shows all four as composers. Come off it, Ringo Starr completing a John Lennon song?

In February 1994, they started work at Paul McCartney's Mill Studio with Paul's choice, Geoff Emerick as the engineer and George's choice, Jeff Lynne, rather than George Martin, as the producer. Lynne changed the erratic speed of John's tape for 'Free As A Bird' and the new vocals and instrumental parts were recorded. To psyche themselves up, they pretended John had left for a holiday and they were completing his track. As so often turned out with Lynne, the final result sounded like ELO or, more significantly perhaps, a Travelling Wilburys outtake. They all worked on 'Real Love' and recorded, inevitably, a medley of rock'n'roll songs.

Surely if John Lennon thought highly of 'Free As A Bird', he would have included it on his comeback album, although, admittedly, he was reduced to seven songs because of Yoko's contribution. Half the fun with John Lennon was that you could never predict what he might think. From a technical perspective, he'd probably have enjoyed George's slide guitar, but Paul McCartney's middle eight sounds just like the bits of The Beatles that John hated. Overall, the end result would surely have jarred with him, the way Phil Spector's arrangement for 'The Long And Winding Road' did with Paul McCartney. Indeed, could this be McCartney's revenge?

44. The Anthology TV series and subsequent book are the final words on The Beatles.

For a variety or reasons, not least the individual Beatles' changing views, the *Anthology* project was on and off for over four years, eventually being screened in 1995. The three remaining Beatles, Paul, George and Ringo, intended the *Anthology* TV series and its offshoots to be the final word on the subject. They would comment on all aspects of The Beatles' career and nothing would be wasted: expanded versions of the series would appear on video and a book would include the full text of their interviews. The result with its myriad of archive clips and the subsequent coffee-table book were very impressive but for completists, they left much unanswered.

The main strength of the series is also its main fault. The episodes concentrate on the reminiscences of Paul, George, Ringo, George Martin, their road manager Neil Aspinall and their second publicist Derek Taylor with earlier interview material from John. This works very well but to an extent, The Beatles in the 1960s were living in a vacuum. They were in a sealed unit whilst on tour and much of the action was taking place out of their sight. For example, they weren't personally involved in the controversy surrounding their appearance in the Philippines and can only comment on what they know. As John Lennon said so perceptively: "We always called it the eye of the hurricane. It was calmer right in the middle than on the peripheries." Or as their first publicist Tony Barrow put it in *The Beatles Book*, "Because the boys were so busy being Beatles and looking inwards at themselves throughout the 60s, they missed much of what was happening outside their tiny, protected universe."

Barrow describes their concerts in Tokyo. The Beatles praised the high-powered security, but didn't appreciate why it was there. Barrow says: "They thought the extraordinary Japanese security activity was to protect them from their fans. In fact, it was to protect them from the very real possibility of being shot dead by extremist snipers." An extremist student faction had threatened to assassinate The Beatles, and Brian Epstein kept it from them as he thought it would cause 'needless stress'.

There is an element of hindsight, particularly when George says that Ringo was destined to be a Beatle. The series director, Bob Smeaton, said: "Pete Best has had a hard enough time as it is. We can't go and make it any worse for him." Why not? Let's have the truth. Sometimes the truth hurts.

Being made by Apple Productions, *Anthology,* understandably, shows them in as good a light as possible and they have emphasised the positive sides of their time as Beatles. Drugs are not discussed to any great degree, and John's heroin addiction is glossed over: the opinion of his partners would have been invaluable here. Also, the remaining Beatles had become middle-aged adults with families and they didn't want to itemise the shenanigans of their youth. In the end, there is nothing in the book that they are not happy to see in print.

The series would have been better if other insiders had also been interviewed - Tony Barrow, Pete Best, Pete Shotton, Bob Wooler, fellow NEMS performers, wives and girlfriends and their fan-club secretaries, for starters. This might have diluted the impact of The Beatles' own presence, but who decreed that the TV series or the book had to be a certain length? Surely each episode could have been 20 minutes longer to accommodate additional material.

At the end of the day, this was a commercial enterprise. The intention was to make millions from the TV series, videos and the three double-CDs of unissued material. Even if we didn't learn very much, we should be grateful that it wasn't a complete whitewash and be thankful for small Merseys.

45. Paul McCartney and Yoko Ono have always been on bad terms.

Oddly, Paul McCartney met Yoko Ono before John Lennon did. She called unsolicited at his house and asked for an original manuscript to give to John Cage for his fiftieth birthday. McCartney told her that he kept his original manuscripts so she then asked John and he gave her *The Word*.

Paul McCartney got on well with Cynthia and so he was understandably disappointed when John Lennon took up with Yoko Ono. John would bring Yoko to the recording sessions, which antagonised them all. He recalled in *Many Years From Now*: "I remember later John and Yoko looking at each other for hours in the studio because it became a thing for bonding."

He found it difficult to be creative with Yoko always being at John's side: "I might want to say something like, 'I love you, girl', but with Yoko watching I always felt that I had to come out with something clever and avant-garde."

John wanted Allen Klein for a manager and Paul, Lee Eastman and the disagreements didn't help their relationship. The lawsuits to dissolve The Beatles would follow.

McCartney included a questionnaire with his first solo album:

Q. What do you feel about John's peace effort? The Plastic Ono Band? Giving back the M.B.E? Yoko's influence? Yoko?
A. I love John and respect what he does - it doesn't give me any pleasure.

Q. Will Paul and Linda become a John and Yoko?
A. No, they will become Paul and Linda.

In a press interview to Ray Connolly, he added, "John's in love with Yoko, and he's no longer in love with the other three of us."

In 1982 both Yoko and Paul were agreed that they wanted control of the Lennon and McCartney songbook. Paul wanted Yoko to buy the catalogue with him, she said no and it later got snapped up by Michael Jackson.

In 1983 Yoko took Sean on his first visit to the UK. Yoko met up with the surviving Beatles to discuss business. They all met at the Dorchester Hotel but the meeting was civil with little achieved. However, it is clear that both Yoko and Paul wanted to maximise the profits from The Beatles' legacy. For a time, they had reasonably positive conversations and then, on 11 March 1995, the unexpected happened. Yoko and Sean came to the UK and they met up with Paul and Linda and their children at Paul's recording studio. Together, they jammed on 'Hiroshima, It's Always a Beautiful Blue Sky' with Yoko taking the lead vocal. After the session, Paul gave the recording to Yoko. The track has never been released, but it was never intended for that.

In recent years the relationship has slid back. Paul asked Yoko if 'Yesterday' could be credited as a McCartney - Lennon composition, but was refused. He has continued his campaign however, crediting Beatles compositions on a 2002 live solo album as just that.

In 2002 they both met the Queen on the same day in Liverpool - Paul to show the Queen his paintings, and Yoko to show the Queen the John Lennon International Airport. Paul and Yoko did not meet, the given reason being that Paul was due at a recording session. But would Paul have wanted to meet Yoko at the John Lennon International Liverpool Airport, whose very name diminished his contribution in favour of John? Still, John wrote "Above us only sky" and the best McCartney could offer an airport would be "Man, I had a dreadful flight".

46. John Lennon was an only child.

Two Liverpool people, Alfred Charles Lennon (born 1912) and Julia Stanley (born 1914) were married at the Mount Pleasant Registry Office on 3 December 1938. Their son, John Winston Lennon, was born on 9 October 1940 at the Oxford Street Maternity Hospital. Freddie and Julia separated in 1946, but did not divorce. John Lennon had been their only child. However, John Lennon was not an only child; he had two half-brothers and three half-sisters.

Julia Lennon lived with John Dykins and their daughters were Julia (born 1947) and Jackie (born 1949). Both Julia and Jackie followed the Beatles' progress and although John made no attempts to hide their existence, they remained in the background. In 1985, they broke their silence and told of their relationship to John. Julia is a schoolteacher and, under the name of Julia Lennon, she appears at Beatle Conventions. The family likeness is startling, admittedly helped by her hairstyle and JL glasses. In 2000 she and John's cousin, Stanley Parkes, unveiled an English Heritage blue plaque at John Lennon's childhood home at 251 Menlove Avenue in the Liverpool suburb of Woolton.

In 1967, amidst considerable controversy, Freddie Lennon married 19 year old Pauline Jones. They settled in Brighton with John's help and they had two sons, David Henry (born 1969), and Robin Francis (born 1973). John, however, showed little interest in the family - he never met Robin - and when Freddie died in 1976, John's offer to pay for the funeral was refused.

During the war, Julia had had a liaison with a serviceman, Taffy Williams, and their child, Victoria Elizabeth Lennon was born in June 1945. The father's name was not given on the birth certificate and through the Salvation Army, the child was adopted by a Norwegian sailor and his wife. During the 1960s, John tried to discover where his half-sister was but to no effect. Her identity, which had been hidden under the name of Ingrid Pedersen, was revealed in 1998.

47. The Beatles were the first British group to perform American R&B.

The Beatles made their name in Liverpool with their enthusiastic covers of relatively obscure American songs by Arthur Alexander, The Coasters, The Isley Brothers, The Shirelles and the like. This was also a feature of their first two albums, *Please Please Me* (6 covers) and *With The Beatles* (also 6 covers), both being released in 1963. In Liverpool, the local bands had plundered the same repertoire but several non-Liverpool acts were also covering R&B songs on stage – Blues Incorporated (London), Bern Elliott and the Fenmen (Medway towns), Alan Price Combo (Newcastle), Dave Dee and the Bostons (Salisbury) and Dave Berry and the Cruisers (Sheffield). The Mann-Hugg Blues Brothers even took their repertoire to Butlin's in Bognor Regis. However, once The Beatles became known, nearly every UK beat group was clambering onto the R&B bandwagon.

The Beatles and their compadres were thought to be setting new standards and although they were in terms of quality performances, many of the R&B songs had been covered by UK bands in the early 1960s. For example, there was 'Slippin' 'n' Slidin'' (Dickie Pride, 1959), 'Hey Miss Fannie' (Dean Webb, 1959), 'Sea Of Love' (Marty Wilde, 1959), 'A Hundred Pounds Of Clay' (Craig Douglas, 1961), 'Sweet Little Sixteen' (Michael Cox, 1961), 'When I Get Paid' (Cliff Bennett, 1961), 'When My Little Girl Is Smiling' (Jimmy Justice, 1962) and 'I Sold My Heart To The Junkman' (Lyn Cornell, 1962).

Although the beat groups mocked them, Cliff Richard and the Shadows rescued many American songs from total obscurity - 'Rockin' Robin', 'My Babe', 'Apron Strings', 'Willie And The Hand Jive', 'Mumblin' Mosie', 'What'd I Say' and 'Don't Bug Me Baby'. In 2002, EMI released a concert performance by Cliff Richard and the Shadows at the ABC Kingston, recorded some 40 years earlier. Cliff performs 12 songs, five of them his own, a Lonnie Donegan hit, and covers from Ray Charles, Fats Domino, Bobby Freeman, Bill Haley (twice) and Jack

Scott. With the exception of 'The Young Ones', The Beatles could have happily performed the whole set.

The band that was Mersey Beat before Mersey Beat came round was Johnny Kidd and the Pirates. Kidd's outfit had the aggression of the Beatles, and their September 1962 single that combined Arthur Alexander's 'A Shot Of Rhythm And Blues' and Bo Diddley's 'I Can Tell' is up to anything The Beatles recorded in 1963. Johnny Kidd and the Pirates recorded fine covers of 'Linda Lu', 'I Just Want To Make Love To You' and, tellingly, 'Some Other Guy'. His own rock'n'roll songwriting, 'Shakin' All Over', 'Please Don't Touch' and 'Please Don't Bring Me Down', could match Lennon and McCartney's, but he wasn't encouraged to pursue his talent and, astonishingly, never released an album during his lifetime.

48. Marijuana plants are shown on the cover of 'Sgt. Pepper's Lonely Hearts Club Band'.

Whatever else the Beatles did, they knew how to absorb influences and then improve upon them. Other bands may be more representative of the hippie era or psychedelia, but *Sgt. Pepper* is taken as the epitome of the Summer of Love and, despite its many other styles, it is also the best-known example of psychedelia, particularly with 'A Day In The Life' and 'Lucy In The Sky With Diamonds'

The proposed artwork for the album was designed by the Dutch design duo, Simon and Marieke, collectively known as The Fool. The art dealer, Robert Fraser, saw their work and told the Beatles that it would be regarded as "just another psychedelic record" and suggested that they use the leading Pop Art painter, Peter Blake, instead. The Fool, incidentally, went on to work for Apple and painted the front of their building.

Commenting on the album, Peter Blake says: "The album broke so much ground, not particularly because of me. The Beatles were at their absolute peak and I was quite inventive. If we decided to do something, they could go to EMI and say, 'This is what we want to do'. If EMI refused, they would say, 'Then you don't get the record.' They were very powerful which meant we could break through lots of barriers. One thing was the words on the back, another was that it was going to be a double-album. It ended up as one record in a double-sleeve. They thought that there would be more material but there wasn't enough, so we then put this sheet of things you could cut out like the sergeant's stripes, which went into the other part of the packet."

The Beatles already had the title, *Sgt. Pepper's Lonely Hearts Band*, and Blake suggested that they should be playing a concert in a park. They were posing for a photograph and behind them was a crowd of fans who had been at the concert. The cut-outs could represent anybody and so the Beatles, Robert Fraser and Blake himself compiled lists of significant cultural, political or religious personalities. In a strange pairing, both

Jesus Christ and Adolf Hitler were removed at EMI's insistence. Brian Epstein was not wholly in favour of the cover and wrote a note, "Brown paper bags for *Sgt. Pepper*", which was ignored.

Much has been written about marijuana plants being on the front of the sleeve, but Peter Blake says, "There's a whole mythology around this, which is extraordinary. As far as I'm concerned, it's all chance. Someone once said that there were marijuana plants and if they were, it was completely a joke on me, but I have been told that they are not marijuana plants but house plants. The figures were set up at the back, then there was a stage for the Beatles to stand on, and in front of that, at an angle, was a flowerbed. That was subcontracted to a firm that came in and made up the flowers, so if there were any marijuana plants - and I don't think there were - they put them in. A young boy who was helping out said, 'Can I do a guitar in hyacinths?' It seemed a nice, simple, lovely idea, so we said, 'Yes, that's fine.' If you look at the little white guitar, you can read, 'Paul?', which was brought up at around the time of the rumours that Paul was dead: you know, Paul question-mark - Is Paul dead?"

49. The Beatles dominate the sales figures for the UK's top-selling singles.

Astonishingly, they don't. Many lesser acts have recorded bigger selling singles.

UK sales over 4 million
- 'Candle In The Wind 1997' – Elton John (1997) 4.9 million. More than 1 in 10 UK adults bought the single, which was effectively the official Diana memorial product.

UK sales over 3 million

- 'Do They Know It's Christmas' – Band Aid (1984) 3.6 million. Paul McCartney appears on the B-side with a goodwill message.

UK sales over 2 million

- 'Bohemian Rhapsody' – Queen (1975) 2.1 million.
- 'Mull Of Kintyre' – Wings (1977) 2million. The UK's first two-million seller and Paul McCartney outstripping all his efforts with The Beatles.

UK sales over 1.5 million

- 'Rivers Of Babylon' / 'Brown Girl In The Ring' – Boney M (1978)
- 'You're The One That I Want' – John Travolta and Olivia Newton John (1978)
- 'Relax' – Frankie Goes To Hollywood (1983)
- 'She Loves You' – Beatles (1963)
- 'Unchained Melody' – Robson and Jerome (1995)
- 'Mary's Boy Child' – Boney M (1978)
- 'Love Is All Around' – Wet Wet Wet (1994)
- 'Evergreen' / 'Anything Is Possible' – Will Young (2002)

- 'I Just Called To Say I Love You' – Stevie Wonder (1984)
- 'I Want To Hold Your Hand' – Beatles (1963)
- 'Barbie Girl' – Aqua (1997) (!!!)
- 'Believe' – Cher (1998)
- 'Perfect Day' – Various Artists for Children In Need (1998) No Beatle involvement.
- '(Everything I Do) I Do It For You' – Bryan Adams (1991)
- 'Tears' – Ken Dodd (1965)
- 'Can't Buy Me Love' – Beatles (1964)
- 'Summer Nights' - John Travolta and Olivia Newton John (1978)
- 'Two Tribes' – Frankie Goes To Hollywood (1984)

A further 54 singles have sold over a million in the UK and they include 'Imagine' (John Lennon), 'I Feel Fine' (Beatles) and 'We Can Work It Out' (Beatles). Only five Beatle records in 76 million is not great going, considering the eminence of the group: still, Elvis only has one UK million-seller, 'It's Now Or Never'.

50. 'Yesterday' was the first occasion on disc when The Beatles employed additional musicians.

At the very beginning of The Beatles' tenure with EMI, a session drummer, Andy White, was wheeled in to assist on 'Love Me Do' and its 'PS I Love You' B-side. Next, the person responsible for hiring White, producer George Martin, was loud and clear on the debut album, contributing piano to 'Misery' and celesta - a keyboard instrument of greater antiquity - to 'Baby It's You'.

He figured in much the same capacity on further releases - notably the menacing piano section of 'Money' on *With The Beatles*, and joining Lennon and McCartney on the same instrument for *Beatles For Sale*'s 'Rock And Roll Music'.

The Beatles' immediate entourage also helped out in the studio. Road manager Mal Evans, for example, was waved in to add Hammond organ to 'You Won't See Me' on 1965's *Rubber Soul*.

However, on the soundtrack side of *Help!*, EMI house arranger Johnnie Scott was brought in by George Martin to play two flutes on coda to 'You've Got To Hide Your Love Away', a far less conspicuous embellishment than the string quartet that enhanced side two's 'Yesterday'. The Beatles' third all-acoustic number (the second was 'I've Just Seen A Face') was completed in June 1965, four months after the Scott track - when a version of 'Yesterday' with 'holy' electric organ was rejected.

On the not-too-distant horizon lay horn sections (e.g. 'Got To Get You Into My Life'), Indian musicians ('Within You Without You'), full orchestras ('A Day In The Life'), as well as wives, girlfriends and musical confreres getting in on the act. Years before, The Beatles had had guest singers in Horst Fascher, the Star-Club's general manager - and his brother Freddie - who sometimes ventured on stage to commandeer the central microphone with some of the groups that worked there.

Some of the brothers' turns with The Beatles - which included lead vocals on 'I Saw Her Standing There' - took place during their final season at the club in December 1962. The entire alcohol-fuelled set was recorded by Kingsize Taylor on a domestic machine, and most of it released - to The Beatles' displeasure - fifteen years later by Lingasong.

51. Paul McCartney was the only vegetarian Beatle.

At a press conference during The Beatles' 1964 tour of Australia, one barrel-scraping journalist asked George Harrison to list his preferred meats. "Beef, pork...," replied George, too nonplussed to crack back with a Fab Four witticism, "oh, and mutton, yes."

When filling in the *New Musical Express*'s 'Lifelines' questionnaire early in 1963, George, Paul and Ringo had all chosen chicken, lamb, and steak cuisine as their 'favourite foods' while John went for non-committal 'curry and jelly'.

Lennon had acquired such a comparatively exotic taste via Pete Best's Indian mother and, later, in a Britain where most restaurants that served a late-night square meal were Indian or Chinese. Otherwise, during that year's travelling life of snatched and irregular meals, The Beatles' palates had been coarsened by chips-with-everything in wayside snack bars.

It had been the same in meat-happy Hamburg where *Bratwurst* sausage was the equivalent of fish-and-chips, and menus in establishments like Der Fludde, Harold's Schnellimbiss and Zum Pferdestalle - which translates as 'the Horses' Stable' - favoured horsemeat steaks, *Labskaus* - a *melange* of corned beef, herrings, mashed potato and chopped gherkins, topped with a fried egg - and *Deutsch bifsteak*. A search for a nut roast would be fruitless as all over Europe, in the early 60's vegetarianism was regarded generally as an eccentricity and an inconvenience for dinner party hosts.

None of The Beatles had, therefore, ever seriously considered adopting vegetarianism, even when they had the means to order more than beans-on-toast. On the run around the world, gourmet dishes with specious names - *trepang* soup, veal Hawaii, *furst puckler* - pampered stomachs yearning for the greasy comfort of cod and chips eaten with the fingers.

'Long Live Ze King' [see chapter 31]

Die 20 beliebtesten Beatgruppen

Dave Dee, Dozy, Beaky, Mick & Tich   82,034

Herman's Hermits   17,345

Sonny & Cher   9,688

Los Bravos   6,641

Tief atmen und nicht bis drei, sondern bis 20 zählen. BRAVO präsentiert die 20 Beatgruppen, die Ihr bei der Otto-Wahl 1967 als Eure Favoriten gewählt habt. Es war die spannendste Wahl der letzten Jahre. Das gute alte Europa blieb Sieger. Nicht weniger als zehn englische, drei deutsche (!) und eine spanische Gruppe teilen sich mit fünf Bands aus den USA und einer aus Australien die Plätze. Die Gold-Sieger Dave Dee & Co. findet Ihr auf der Rückseite in Farbe und im Riesenformat zum Aufhangen!

This was one of DDDBMT's greatest moments, winning the German magazine Bravo Golden Otto award (the Beatles had won it the previous year). Germany at the time was the World's third largest record market. The poll was conducted from readers votes, and DDDBMT received a staggering 82,034. We have left the intro in German, so out with your dictionaries. The remaining positions of the top 20 were ....13 The Who (3,258)....14 The Rattles (2,111)......15 The Rivets (1,088).........16 The Mama's & Papa's (1,017).....17 The Small Faces (839) ...18 The Monkees (541) .19 New Vaudeville Band (417).....20 Easybeats (352).
The above info was taken from Bravo No. 14   27 March 1967. At the time 'If Music Be The Food Of Love...' was at position 3 in the album chart.

'Not always on top!'   [see chapter 94]

Reprinted courtesy of Bravo Magazine 1967

'On Second Thoughts' [see chapter 91]

'Above Us Only Sky' [see chapter 45]

'And The Best Drummer In The Beatles Is…'
[see chapter 75]

'Academic Failures?' [see chapter 55]

'Sage Or Onion?' [see chapter 78]

'C'mon Luv, Rattle Yer Necklace'
[see chapter 60]

'George Who?' [see chapter 71]

'But Officer, We've Never Even Met Bob Dylan' [see chapter 13]

'Would The Real 5th Beatle Please Stand Up'
[see chapter 64]

Nevertheless, after the decision to quit touring, Lennon was the first, apparently, to at least try a meat-free diet - though wife Cynthia and son Julian didn't then. Later, he - and Yoko Ono - backslid, justifying himself in 1980 with 'We're mostly macrobiotic - fish and rice and whole grains - but sometimes I bring the family out for a pizza. Intuition tells you what to eat. We went through vegetarianism and macrobiotic, but now, because we're in the studio, we do eat junk food.'

By the time George returned from his trip to India in autumn 1966, he too had become vegetarian, even going through a phase of eating with his hands, Indian style. As well as the expected meatless curries, his kitchen also served, say, *pakoras* (pastries stuffed with cauliflower and peas, deep-fried in *ghee*) and vegetable *samosas*.

In preparation for the visit to the Maharishi's *ashram* in the Himalayas, Ringo too had a go - 'because we knew there wouldn't be any meat over in India' - though his input was more egg-and-chips than *pakoras*. His choice was limited further by inherited digestive maladies that included an aversion to any food with the faintest tang of onion or garlic. Starr stuck it out for only a few weeks, but when he and the surviving Beatles met in 1994 to record the supplementary *Anthology* tracks, he professed to have resumed vegetarianism.

Far and away the most publicly pledged Beatle, however, is Paul, who experienced a revelation when tucking into a meat-based main course with his family, while at the same time gazing out at an idyllic rural scene of lambs gambolling round their mothers in a meadow. Embracing vegetarianism almost immediately, he and, especially, his late wife Linda, became evangelical about the subject. At his insistence, for example, the catering at his Liverpool Institute For Performing Arts is exclusively vegetarian - while Linda wrote a best-selling book of recipes, and her picture remains the emblem of a still-expanding Linda McCartney range of vegetarian products stocked in supermarkets all over the globe.

52. 'Revolution 9' was a self-indulgent waste of needle-time.

The Beatles were all determined self-improvers. By 1967, the pioneering tonalities of Luciano Berio, John Cage, Arnold Schoenberg, Krzystof Penderecki, Edgard Varese, Karlheinz Stockhausen – the last included on the *Sgt. Pepper* montage - and other modern classical composers were as likely to blast from their car stereos as Ravi Shankar, Bob Dylan and the Top 40.

This interest manifested itself in the melange of tape loops that formed the instrumental interlude of 1966's 'Tomorrow Never Knows'; the avant-gardenings of 'Carnival Of Light' - The Beatles' contribution to a psychedelic 'happening' at London's Roundhouse - and, most conspicuously, on 'Revolution 9', the penultimate (and longest) track on 1968's *The Beatles* at a time when the 'serious' likes of Terry Riley, Steve Reich, percussion virtuoso Stomu Yamash'ta and Apple's own John Tavener were being promoted almost like rock stars. Included on the double album at the insistence of John Lennon - who created almost all of it with Yoko Ono - only the recurring 'number nine' announcement lends 'Revolution 9' even shadowy orthodox form - though Lennon was to aver that "It has the basic rhythm of the original 'Revolution' [the song that begins side four of *The Beatles*] going on with some twenty tape loops we put on, things from the archives of EMI. There were about ten machines with people holding pencils on the loops. I did a few mixes until I got one I liked."

This patchwork of noises that the man-in-the-street wouldn't think of as musical is comparable to Varese's 'La Poeme Electronique' - a montage of sound commissioned as part of an exhibit at the 1958 World's Fair in Brussels - that was also a sound-painting assembled literally second by second from seemingly random sources. 'Revolution 9' was lauded too by Barry Miles in the *International Times* as a send-up of Cage's 'Fontana Mix', an eleven-minute 'chance operation' tape collage recorded in 1958, and a classic of its kind like his more famous 'silent piece', '4'33"', which requires a pianist to sit before a keyboard without touching it for that length of time. Coughs, the rustling of programmes and the huff of footsteps walking out of the auditorium are part of the performance.

There is also an affinity between Cage's work, 'Revolution 9' and 'conceptual' exhibitions of Ono, a Tracey Emin *du jour*. Among these were an all-white chess set; an apple with a £200 price tag, and her 'happening' in Liverpool's Bluecoat Chambers, where she'd had different members of the audience picking up pieces of a jug she'd just smashed. Moreover, Ono's vocal gymnastics owed much to the free choral babbling and odd tone clusters of Schoenberg and Penderecki. 'Once I heard her stuff,' said Lennon, 'I got intrigued, so I wanted to do one. I spent more time on "Revolution 9" than I did on half the other songs I ever wrote.'

'Revolution 9' – "an aural litmus of unfocused paranoia" concluded *Rolling Stone* - reached a far, far wider audience than all its avant-garde antecedents combined - antecedents of which most of its consumers were unaware. Hence its dismissal as 'rubbish' by those who were bored, irritated and, at times, inadvertently amused by what they heard only as aural scribble between 'Cry Baby Cry' and 'Goodnight'. Others - including one of the authors [AC] - weren't so sure, and listened again - and again and again - until 'Revolution 9' reached out and held them forever.

53. No Beatle ever appeared in a TV commercial.

During the ITV broadcast of the first part of the *Anthology* documentary in 1995, the moments preceding the first commercial break were filled with The Beatles' 1962 spot at the Cavern for the channel's topical *Know The North* magazine. In the very last second, someone in the audience bawled 'We want Pete!' - and, within the minute, there he was - or, at least, his middle-aged self as the central figure in a lager advertisement.

Yet the first - and only other - Beatle to palm cash for endorsing merchandise on television was Best's successor, who extolled the virtues of a brand of leisure wear in a series of seven Japanese commercials in the early 1980s; appearing in dubbed sketches, composing four short ditties (all entitled 'Simple Life') and, relaxing on a sofa, just ruminating generally about 'Renown' T-shirts, slacks *et al*.

For a rich man bathed, as he often was then, in pampered tedium, the process was an intriguing and challenging diversion: the sloganising, the gimmicks, the hype, the cramming of everything the merchandiser wanted said about the product into less space than a two-minute single.

It was also easy money. Not long before he entered an Arizona clinic in October 1988 for treatment for his chronic alcoholism, Starr banked a huge cheque for five days in the Bahamas for a Sun County wine commercial - though he felt uncomfortable about this after his victory over the demon drink.

His next venture into television advertising was in the early 1990s when, on behalf of Oldsmobile Cutlass cars, he (or a lookalike stunt man) slid down a banqueting table and out of a twelfth-floor window. Then Ringo sat himself in a vehicle, driven by daughter Lee, by now quite a young adult with her purple-dyed hair.

Though Starr is the 'poorest' ex-Beatle, the motivation for his involvement in these projects were because, as he told *Rolling Stone* in 1981: "most of the time, I want to do them, which isn't necessarily right, but I like to have a good time." In spring 1996, Ringo - still on the wagon - uttered just one line in a Japanese commercial for Ringo Suttar natural juice. Into the bargain, he didn't even have to go to Japan to do it. He simply boarded a first-class flight from California to Vancouver, to be filmed in front of a blown-up photograph of Mount Fuji. The fee of half a million pounds was a mere bagatelle.

54. Lennon and McCartney were The Beatles' only songwriting team.

Accumulated since their partnership began in the late 1950s, John Lennon and Paul McCartney's ever-swelling stockpile of songs could - even by 1962 - fulfil EMI's contractual requirements many times over. Ringo Starr and George Harrison were, therefore, under no commercial pressure to write songs themselves.

However, there was a time when it was 'Harrison-McCartney' rather than 'Lennon-McCartney'. Before either Paul or George joined The Quarry Men, Buddy Holly and the Crickets appeared at the Liverpool Empire on 20 March 1958. Among Holly's creative talents was an ability to compose - with various Crickets - simple but atmospheric songs tailored to his elastic adenoids.

George was in complete concord with Paul in a liking for Buddy Holly, and was, therefore, at least prepared to listen to his schoolfriend's suggestion that they too attempt to pen their own songs - though, to Harrison, nothing could be up to US standards. Yet he didn't mind being McCartney's sounding board. An effort that survived their recruitment into John Lennon's skiffle group was 'Hey Darlin'', an opus much in lovelorn Everly Brothers mould. With slight help from George too, Paul's 'In Spite Of All The Danger' - sung in *shooby-doo-wah* style - was recorded on a Quarry Men demonstration disc.

This was the tide-mark of Paul's collaboration with George, for whom songwriting was incidental to his self-image as a rock 'n' roller. Also, made to feel intellectually (as well as chronologically) inferior to Paul - soon to sit his 'A' levels - and Art School John, he felt then that he had neither the knack nor the inclination to compose. Where did it get you anyway? The Dusty Road Ramblers' 'Sweet Liverpool' was a rare example of a local outfit performing a home-made piece in public, but, as Harrison and everyone else knew, if anything other than the familiar was attempted, dancers would be inclined to either sit it out or go to the toilet. It just wasn't done in the 1950s.

Nevertheless, it was George who came up with the first Beatles original to be considered for release on disc. John too received a credit for 'Cry For A Shadow', an instrumental taped during the group's May 1961 session in Hamburg, for which they'd been hired ostensibly as Tony Sheridan's accompanists. Much like a Shadows out-take, it was more in keeping with current trends than anything Lennon and McCartney had on offer - so much so that producer Bert Kaempfert allowed The Beatles to record it as a possible single in their own right.

It was not, however, to be issued until it had acquired historical importance, even climbing into the Australian Top Ten as an A-side.

There have been only four other multiple songwriting credits for Beatles other than than 'Lennon-McCartney' (or 'McCartney-Lennon' as it was at first). 'Lennon-McCartney-Starkey' were responsible for *Rubber Soul*'s unremarkable 'What Goes On' ("resurrected with a middle-eight thrown in with Paul's help to give Ringo a song"). With their works being covered now by everyone from international stars like Matt Monro and Peter Sellers to banjo bands and barbershop quartets, John and Paul could afford to be generous.

Finally, 1967's 'Flying', the instrumental on the *Magical Mystery Tour*, was attributed to all four members of the group - as was 'Dig It' from Let It Be plus 'Free As A Bird' and 'Real Love', the spin-off singles to the *Anthology* series.

As a postscript, George and Ringo began composing together - though no fruit of this partnership appeared on disc until after disbandment, notably 1973's 'Photograph', a million-seller for Starr. Moreover, it must have been sweet indeed for George in the late

1980s to hear of Paul's - ultimately unfulfilled - desire to compose with him again. After Lennon, personnel from Wings and 10cc's Eric Stewart, McCartney had teamed up more recently with Elvis Costello. Paul looked at it like this: "George has been writing with Jeff Lynne; I've been writing with Elvis, so it's natural for me to want to write with George." Well, it had been a long time since 'Hey Darlin'.

55. The Beatles were all 'academic failures'.

In 1967, George Harrison confided to a scribbling journalist that he thought The Beatles, overall, were 'academic failures'. Yet the five members - George, John Lennon, Paul McCartney, Stuart Sutcliffe and Pete Best - who arrived in Hamburg in 1960 had all passed the Eleven Plus examination to gain a place at a grammar school, rather than the secondary modern, where 'failures' went.

This was a desirable social coup for ambitious parents. When the ITV soap-opera *Coronation Street* was young, 'Ken Barlow' - then a primary school teacher - was once depicted refusing a bribe to rig Eleven Plus results so that a town councillor's son could attend Market Wetherby Grammar. Fairer was the 'education for all' concept of the comprehensive which, combining elements of both grammar and secondary modern, enabled children to follow what best suited their abilities and inclinations as they developed.

John Lennon and George Harrison may have fared better at a comprehensive. Quarry Bank - where Lennon went - was nicknamed 'the Police State' by pupils at more liberal schools for its draconian affectations and futile rigmarole. Academic streaming was in full force - and so was corporal punishment, administered as often as not with the swish of a bamboo cane on buttocks or outstretched palm.

Within a year of enrolling, John was transformed from a capable if uninvolved pupil to a C-stream hard case and the proverbial 'bad influence' on others. Yet while he failed all his GCE 'O' levels - albeit by only one grade each - in July 1957, the headmaster, William Pobjoy gave him a written testimonial glowing enough to ensure admittance to Liverpool's Regional College of Art that September.

Fresh from the Sixth Form at the time The Beatles began their first season in Germany, Paul McCartney was wondering if his GCE 'A' level results had alighted on his Allerton doormat yet. They had, and he'd received just one certificate - in Art. This was disappointing because at Liverpool Institute High School For Boys - a more liberal establishment than Quarry Bank - Paul had been in the 'A' stream throughout, even winning a school prize for an essay. Like Pete Best and Stuart Sutcliffe, who distinguished themselves similarly at, respectively, Liverpool Collegiate and Prescot Grammar, Paul had considered applying to teacher training college.

Institute masters were to be surprised later that McCartney and George Harrison even knew each other. The academic gulf between them was such that as George and other leavers filed out on their last day at the Institute, an inkling of what his final report would say was detectable in Headteacher Jack Edwards acidic remark that he'd made "no contribution to school life". Sure enough, George read on the bus home that Edwards "cannot tell you what his work is like because he hasn't done any".

A postscript to George's bursting free from the Institute was his return in September 1959, to repeat the 'O' level year, as some mortified teachers assumed. Only an hour in class, however, convinced him that slacking until the following summer among boys a year his junior was an univiting prospect that would give him no more time to "be in a band as opposed to having a job".

Ringo Starr's achievements at school were far more negligible than George's. Ineligible to even sit either the Eleven Plus or 'O' levels – mainly because of lengthy abcensees through illness at primary school – his years at Dingle Vale secondary school were spent in the lowest stream. Progress was marred further by long spells in hospital. When his schooling was over by 1955 at the minimum age of fifteen, all that remained was the formality of returning to Dingle Vale "to get the certificate to prove I'd left. They didn't even remember I'd been there."

56. A kick in the head was the underlying cause of Stuart Sutcliffe's death.

In 1994, Scala Productions, the makers of *Letter To Brezhnev* and *The Crying Game*, brought us *Backbeat*, a bio-pic centred on John Lennon, his fated best pal Stuart Sutcliffe and the latter's German girlfriend, Astrid Kirchherr. While this was also an atmospheric evocation of both the young Beatles and the Hamburg scene, Fab Four trainspotters were able to alight on several liberties taken with known fact.

These were corrected when one of the authors [AC] was commissioned by Pan-Macmillan to write the - now out-of-print - tie-in book with Pauline Sutcliffe, the late Stuart's younger sister. Thus the saga was traced as accurately and as adequately as anyone might reasonably expect.

2001, however, saw the publication - also by Macmillan - of *The Beatles Shadow: Stuart Sutcliffe & His Lonely Hearts Band,* Pauline's subjective re-write of *Backbeat* - which was almost like reading the same book in a parallel dimension. She now claims that John and Stuart's mere scuffle in the movie was actually a full-blooded assault that climaxed with Sutcliffe sustaining a kick in the head which "was what eventually led to Stuart's death".

Now hang on, Pauline. The film blamed some thugs who set upon him and knocked him unconscious outside some Liverpool pub. Some Beatle annals pinpoint a similar occurrence during a punch-up after a booking at Seaforth's Lathom Hall on either 30 January, 4 February or 6 February 1961 - but didn't you and Clayson decide that his death was most likely to have been caused by drugs? This was based on an examination of Stuart by a Dr. Peter Hommelhoff, Director of Medicine in a Hamburg hospital, who decided that the patient's poor state of health was the legacy of too much alcohol and, especially, Preludin. "Cerebral paralysis due to bleeding into the right ventricle of the brain" was noted in the post-mortem report as an apparent confirmation of Hommelhoff's diagnosis rather than any blow to the head.

Hamburg's Reeperbahn - the red-light district where The Beatles worked, on and off, in the early 1960s - was a narcotic ghetto as well as a sexual one. Containing amphetamines, Preludin (and Captigun) were brands of appetite suppressants for dieters. Outlawed during the 1950s in Britain, they were, professedly, available only on prescription in Germany. Nevertheless, unauthorized caches could be obtained with ease, and it was no hanging matter if you were caught with them. Most Hamburg police officers couldn't be bothered with the paperwork.

For all-night assaults on course work, some of the students with whom The Beatles fraternized dosed themselves with more Preludin than that recommended by doctors. For purposes other than fighting the flab too, supplies came to be stocked for employees' use in most Reeperbahn establishments that kept Dracula hours. This ensured that the final session of the night by a given club's resident rock 'n' roll group would be as energetic as the first at dusk. Weeks of youthful energy were burnt up in sixty minutes of metabolic chaos.

In broad terms, the after-effects of amphetamines vary from person to person. Some can take speed every day without paying a price, but Stuart Sutcliffe couldn't. The rocky road to his fatal cerebral haemorrhage on Tuesday, 10 April 1962 was signposted by classic drug withdrawal symptoms. It began with ringing headaches, hyperactivity, black-outs, panic attacks, irritability and long wakeful periods in bed. More sinister were muttered trepidation building to Hitlerian screech; muzzy eyesight as a harbinger of temporary loss of vision; dizziness; swaying and staring vacantly as a prelude to a convulsive fit; nightmare hallucinations ('the horrors') and other disturbances that reduced Sutcliffe to a pathetic isolate.

He'd be seen sitting with Astrid at a club's most secluded table, lost in melancholy and paranoia, his fingers pressed against his forehead, and his lips pressed together as if holding back pain. When his eyes weren't screwed shut, she noticed that their twinkle had gone; a burned-out look was emphasized by purple-black blotches beneath them, like mascara that had trickled and dried.

To those back home who could not see his emaciation and corpse-grey colour that he radiated, the only indication that anything was amiss was in letters that flitted too fitfully from topic to unrelated topic in handwriting that, becoming noticeably larger and more spidery, deteriorated to near-illegibility like Captain Scott's log as its writer died by inches in the Antarctic blizzards.

57. The Beatles were the first Mersey Beat act to reach Number 1 in Britain.

In the early 1960s, four national musical journals - *Melody Maker, New Musical Express, Disc* and *Record Mirror* - published a chart that tabulated each week's best-selling singles. The latter publication relied on a list in the trade periodical *Record Retailer* (now called *Music Week*), operational since 1960. This was the one compiled by the music industry, and accepted as such as the fullest and most accurate. It was to be the main source of raw information when Guinness began publishing editions of *British Hit Singles* in 1977.

Major discrepancies between the five charts were a frequent occurrence - as exemplified by the 1964 week when The Rolling Stones' 'Little Red Rooster' went straight in at the top in the *New Musical Express* while entering at Number 15 in *Melody Maker*.

The sales territory of The Beatles' first single, 1962's 'Love Me Do', was limited initially to loyal Liverpool - where it went straight in at Number One in *Mersey Beat* - until all-important airplay on the wireless began humbly with a solitary spin crackling from Radio Luxembourg in the late evening.

'Love Me Do' slipped into the *Record Retailer* list at twenty-one on 8 December, and hovered on the edge of the Top Twenty until just after Christmas, outselling on aggregate the latest by Mark Wynter and an expedient revival of 'Love Me Tender' by Richard 'Dr. Kildare' Chamberlain. At Number One was Frank Ifield, the latest pretender to Cliff Richard's crown, with a revival of a 1949 country-and-western million-seller, 'Lovesick Blues'.

The Beatles had done well for first timers, but few would assume that they were anything other than a classic local group who'd caught the lightning once and would probably be back on the Liverpool-Hamburg treadmill of engagements by this time next year, even as Brian Epstein negotiated their maiden national tour, second-billed to Helen Shapiro, the kingdom's most popular female singer, according to the most recent *NME* popularity poll.

However, the distant rip-tide of Merseybeat that was to overwhelm Shapiro, Ifield and their sort crept closer as the New Year got underway. In January, *Mersey Beat* announced the impending release of a second Beatles single, 'Please Please Me'. According to *Record Mirror* - and *Record Retailer* - it entered at Number 16 on 2 February, jumping thirteen places the following week. It held the same position for a further seven days before reaching its apotheosis of Number 2, checkmated by Frank Ifield's 'The Wayward Wind'.

A fortnight later, it was down one place, but returned to 2 on 16 March with only Cliff Richard's 'Summer Holiday' in the way. Then it was downhill all the way - 5, 7, 11, 17 and out.

The pattern was similar in the other charts - except that *Melody Maker*, midway through the Helen Shapiro trek, had 'Please Please Me' lording it over 'The Wayward Wind'. In this respect, The Beatles were, indeed, the first Mersey Beat act to reach Number 1 in Britain - as announced by master-of-ceremonies Bob Wooler one lunchtime at the Cavern.

With a little logical blindness and retiming of the truth, The Beatles might be said to have tied at the top with Frank Ifield on aggregate, but we must add the raw information that *The Guinness Book Of Hit Singles* - the Yellow Pages of such matters - has 'Please Please Me' at 2, and confirms that the first disc by a Liverpool group to top all UK singles charts was 'How Do You Do It' by Gerry and the Pacemakers in April 1963. Yet what was becoming discernable as the 'Mersey Sound' or 'Liverpool Beat', would germinate the following month when The Beatles' 'From Me To You' eased 'How Do You Do It' from the top spot.

Seven weeks later, Gerry's second offering, 'I Like It', brought down The Beatles in turn. After The Searchers did similar damage to the Elvis

Presley's latest in August, they, Gerry, The Beatles and Billy J Kramer slugged it out for hit parade supremacy for the rest of the year, interrupted only by 'Do You Love Me' by Essex's Brian Poole and the Tremeloes.

58. The Beatles were a great 'live' act.

The months in Hamburg in the second half of 1960 transformed The Beatles from a clumsy provincial group into a peerless 'live' act. The story goes that, after a week's petrified inertia when they were moved from the Indra to the Kaiserkeller, they had slipped into gear when, purportedly, Allan Williams' exasperated yell of 'Make a show, boys' was taken up as '*Mach schau*' by club regulars. This chant infused each of the outfit's front line with the desire to outdo each other in cavortings and skylarks, eliciting a wild response.

Suddenly, The Beatles found themselves home and dry as involved onlookers - sailors, gangsters, prostitutes, tourists on a night out and teenagers who'd stumbled in from the street - rushed towards the stage or clambered onto crammed tables, worrying when the five flagged, cheering when they rallied, glowing when, ultimately, they went down well. Now that they had the knack, there was no stopping The Beatles, although, as George would recall, "All we really were was thump-thump-thump." Nevertheless, in the days before onstage monitors and graphic equalizers, vocal balance was achieved by simply moving back and forth on the microphone. The three-part harmonies of John, Paul and George were hard-won but perfected in readiness for what lay ahead for them, if not for Pete and Stuart.

As the residency continued, they came to know each other in an almost extra-sensory way whilst discovering how to 'read' an audience. Of course, there were 'good' and 'bad' nights - but there were moments when they were truly tearing it up - the most wailing combo on the planet.

By the time The Beatles returned to Liverpool, they were a hard act to follow. It was there for all to see on the first post-Hamburg date back at the Casbah. The full house remained spellbound until the final chord of the opening number, and the long moment of shell-shocked hush before clapping crescendoed to a bombardment of whistling, cheering, stamping pandemonium.

The group continued to dole out casually cataclysmic performances that their lengthy sojourn in Germany had wrought. The next step up was to ballrooms beyond Merseyside where they became a dependable draw on a par with other proficient units - such as Dave Dee and the Bostons, Sounds Incorporated, Cliff Bennett and the Rebel Rousers - who'd likewise broken loose of local orbits.

"What we generated was fantastic," said John Lennon with quiet pride. "There was nobody to touch us." Nevertheless, he would cite the subsequent tours as a principal reason "why we never improved as musicians. We always missed the club dates because that's when we were playing music."

During the global aftermath of domestic Beatlemania, the group went into further decline through cranking out the same thirty minutes' worth of stale, unheard music night after night into the teeth of the screams.

As bootleg recordings from this period reveal, John, Paul, George and Ringo were taking numbers too fast, transitions from choruses to middle eights were cluttered, and lead guitar breaks wantonly slapdash. Once, George had taken the trouble to tune both his and John's guitars. Now neither could care less about the wavering bars of bum notes and blown riffs. "Don't try to listen to us," sighed John Lennon to a support group at Hamburg's Ernst Merke Halle in 1966, "We're really terrible these days." For devilment, the three front-line Beatles would slam sickening discords while Ringo just as deliberately stamped the bass drum on the off-beat. "By 1965, we were turning into such bad musicians," he groaned in 1991, "There was no groove to it."

They downed tools as a working band at San Francisco's Candlestick Park on 29 August, 1966. No better or worse than any other concert they'd given on that particular US tour, they ran through this final half-hour any old how, with Ringo repeating a verse of 'I Wanna Be Your

Man' and George fluffing his guitar runs as Paul tried to make a show of it. "Nice working with you, Ringo," cracked John shortly before the four piled into the nostalgic finale, 'Long Tall Sally', which had been in and out of the set since before Hamburg.

59. John Lennon and Brian Epstein had a homosexual relationship.

Although all The Beatles were the most heterosexual of males, the vice-like grip Stuart Sutcliffe appeared to have on John - and *vice-versa* - provoked in George and, especially, Paul an apprehension akin to that of a child viewing another sibling as a barrier to prolonged attention from an admired elder brother - and, for a similar reason, Lennon was to be dismayed initially when Sutcliffe and Hamburg photographer Astrid Kirchherr became an 'item' - though, alternatively, this may have been simple jealousy because he fancied her himself.

If Lennon and Sutcliffe weren't exactly David and Jonathan, June Furlong, one of the life models at Liverpool's Regional College of Art, had 'never seen two teenagers as close as those two'. In her book, *The Beatles' Shadow: Stuart Sutcliffe & His Lonely Hearts Band [Macmillan 2001]*, Pauline Sutcliffe theorizes that Stuart and John had oral sex on a bunkbed during The Beatles' first trip to Germany, but if it happened, she didn't witness it. Indeed, her source of this story was Geoffrey Giuliano's *Lennon In America* - and Giuliano was guessing too.

Giuliano and others have also made much of Brian Epstein's homosexuality - often the butt of unpleasant jibes by John over the years - and his erotic attraction to The Beatles, particularly Lennon. Yet in his first autobiography, *Beatle!*, Pete Best states that Brian propositioned him one evening in 1962, "but there had been nothing nasty about it, nothing obscene, nothing dirty. It was a very gentle approach."

When the group - now without Pete - took a fortnight's break from a hectic schedule between 27 April and 11 May 1963, Brian - godfather to the newly born Julian Lennon - persuaded John to join him for a twelve-day break in Spain. Paul McCartney remembers: "John, not being stupid, saw his opportunity to impress upon Mr. Epstein who was the boss of the group. He wanted Brian to know who he should listen to. There was never any hint that he was gay."

Some within The Beatles' circle, however, imagined that the two holidaymakers had an affair - which John denied very emphatically at the time. Brian too insisted that "It is simply not true" when asked about the matter by Don Short of the *Daily Mirror*. In any case, as it was with Pete Best, Epstein "wouldn't have done anything to frighten John off," stressed Brian's personal assistant, Wendy Hanson. "John was a womaniser - and Brian was a very sensitive person. He'd never push himself on anyone."

Nevertheless, ever the iconoclast, Lennon, routinely unfaithful as both a boyfriend and husband, may have decided to experiment for much the same reason as French sex symbol Serge Gainsbourg, who admitted in print that, yes, he'd once had a homosexual experience, "so as not to remain ignorant". In a 1983 autobiography, *In My Life*, Lennon's childhood friend and fellow Quarry Man Pete Shotton wrote that John himself had admitted that there had been a half-hearted attempt at non-penetrative sex with Epstein on one occasion in Spain, perhaps lending credence to Lennon's rationalization that "Well, it was almost a love affair, but not quite. It was never consummated - but it was a pretty intense relationship." This was also implied in 1991's *The Hours And Times*, a sixty-minute celluloid dramatization of the trip - with Lennon played by Ian Hart, the same actor who portrayed him in *Backbeat*.

Since the Spanish jaunt, there was no other indication that what passed between John Lennon and Brian Epstein was anything beyond friendship and business.

60. The expression 'Beatlemania' was first coined after the Royal Command Performance.

Towards the middle of 1963, The Beatles had been superimposed upon the grid of a British media overrun relentlessly with 'serious' news of the Profumo scandal, the nuclear test ban treaty, the Great Train Robbery, racial unrest in Alabama and, to cap it all, the West Indies beating England at cricket. Between radio reports of the kingdom's shame and east-west, black-white tension came the sinless strains of 'From Me To You'. While The Beatles gestured with cigarettes during TV interviews, and let loose the odd mild expletive like 'crap' and even 'bloody', "they were regarded as clean-living boys during the time they were getting established," confirmed Prime Minister-in-waiting Harold Wilson, "whatever may have gone on later" - or before.

Innocent scamps, The Beatles' much-copied mid-air leap on their *Twist And Shout* EP sleeve was the epitome of the antidotal Merseybeat, that was shaking theatres with healthy, good-humoured screams. All pop music was rubbish, but, by God, these Beatles were *British* rubbish. Theirs was a human interest story of Poor Honest Northern Lads Who'd Bettered Themselves. Moreover, they were good copy - plain speaking, coupled with quirky wit delivered in thickened Scouse.

Viewing figures were at their highest when, straight after the precribed hour of religious programmes on 13 October, The Beatles kicked off ITV's *Sunday Night At The London Palladium*, the central height of British showbusiness aspiration, with a teasing burst of 'I Saw Her Standing There' during a single rotation of the Palladium's revolving stage. Before the four reappeared for five numbers that they could hardly hear themselves play, the seated majority of teenagers fidgeted through endless centuries of formation dancing, US crooner Brook Benton, singing comedian Des O'Connor and the celebrated 'Beat The Clock' interlude, in which a woman was scolded by compere Jimmy Tarbuck for producing a large toy beetle from her handbag, thereby starting off another orgy of screaming.

Parents in living rooms might have remarked disparagingly about The Beatles, but children noticed that their eyes were still glued to the set for the traditional finale, when the assembled cast lined up to wave a cheery goodbye as the platform turned slowly once more while the pit orchestra sight-read the show's 'Startime' theme tune. Whenever The Beatles hoved into view, 'Startime' would be swamped in screams that would ebb abruptly as the group was carried off to the back of the stage.

The next day, the media was full of the 'overnight sensation' and its aftermath as a police cordon with helmets rolling in the gutter held back hundreds of clamorous fans who'd chase The Beatles' getaway car. One pressured journalist - the *Daily Mirror*'s Vincent Mulchrone - chronicling this mayhem, came up with the word *Beatlemania*. The phrase stuck - but Beatlemania as a phenomenon was to have less to do with the group itself than with the behaviour of the British public who, once convinced of something incredible, would believe it with an enthusiasm never displayed for mundane fact.

Thus, 'Beatlemania' was the blanket description used too when The Beatles' fabled appearance in the Royal Command Performance three weeks later on 4 November 1963 nudged the weather vane of adult toleration, if not approval, in their direction. Short haircuts would still be imposed upon sons of provincial Britain, and pop would not yet be an acceptable careers option, but parental blood had not run cold over John Lennon's chirpy 'rattle yer jewellery' instruction to the royal balcony.

The general feeling was that John, Paul, George and Ringo - as Harold Wilson was to suggest - were the stock Nice Lads When You Got To Know Them. This present fuss was seen by some sections of the media as just a prelude to The Beatles' future career as 'all-round entertainers' when, like Tommy Steele and Cliff Richard before them, they were overtaken - as they surely would be - by another short-lived 'mania'.

61. Only after Sgt. Pepper was it was deemed OK for an intellectual to like The Beatles.

To workmanlike local groups like Cass and the Cassanovas and Derry and the Seniors, The Silver Beatles had been derided as 'posers', what with Lennon and McCartney's pretentions as composers, and their and Stuart Sutcliffe's use of long words and mention of the likes of post-Impressionist painter Modigliani and the Danish philosopher Kierkegaard into conversations.

They'd once been involved too in a fusion of poetry and rock with beat poet Royston Ellis, who'd judged them to be 'more of the bohemian ilk than other young northerners of the time.' To a degree, John, Paul, Stuart - and George - played up to it. In one incident, they dumbfounded a member of another outfit in the dressing room by pretending to be reading Russian poetry to each other, each intoning and murmuring appreciatively in mock seriousness.

The Beatles' general 'arty' aura was a subliminal lure for Hamburg's young aesthetes who, perhaps via some complex inner debate, gave into a self-conscious conviviality as they tuned into the epic vulgarity taking place on stages in the Kaiserkeller, Top Ten and elsewhere in the Reeperbahn mire.

Yet in a wider world, British pop stars - as opposed to British pop *music* - had started to move up in highbrow circles on their own soil, following Adam Faith's intelligent and eloquent showing on BBC television's inquisitorial interview programme, *Face To Face* in 1960.

Adam was the first from the world of pop to experience such a grilling, and, because he gave a good account of himself, he paved the way for further 'articulate' pop spokesmen such as ex-Oxford undergraduate Paul Jones and Spencer Davis with his BA in German.

However, the notion of the music as a viable means of artistic expression wasn't taken seriously amongst prominent intellectuals until the coming of The Beatles, unless you counted the earnest fascination with the brashest of junk culture by Andy Warhol, Peter Blake - designer of the *Sgt. Pepper* montage - Eduardo Paolozzi, Richard Hamilton and other pioneers of Pop Art who listened avidly to one-shot gimmicks, dance crazes and whatever else dominated turn-of-the-decade Top Forty radio.

Initially, 'quality' newspapers like *The Times* and *The Observer* concerned themselves almost exclusively with the hysteria that accompanied Beatles performances on the 'scream circuit', putting sniffy inverted commas around their name, followed by "the Liverpool 'pop' group" or similar explanatory phrase.

Then William S Mann - who wrote for *The Gramophone* and usually covered classical music for *The Times* - entered the fray after a perhaps rather patronising fashion on 27 December 1963. The day after a prosy *Times* end-of-year cultural summary - attributed to 'Our Music Critic' - was published, Ringo Starr admitted that "we didn't understand what all this stuff about Aeolian cadences was about". Mann, who also wrote of Lennon and McCartney's 'sub-mediant key switches', 'chains of pandiatonic clusters' and 'melismas with altered vowels'; noticed a similarity between the chord progression in 'Not A Second Time' (from *With The Beatles*) and those in the coda to Mahler's 'Song Of The Earth' [*Das Lied Von Der Erde*], and even cut, dried and dissected George Harrison's maiden opus, 'Don't Bother Me' ("harmonically a good deal more primitive, though it is nicely enough presented").

Finally, he lauded John and Paul as "the outstanding composers of 1963" - two days before Richard Buckle of the *Sunday Times* had them as "the greatest composers since Schubert".

On the horizon were a random Beatles B-side, 'Yes It Is', analysed in *Music And Musicians* magazine, and Fritz Spiegl's *Eine Klein Beatlemusik*, a 1965 album of their hits arranged in the style of Mozart.

Although McCartney and Lennon would still be damned with such faint praise as "reasonable good 'amateur' composers, greatly assisted by the poverty of British composing standards" in the *Sunday Times* as late as 1966, the die had been cast, and the elevation of The Beatles from merchants of ephemera to attracting the sort who read the likes of Mann and Buckle as gospel, was in motion long before *Sgt. Pepper*.

62. The Beatles' US chart success was immediate.

The Beatles first penetrated the US *Hot 100* by proxy when, during a break in a 1963 British tour, Del Shannon booked a London studio and some session musicians for a cover of 'From Me To You', purely for the North American market. It was issued on the Bigtop label, and entered the *Hot 100* at Number 86 on 6 July, climbing nine places over the next fortnight.

Progress for Beatles records in their own right was negligible until 'I Want To Hold Your Hand' reached the Top 40 on 1 January 1964 - though everything issued previously was to sell millions when repromoted. Nevertheless, the first four singles and the *Please Please Me* long-player (minus two tracks and retitled *Introducing The Beatles*) were not deemed worthy of release by Capitol as, declared Jay Livingstone, a senior executive, "We don't think The Beatles will do anything in this market," unmindful as he was of whatever was gripping a backwater like Britain.

So it was that 'Love Me Do' was issued by Tollie; 'Please Please Me', 'From Me To You' and the album by Vee-Jay - a Chicago company that usually traded in black music by the likes of Jimmy Reed, Billy Boy Arnold and Betty Everett - and 'She Loves You' by Swan. Thanks in a perverse way to Del Shannon's version, 'From Me To You' crept by association to Number 116 towards the end of the summer, and that appeared to be that for The Beatles in the USA.

Further headway seemed an impossible dream when, in September 1963, George Harrison spent just over a fortnight at the home of his married sister Louise Caldwell, in Benton, a small Illinois mining town. The first Beatle to set foot in the United States, he also spent a day *en route* sight-seeing in New York, conspicuous only as another long-haired Englishman.

As his face hadn't been plastered over magazine covers in the States as it had been at home, he was treated at journey's end as Mrs. Caldwell's brother, some sort of musician, unrecognised, unphotographed and unpestered as he wandered the streets of Benton. How unexpectedly pleasurable it was to be a nobody again, not to have to steal into a cinema - one of these 'drive-ins' - after faded dimmers had guaranteed shelter from the stares and approaches of fans.

An interview on local radio and even a stage appearance with The Four Vests, Benton's boss group, had the impact of a feather on concrete, and Harrison was to return to Britain with a funny story about the aftermath of his night with the Vests when someone told him that 'with the right kind of backing, you could go places.' This judgement proved correct, and the next the good people of Benton saw of George was on the nationally-networked *Ed Sullivan Show* the following February.

Some would opine that The Beatles' success in this most vital market of all was because - like Bobby 'Boris' Pickett's 'Monster Mash' novelty - it was an antidote to the depressing Christmas that followed the Kennedy assassination. John Lennon's more forthright theory was that "kids everywhere go for the same stuff, and seeing as we'd done it in England, there was no reason why we couldn't do it in America."

Within months, 'I Want To Hold You Hand', 'Love Me Do', 'Please Please Me' and 'She Loves You' had all topped the national chart. Even the B-sides of the first two made the Top 40 - though 'From Me To You', the one that had climbed highest of all before 1964, could only manage Number 41.

63. *The Beatles weren't bothered by copyists.*

After the Olympic torch of Mersey Beat had been carried to every nook and cranny of the British Isles, you didn't have to look far for the principal blueprint. Moaning about it to *Melody Maker* in August, John Lennon had noticed that Gerry and the Pacemakers suffered 'terrible copying' too, but far more groups had been formed in The Beatles' image, 'pinching our arrangements and and down to the last note at that.' While some used insectile appellations - Termites, Moths, Grasshoppers *ad nauseum* - others would work the word *beat* into their titles - Beatstalkers, Counterbeats, Beat-Chics, Beat Merchants and so on.

Youth club combos in the sticks wore collarless suits and moptops that resembled spun dishmops whenever they shook their heads and went 'oooooo', and there'd be announcements in tortuous Liverpudlian accents by either 'John' or 'Paul', and an unsmiling lead guitarist who, in imagination at least, played a black Rickenbacker through a Marshall amplifier, just like George Harrison.

By mid-1964, British beat had gone international, and this large scale re-run of the hysteria at home also embraced myriad domestic 'answers' to The Beatles. From the sub-cultural woodwork crawled legion mimics who'd grown out their crew-cuts or acquired wigs, and taught themselves apposite slang - 'fab', 'gear', 'wack' and so on. A New Jersey quartet, The Knickerbockers actually scored in the US Top Twenty with 1966's 'Lies', an uncannily precise duplication of the salient points of The Beatles' overall sound.

No such luck befell more hastily assembled soundalike discs by the likes of The American Beatles, The Bug Men, John and Paul, The Manchesters, The Wackers and The Beatlettes (with 'Yes You Can Hold My Hand') - mostly by session musicians who probably bitched during coffee breaks about this Limey combo 'everyone's talking about'.

For The Beatles themselves, however, the most irritating repercussions of copying were isolated instances of local talent checkmating their originals in the charts. Off-the-cuff examples are Mississippi's Gants' lead singer, Sid Herring, sounding as Scouse as Lennon on a debut disc that xeroxed The Beatles' 1966 B-side, 'Rain' - and a New Zealand ensemble, Ray Columbus and his Invaders, who issued a version of 'I Wanna Be Your Man' which sold more than those by both The Beatles - on a New Zealand-only A-side - and The Rolling Stones combined.

Yet the British Invasion petered out, and so did the Beatles impersonators who'd sprung up in its wake. Nevertheless, the phenomenon was to rear up again with *John, Paul, George, Ringo - And Bert*, a musical play by Willy Russell, which shattered box-office records at Liverpool's Everyman Theatre in summer 1973. Its stylized portrayal of The Beatles' fable through the eyes of Bert, a fan, was uncannily close to the bone. Contrasting withn 'Pete Best', sacked and alone beneath the proscenium, was a comedy scene of 'George' trying to blow through a sitar when still new to Oriental music. When it reached the West End, the proper George looked in, primarily to see an old friend, Arthur Kelly, who was playing 'Bert'. 'George found it hard to watch,' perceived Derek Taylor, 'and I found it hard work sitting with him. It was a genuine form of suffering for him.'

The drama's climax involved Bert, who'd grown up to become a Gary Glitter-esque entertainer, deputizing for a disbanded Beatles who'd just chickened out of a reunion appearance. George didn't see this scene, having shuffled out during the interval. However, in his capacity as a movie mogul, Harrison was to finance 1978's parodic *All You Need Is Cash*, a spin-off of Eric Idle's BBC 2 series, *Rutland Weekend Television*. In it, 'The Rutles' - with Idle himself as 'Paul' - run a gauntlet from an Arthur Scouse sending them to Hamburg's Rat Keller, their rise to fame, *Sgt. Rutler's Darts Club Band*, formation of Rutler's Corps and the split following *Let It Rut*. Get the picture?

Backbeat - a silver screen perspective on John, Paul, George and Pete in Hamburg - loomed on a distant horizon then, but 'Beatle conventions' had been fixtures in cities throughout the world for years. Entertainers at these functions included units that were, if anything, even more contrived than The Beatlettes, The Knickerbockers *et al*, with their big-nosed drummers, moon-faced bass players and handles like 'Walrus', 'Cavern', 'The Blue Meanies' and 'Abbey Road'.

Other tribute bands' ambitions extended beyond the conventions - as illustrated by the raw statistic that there are nigh on two hundred such professional entities operational in Britain alone. On a global scale, however, the most famous are The Bootleg Beatles - maybe the most accurate copycats anywhere - formed from the cast of the West End musical, *Beatlemania*.

Via cleverly co-ordinated costume changes, The Bootleg Beatles cover every phase from the enlistment of Ringo to the end of the Swinging Sixties, but others of their ilk focus solely on particular periods, even paying homage to solely one Beatle - as do Hari Georgeson and Starrtime. The Silver Beatles' *raison d'etre*, however, is the ramshackle grandeur of the post-Pete Best Cavern era. In this respect, they are almost flawless in that the only faults are either minor or inavoidable - as instanced by ropey mouth-organ blowing from 'John', inappropriate plumminess from 'Ringo' during 'Matchbox' and - the most common problem of the clone groups - a right-handed 'Paul'. These may be distracting for some onlookers, but others might find them no more problematic than, say, the real Lennon's loosened tie, Paul's frequent five o'clock shadow - and, of course, the wavering tempos and fluffed riffs that the Fab Four themselves delivered on stage.

When The Silver Beatles featured in *With A Little Help From Their Friends*, the 1996 Beatles tribute package starring Cynthia Lennon, there was a peculiar sketch in which, to a delighted cheer, matronly Cynthia was embraced by Andy Powell as youthful 'John' in his high-buttoned suit.

While it's futile to hypothesise on the actual John's beyond-the-grave opinion about this and like ventures, his former colleagues seem to accept copyists as life's small change. George was vaguely intrigued when one Bootleg Beatles watcher was able to confirm actor Andre Barreau's 'George' was authentic down to 'the Liverpool leg', Harrison's rhythmic twitching of the said limb as if grinding a cigarette butt with the heel. He actually witnessed a performance at a party thrown by Dave Gilmour, and enjoyed a chat with The Bootleg Beatles afterwards, even demonstrating to them the correct chords to 'Free As A Bird'.

On the surface, Paul didn't seem to mind much either. He was, for example, quite amenable to being photographed with The Blue Meanies. Nevertheless, McCartney had pulled strings, allegedly, to prevent *John, Paul, George - And Bert* being seen in the USA. He also raised an objection that, in *Backbeat*, 'John' rather than his character sang 'Long Tall Sally', and seemed generally to be as bemused as Harrison that anyone should make a living impersonating The Beatles.

Ringo, however, remains quiet and dignified about the subject.

64. After the group became famous, there was no true 'Fifth Beatle'.

To many who heard him play with them, Pete Best will always remain a Beatle - and so will Stuart Sutcliffe. However, on the other side of the 'Love Me Do' watershed, Neil Aspinall and Mal Evans, as principals of the road crew, came to be as synonymous with the group too, almost to the same degree as Brian Epstein - whose death in 1967 provoked George Harrison to comment, 'Brian was one of us, one of the boys, as you might say.' He'd have liked to have been.

Over the years, less plausible candidates have nurtured a close enough affinity to John, Paul, George and Ringo to be rated - by either themselves or those with vested interest - as a 'Fifth Beatle'. Off-the-cuff examples of what is a faintly ludicrous notion anyway, are New York disc-jockey Murray the K (later, 'the Sixth Rolling Stone' too) - because he almost-but-not-quite blagged his way into rooming with George Harrison during the first US visit - and Jimmy Nicol, Ringo's replacement at four venues during a world tour later that year.

Then there was Harry Nilsson, referred to in *Beatlefan* and further post-1970 fanzines as a 'quasi-Beatle' - and Klaus Voorman, who, like the stock Hollywood chorus girl thrust into a sudden starring role, was a central figure in spurious rumours about The Beatles' reformation. See, as Paul was *persona non grata*, the other three were going to try again with their old Hamburg friend - and former Manfred Mann bass player. 'New Beatle Klaus Goes Into Hiding!' *Melody Maker* had front-paged on 27 March 1971 when he and his wife had spent a few days at George Harrison's spread in Henley-on-Thames.

John, *Klaus*, George and Ringo were not to be - but Paul, George, Ringo and the ghost of John were to be heard on disc in 1996 when 'Free As A Bird' and 'Real Love' took shape. These were produced by Jeff Lynne rather than the now rather elderly George Martin. And it's Martin who, perhaps more than even Brian Epstein, has a legitimate claim to be the Fifth Beatle, in the sense that their music would have sounded very different without him.

His efforts as the group's artistic midwife "represented the highest examples of recorded art from every standpoint," gushed fashionable 1970s producer, Richard Perry. Nevertheless, when The Beatles entered his life in 1962, George had been long steeped in UK record industry conservatism. This was a culture that frowned on a jazz drummer removing his jacket during a record date, and stuck to Musicians' Union-regulated session times with prescribed tea breaks and an hour off for lunch. Yet, with Martin's approbation, this was to be challenged when The Beatles, having proven themselves as sound an investment for EMI as Elvis Presley had been for RCA, were able to run over into the small hours and created what George Harrison was to describe as "new meanings on old equipment".

From the beginning, George Martin involved the group in the technical side of studio methodology. One of the least dogmatic of British recording managers, he was also prepared to accommodate the most radical suggestions - initially, The Beatles' preference for a Lennon-McCartney original - 'Please Please Me' - to the perky and 'professional' 'How Do You Do It' that Martin considered ideal for them. Its predecessor,'Love Me Do', had been presented as, recalled Lennon, "a slower number like Billy Fury's 'Halfway To Paradise', but George Martin suggested we do it faster. I'm glad we did." He confessed later, "We all owe a great deal of our success to George, especially for his patient guidance of our enthusiasm in the right direction."

As dirge-like in embryo as 'Love Me Do', the arrangement of the 'Please Please Me' follow-up was, on Martin's instructions too, simplified and accelerated, with tight harmonies, responses behind Lennon's lead vocal - and, reported *Mersey Beat*, "intricate drumming effects". Indeed, The Beatles' unique drum sound was down to George Martin's miking experiments with varying degrees of acoustic overspill and practice of swathing the tom-toms in dishcloths and even blankets to achieve the 'pudding effect', as it was jargonised.

Such explorations became less tentative when EMI, acceding to The Beatles' every desire, allowed them unlimited Abbey Road time and, like unrestrained children in a toy shop, the freedom to requisition all manner of auxiliary instrumentation - and, later, musicians - as well as fiddle about with whatever weird-and-wonderful implement was either lying about their favoured Studio Two or staring at them from one of the complex's storerooms.

In this workshop-playroom ambience, George Martin was quite amenable to, for example, an Arabian bongo pepping up 'Don't Bother Me' on *With The Beatles*; Ringo swatting a packing case in place of snare on 'Words Of Love' from 1964's *Beatles For Sale*, and the hiring of a string quartet for 'Yesterday'.

Little would seem strange after George Martin declared his independence from EMI in 1965 via the formation of his Associated Independent Recording (AIR) production company, and reached his apotheosis as a console boffin during the making of *Sgt. Pepper's Lonely Hearts Club Band* .

Engineers muttered darkly but said nothing out loud when, say, dials went into the red or Martin razored a tape of Sousa marches to pieces and ordered someone to stick it back together any old how for the instrumental interlude in 'Being For The Benefit Of Mr. Kite'. Elsewhere, vocals floated over layers of treated sound, and gadgetry and constant retakes disguised faults. A mere ten hours - the time spent recording the four's first *LP* - was no longer considered adequate for one Beatles *track* by 1967. This was exemplified the following year when 'Not Guilty' - a George Harrison number remaindered from *The Beatles* - ran to a marathon 100-odd takes.

Throughout the subsequent *Let It Be* project, The Beatles subjected George Martin - no longer the imposing figure he'd been in 1962 - to the same oafish discourtesies they were rendering each other. This was among reasons that he became as sick of *Let It Be* as they did.

Nevertheless, the team - John, Paul, George, Ringo and George - rallied for the *Abbey Road* finale - which the discerning Frank Zappa regarded as "probably the best mastered, best engineered rock 'n' roll record I've heard," albeit adding "which has nothing to do with the material on the album."

George Martin stuck it out to this bitter end because he loved The Beatles' music enough to use his own George Martin Orchestra for the self-explanatory long-player *Off The Beatle Track* in 1964, and to supply apposite incidental music for the *Yellow Submarine* movie.

Yet Martin also qualifies as Fifth Beatle for what he *didn't* do. He wasn't concerned with inflating songs with gratuitous frills or heavy-handed orchestrations. Back in 1962, he'd dismissed the notion of either singling out one of The Beatles as nominal 'leader'. Neither had he foisted his own compositions on The Beatles as, say, Pye's Tony Hatch did on The Searchers or Decca's Tommy Scott on Twinkle and Them, taking advantage of a young group still too much in awe perhaps of the condescending voice calling them to order via the control-room intercom to splutter, "We'd rather not, sir."

65. On their first national tours,
The Beatles always stole the show.

On their maiden round-Britain tour, the main attraction was, technically speaking, Helen Shapiro apart from two dates when she was indisposed, and Danny Williams and Billie Davis - UK vocalists with a backlog of hits and a current chart strike - were drafted in to pad out the something-for-everyone bill. All three were backed by the all-purpose Terry Young Six, who kicked off each night's proceedings fronted by hip-shakin' Terry.

By the final night - 3 March 1963 - Helen was still closing the show, but the *de facto* headliners were The Beatles for whom considered applause had unfurled into screams. She hadn't a prayer from the start. Her last two singles had flopped badly and there'd been dispiriting press articles which discussed whether she was 'A Has-Been At Sixteen', while The Beatles, buoyed mid-tour by a Number 2 hit with 'Please Please Me', were, according to Barry Booth of Terry Young's combo, "very new news. There were buzzes of conversation about this new quartet. The unusual spelling of 'Beatles' was causing comment."

In less than a week after the Shapiro jaunt, The Beatles were supporting Tommy Roe and Chris Montez - also accompanied by Terry Young's sextet - on another 'scream circuit' trek. Despite going off the boil at home, the boy-next-door North Americans each went through the motions on opening night in East London with stock 'wonderful-to-be-here' vapourings and, sneered the *New Musical Express,* - perhaps unfairl*y* - "no semblance of a stage act".

Worse, Chris and Tommy were obliged to conduct themselves with observed good humour when, well before the final night, the running order was reshuffled as crowd reaction dictated that the home-grown Beatles play last, even on the three stops where they appeared as a trio, owing to John's absence with 'flu.

The next such expedition in May wasn't, however, a similar walkover for John, Paul, George and Ringo. According to contract, top of the bill was the long-awaited Roy Orbison - who, bar the remote Elvis Presley, was to command the most devoted British following of any US pop star - supported by The Beatles, Gerry and the Pacemakers, The Terry Young Six and various all-styles-served-here small fry. Arriving at Slough Adelphi, a jet-lagged Roy had barely sat down when Lennon and Brian Epstein asked if he'd got a minute. It was like this: "They said, 'How should we bill this? Look, you're getting all the money, so why don't The Beatles close the show?' I don't know whether I was getting that much more than they were. It wasn't that much - and the tour had sold out in one afternoon."

No-one could pretend that Orbison was the foremost cause of this quick profit. The Beatles' 'From Me To You' would be a Number 1 fixture for the duration of the tour. Shrieking pandemonium and chants of "We want The Beatles!" would greet even compere Tony Marsh's attempts to keep order.

In the wings, Orbison - at twenty-seven, rather an elder statesman of pop - steeled himself to face facts before someone else's audience. Yet he was to be no lamb to the slaughter like Roe and Montez. Battle-hardened by more than a decade in the business, he proved still able to work that old magic without obvious effort, enough to disconcert any British beat group, chart-riding and frantic, on the same bill.

All he had to do was stand his ground with his black guitar and sing the nine hits he'd racked up since 1960. Indeed, he was required to reprise 'Running Scared' mid-set while the sustained and rabid cheering - rather than screaming - after his 'In Dreams' finale was such that impresario Tito Burns at the back of the hall bore witness that "after thirty minutes - he was booked to do fifteen - we still couldn't get The Beatles on. This was the first time I'd seen a standing ovation in Slough."

Thus was set the pattern for the rest of the three weeks that Orbison preceded The Beatles on stage. "He'd slay them, and they'd shout for more," sighed Ringo, "In Glasgow, we were all backstage listening to the tremendous applause he was getting. He was just standing there, not moving or anything."

Typifying the underlying good nature of British pop's most optimistic period was Roy's initiation into its spirit: "I remember John and Paul grabbing me by the arms and not letting me go back to take my curtain call. The audience was yelling, 'We want Roy!' and there I was, held captive by The Beatles, who were saying 'Yankee, go home.' So we had a great time."

66. *Stuart Sutcliffe was a minor talent whose posthumous reputation owes everything to his association with The Beatles.*

The Fab Four's long shadow provided Stuart Sutcliffe's posthumous career with both the best and worst start. In 1964, his first major retrospective in Liverpool's Walker Gallery was attended by coachloads of Beatle fans with only the vaguest notion of what they had come to see. They may have shared the *Liverpool Daily Post* reviewer's "impressive and moving experience" - but, to them, Stuart was less an artist than The One Who Died, the auburn-haired one when the others were dark, the one whose name is less likely to trip off the tongue than even Ringo Starr's predecessor, Pete Best.

Touchingly, Sutcliffe's image was to be included among more fabled celebrities on 1967's *Sgt. Pepper's Lonely Hearts Club Band*'s album sleeve montage. Before that year was out, The Beatles also made veiled reference to their departed colleague in the *Magical Mystery Tour* soundtrack package. Finally, during the 1990s, small fortunes changed hands for Sutcliffe oil paintings, not in the murmur of museums or art gallery committee rooms but in the unrefined bustle of pop memorabilia auctions.

Consequently, regardless of how regrettable a loss he was to the world of fine-art, as a figure in time's fabric, Stuart Sutcliffe's period as a Beatle is still central to most considerations of him. Moreover, there remains division over whether he was gifted - even brilliant - in absolute terms or merely a minor talent in saga of John, Paul, George and Ringo.

Before he entered The Beatles' orbit, Stuart had been a pupil at Prescot Grammar School where he became as well known for his ability to duplicate any known artistic form as the school bully and football captain were in their chosen spheres. The sixteen-year-old's skills were precocious enough for enrolment at Liverpool's Regional College of Art in autumn 1956 at below the normal age of admittance.

He was soon recognized as a being apart from his fellows, as he homed in on details that others in a given class might be too lackadaisical to consider or even notice. Art history lecturer Nicholas Horsfield noticed that Sutcliffe was also more *au fait* than most with the historical traditions and conventions of fine art, and his cultivation of a personal style more advanced. Though painting was to be the main content of his work, he proved no slouch at collage, life studies, charcoal drawing and other areas in his intermediate years. Three-dimensional work held no terror for him either. Neville Bertram, his sculpture tutor, recalled a Sutcliffe wood-carving of "a mother and child that could have been a Henry Moore" - while department head Philip Hartas maintained that "he could have been a sculptor as easily as he could have been a painter."

"It wasn't until I heard about how clever he was that I became interested in his work," conceded Arthur Ballard, the most omnipotent of post-war Merseyside painters, "I had met other gifted students who were more competent in the disciplines, and probably much better technicians than Stuart, but few if any had that particular kind of spark that was genius."

Ballard was, therefore, disappointed when, with the proceeds of the sale of one of his paintings - to no less than the son of the very founder of the biennial John Moore's Exhibition of Contemporary Arts - Sutcliffe made a down-payment on a bass guitar and joined what became The Beatles. Disappointment turned to rage when Stuart took a sabbatical from college when the group went to Hamburg in 1960. "A potentially brilliant artist was lured away from what he was most serious about and really wanted to do," sighed Arthur, "for twenty pounds a week."

Nevertheless, Ballard provided a testimonial when Stuart, his tenure with The Beatles almost up, recommended his studies at Hamburg's State School of Art - *Staatliche Hochschule* - in 1961. He was able to proceed immediately to a Master Class in painting and sculpture supervised by visiting professor Eduardo Paolozzi, a leading pioneer of British Pop Art.

Though it wasn't all smiles between Sutcliffe and Paolozzi, termly reports were golden: "One of my best students. He is working very hard and with high intelligence." When both he and Stuart were gone from Hamburg, Paolozzi would praise his former student as "slightly ahead of the rest of the class. Whatever he did, he'd take things a little bit further than anyone else. Stuart would always be the most imaginative, the most daring. He had brains and he wasn't inhibited."

Praise indeed - but Paolozzi would be less charitable later: "In my period, he wasn't interested in learning. He just wanted to do his own thing."

Yet this strategy yielded a renaissance in Stuart Sutcliffe whose most enduring work lay ahead of him. He found that the lay-off since leaving the Liverpool college had wrought in him a shaper technical assurance and a more subtle sense of colour. Decades after the oils had dried, poet-painter Adrian Henri, speaking at a 1990 Sutcliffe retrospective at Liverpool's Bluecoat gallery, acknowledged that "Some of the self-directed Hamburg abstracts look as good today as when they were painted and as relevant. His posthumous reputation doesn't need the glamour of his former band to enhance it."

Stuart's former Beatles colleague, Paul McCartney, has been but one pop star actively involved in fine art. David Bowie, The Who's John Entwistle and Rolling Stone Ron Wood have more than dabbled too, but comparison of Stuart Sutcliffe to such luminaries is superficial. He belonged to an older romantic tradition that encompasses the brief and unquiet lives of such as Raphael, Van Gogh, Seurat and Modigliani.

"Artists whose lives are cut short are interesting," agreed Nicolas Horsfield, "In most cases, the artist had fulfilled himself. Part of Van Gogh's suicide was because he realized this, and he feared success. Raphael, of course, has fulfilled himself. Seurat, who died at thirty-eight, had not, and it's fascinating to wonder how he might have changed. Stuart's work ended abruptly at a much earlier stage, sixteen years earlier than Seurat. All Seurat's development took place in that sixteen years - which were denied to Stuart."

67. The Beatles resulted from "an English Grammar School interpretation of rock 'n' roll".

As telegraphed in their very name, The Quarry Men's mainstays were members of Quarry Bank Grammar School. Later members were recruited from Bluecoat Grammar and Liverpool Institute High School for Boys. That may have been why George Harrison suggested that The Beatles resulted from "an English Grammar School interpretation of rock 'n' roll" - implying that theirs was somehow a more 'intellectual' approach, compared to other Merseybeat exponents.

Yet The Quarry Men weren't skiffle purists. Nor were they inclined to research far beneath skiffle's chewing-gum-flavoured veneer to its blues and hillbilly nitty-gritty. From the beginning, their repertoire also embraced rock 'n' roll direct from the hit parade - and it was this element that had impressed Liverpool Institute pupil Paul McCartney when he'd attended that historic performance at Woolton summer fete in 1957.

'No Other Baby', a B-side by The Vipers - perhaps second only to Lonnie Donegan in the UK skiffle hierarchy - was to be revived by McCartney on 1993's *Run Devil Run*, but, by 1960, when The Quarry Men had evolved into The Beatles, nearly every non-original in the set was a kowtowing to Elvis Presley, Chuck Berry, Jerry Lee Lewis, Little Richard and Buddy Holly plus lesser North American giants of classic rock. During the subsequent era of well-scrubbed boys-next-door, items like Bobby Vee's 'Take Good Care Of My Baby' and Tommy Roe's 'Sheila' were delivered more or less straight too - with little to indicate that The Beatles' take on these was any more 'scholarly' than those of Rory Storm and the Hurricanes, Gerry and the Pacemakers, Kingsize Taylor and the Dominoes or any other local act containing members from every kind of academic background.

Low in the hierachy of regional popularity then were The Four Jays - later, The Fourmost - who made much of the twenty-eight GCE passes they had between them. Their stage act embraced an element of conscious comedy plus a rather polite approach to the numbers that everybody else did - but not too polite, otherwise they'd have risked being lynched in some of the rougher suburban palais. Nevertheless, if anything, theirs, not The Beatles', was perhaps the closest Liverpool came to "an English Grammar School interpretation of rock 'n' roll".

While The Beatles and The Fourmost - The Searchers too - became distinctive through their adaptations of songs by US girl groups (notably The Shirelles) to a different set of hormones, items like Richard Barrett's 'Some Other Guy', Chan Romero's 'Hippy Hippy Shake' and 'Twist And Shout' from The Isley Brothers became Merseybeat 'standards' by the early 1960s. The party line now was to make each of them *not* sound like any other group's arrangement. Hence the calm precision of The Searchers' 'Twist And Shout' and The Beatles' frantic work-out of the same, just one step from chaos.

The Beatles scarcely bothered with items by British stars, who, in any case, tended to cover American records. Only a handful of discs peculiar to UK artists were deemed as up to US standards. Among these were Johnny Kidd and the Pirates' atmospheric 'Shakin' All Over', 'Apache' from The Shadows and 'A Picture Of You' by Joe Brown and the Bruvvers. There were also game attempts at specific audience requests such as Frank Ifield's 'I Remember You', the finale of the 1977 album, *Live At The Star-Club, Germany, 1962*. Moreover, sniffing the wind in 1960, The Beatles had been writing instrumentals in the style of The Shadows, and, much as John Lennon professed to despise their showbiz polish, as a guitarist, he'd "vamp like Bruce Welch [The Shads'rhythm guitarist] does".

Finally, when warming up each day during the fraught recording of *Let It Be*, John, Paul, George and secondary modern Ringo reacted instinctively to the preludial "Weeeeeell" that had pitched them into a majority of twelve-bar rockers born of an alien idiom back in the old days when The Beatles - like most other UK entertainers - were obliged to make the most of a second-class and, arguably, counterfeit status to the US rock 'n' rollers who'd shown them the way.

68. Wives broke up The Beatles.

"I don't think you could have broken up four very strong people like that," conjected Yoko Ono in 1980, "There must have been something that happened within them - not an outside force at all." The new brides of John Lennon and Paul McCartney were among the catalysts, but the disbanding of The Beatles was caused by matters less specific, connected with their own inner natures and desires - and when it dawned on them that not everything they did was great.

When auditioning to join The Texans - later, Rory Storm and the Hurricanes - in 1957, fourteen-year-old George Harrison had played and sang Gene Vincent's arrangement of a song from the 1920s, 'Wedding Bells'. Its hookline ran "Those wedding bells are breaking up that old gang of mine."

"The old gang of mine was over the moment I met Yoko," agreed John Lennon. Forgetting about both previous *amours* and his first wife, he continued: "It was like when you meet your first woman, and you leave the guys at the bar and you don't play football anymore and you don't go play snooker and billiards. Maybe some guys like to continue that relationship with the boys, but once I'd found *the* woman, the boys became of no interest whatsoever, other than they were like old friends - but it so happened that the boys were well known and not just the local guys at the bar."

Like most of their fans, The Beatles' authorized biographer, Hunter Davies, still blamed - and continues to blame – "the arrival in John's life of Yoko Ono" for the end of the group. At the time, a perturbed *Beatles Monthly* had passed her off as John Lennon's 'guest of honour' after he brazened it out by escorting her to London's Old Vic theatre on 18 June 1968 to catch an adaptation of his slim 1964 volume, *In His Own Right*. *Two Virgins*, the Bed-Ins and further 'happenings' were to follow swiftly.

Of all the other Beatle couples, Ringo Starr and his wife Maureen swooped most unquestioningly to Lennon's defence. The *Two Virgins* sleeve was, concluded Ringo, "just John being John. It's very clean." Yoko became "incredible". No-one doubted it either. "We'd be pleased when people realize that she's not trying to be the fifth Beatle," Starr continued - though, when waiting to console Yoko before Lennon's cremation twelve years later, he was overheard to mutter, "It was her who started all this." This indicated an adjustment of his previously stated opinion, as late as 1971, that her and John's amour had not taken priority over group commitments. "Ringo was a little confused," deduced Klaus Voorman, "because John's closeness to Yoko was sad to him. John and Yoko were one person, which was difficult for him to accept."

George Harrison, however, wasn't confused at all. One day at Savile Row, he could no longer contain his resentment. He burst into the couple's office and came straight to the point. Naming Bob Dylan among those with a low opinion of uncool Yoko, Harrison went on to complain about the present 'bad vibes' within The Beatles' empire that were co-related with her coming. "We both sat through it," said John. "I don't know why, but I was always hoping they would come around."

Having let off steam, George - whose own marriage was floating into a choppy sea - did try to come around. He and John were the only Beatles heard on Lennon's then-unissued 'What's The New Mary Jane', which, though it had lyrics and a tune, was closer in concept to 'Revolution 9' than it was to a Bona Fide song like, say, 'Birthday' (on which Pattie Harrison and Yoko had provided backing vocals).

With all pretensions The Beatles' four-man brotherhood now gone, Yoko's constant and baleful adherence to John at Abbey Road entitled Paul McCartney to bring along girlfriend Linda Eastman, who was from a family of US showbusiness attorneys. While Linda and the older Yoko had both attended school in the same smart New York suburb, they didn't have much in common, although they were both to marry their respective English *beaux* during the same month of 1969.

There were moments of congeniality, but generally lukewarm rapport between the chief Beatles' immovable women was one of Ringo's "little niggly things" - one of them - that cropped up as the group worked through *The Beatles* and then *Let It Be*. "The most miserable session on Earth," scowled John.

The atmosphere was, however, far worse at business meetings. To disentangle Apple's disordered threads, Lennon persuaded Starr and Harrison to join him in championing Allen Klein, while McCartney advocated his own father-in-law, Lee Eastman.

As if children of parents who stay together just because neither has yet quite enough motivation to leave, Ringo and George - who'd both quit briefly already - were waiting for one of the other two to marshal his words and dare the speech everyone knew he'd been agonising over for months. All four prepared for the eventuality after their individual fashions, with Starr consolidating his then promising film career and, like McCartney, recording a solo album; John with his new *Plastic Ono Band* and espousal of various causes, and Harrison, apparently attempting to compose a stage musical with Derek Taylor and the soundtrack to a western starring Ginger Baker (!). Neither of these Harrison projects came to fruition, but it was George, his own marriage all but over, who was to emerge in the first instance as the most engaging and commercially operable ex-Beatle.

69. John Lennon was, technically, a poor vocalist.

By European *bel canto* standards, the adult John Lennon 'couldn't sing' - not 'real singing' as sonorous as Roy Orbison's supple purity or Elvis Presley when he tried hymns. Though briefly a choirboy at St. Peter's, Woolton's Parish Church, Lennon's voice lost vowel purity and nicety of intonation, probably because while it was either still breaking or just freshly broken, he was endeavouring consciously to sound like the rock 'n' roll newcomers he admired. As Gene Pitney's polished tenor would be warped to an electric drill-like whine - albeit an oddly appealing one - so John's chorister soprano was corrupted for all time by, say, the hollered arrogance of Jerry Lee Lewis, neo-hysterical Little Richard and Gene Vincent, 'The Screaming End'.

Come 1960, and he'd spat out the nicely-spoken Lancashire plum forever, and had acquired a baritone that was bashed about and lived-in: in other words, the voice of a great rock 'n' roll vocalist. It got more strangled as he broke sweat, and his adolescent spots rose through the lacto-calomine and turned red. He was probably nothing without the PA system, but when John got intense, every sound he dredged up was like a brush-stroke on a painting. Backing off until the microphone was at arm's length, just a sandpapery quiver during a dragged-out note could be as loaded as a roar with it halfway down his throat.

Yet - as demonstrated by the coda of 1968's 'Happiness Is A Warm Gun' - he could swerve cleanly into falsetto, having already built from muttered trepidation to strident intensity earlier in the song, tackling its surreal lyrics without affectation.

The following year, he was to win a *New Musical Express* poll in which other famous vocalists had each been asked to nominate their own three favourites.

Yet John Lennon, immodest about other matters, was genuinely unconceited about his singing to the point of insisting to George

Martin, "I can't say I ever liked hearing myself." It made him wary of compliments about such disparate items on The Beatles' first LP as downbeat and sensitively handled 'Anna' to 'Twist And Shout' on which he almost ruptured his throat with a surfeit of passion.

"I could never understand his attitude," sighed Martin, "as it was one of the best voices I've heard. He was a great admirer of Elvis Presley's early records, particularly the 'Heartbreak Hotel' kind of sound, and he was always saying to me, 'Do something with my voice. Put something on it. Smother it with tomato ketchup. Make it different.'

"He was obsessed with tape delay - a sort of very near-echo. I used to do other things to him, and as long as it wasn't his natural voice coming through, he was reasonably happy - but he'd always want his vocals to get special treatment. However, I wanted to hear it in its own natural quality."

From 'Instant Karma' to 1980's '(Just Like) Starting Over', Lennon's self-doubt persisted as an ex-Beatle who allowed Phil Spector and, co-producer of *Double Fantasy*, Jack Douglas to smother his vocals in what became a trademark echo, not only in the mix but even as he sang them onto tape, refusing to open his mouth unless this was so.

"After he left me, he did all his own distortion to his heart's content," lamented George Martin, "and I didn't like that. After all, the raw material was so good."

70. Mark Chapman murdered John Lennon
to become famous.

The worst aspects of Beatles idolatory are likely to be represented forever by the homicidal Mark David Chapman - with Britain's own Michael Abram, George Harrison's would-be assassin, a close second.

When the group landed in New York in 1964, Chapman was eight and living with his parents and younger sister in Atlanta, Georgia. He compiled the first of many scrapbooks that kept track of The Beatles' ever-unfolding career. By the time Chapman reached adolescence, every nook and cranny of his bedroom was crammed with Beatles memorabilia and merchandise: pictures of them all over the walls, and piles of records with label variations, foreign picture sleeves and the canons of associated artists: the Word made vinyl in the comfort of his own home. His function then was to remain uninvolved directly, just absorb the signals as they came.

For hundreds, thousands of hours, he'd filed, catalogued and gloated over his acquisitions, finding much to notice, study and compare. Wanting to learn everything possible about the group, no piece of information was too insignificant to be less than totally intriguing. Chapman could dwell very eloquently and with great authority on his interest, but couldn't grasp why fellow pupils at Columbia High School were not as captivated. The ones kind enough not to look fed-up regarded the rather pudgy youth in John Lennon glasses as otherwise "just a real quiet, normal guy".

When he graduated in 1973, Chapman had experienced both LSD and, fleetingly, the glory and the stupidity of being in a pop group. In keeping with a mood of the early 1970s, he was now professing to be a born-again Christian. Two years later, he was working amongst Vietnamese refugees on a reservation in Arkansas, pleasing his superiors with his diligence and aptitude for the most onerous of tasks. No longer outwardly living his life through The Beatles, it was a period that Chapman would recognise as the nearest he'd ever come to contentment.

1978, however, was a climactic year for him. His parents divorced, he parted with one girlfriend and met another (whom he was to marry on the rebound), and his flat - so he claimed - was burgled, necessitating a successful application for a gun permit. He sank into a deep depression that drove him to two suicide attempts. The old Beatles craving reared up with a vengeance too to the degree that he evolved a mind-crushing fixation about John Lennon.

By autumn 1980, he had decided that the chief Beatle's control of his life could not remain remote - especially now that Lennon was re-entering public life after the release of a new album, *Double Fantasy*, and was available for interviews again with the unblinking self-assurance of old.

Chapman may have preferred John's to remain an ever-silent 'no return' saga. Perhaps he felt uncomfortable about a comeback that might make Lennon no longer his unknowing intimate, but common property again. Therefore, he finished his last shift as a security guard in Hawaii - signing off as 'John Lennon' - and appeared in New York as if from nowhere early in December 1980.

Outside the Dakota, he looked upwards, wondering what was busying those rooms at that very moment. For hours daily, he stood on that pavement, feeling endlessly patient.

Then something incredible happened! Twilight was falling on Monday 8 December when John - with Yoko Ono - strolled out of the building.

Assuming that all he had to do was autograph another copy of *Double Fantasy*, John Lennon walked on. Before the day was done, he'd be back on that same spot, open-mouthed with his life puddling out of him. Yards away, Chapman would be standing with a smoking revolver in his hand.

Most people felt that John Lennon was killed simply because Chapman - who'd also been sighted sniffing round Bob Dylan too - was as nutty as a fruitcake. This opinion was fuelled from the start by those of the police officers who detained the suspect at New York's Twentieth Precinct station. Yet Mark Chapman was to be confined not to a mental institution but gaol when, rather than seize the opportunity to deliver a headline-grabbing speech from the dock, pleaded guilty without fuss, saying tacitly that "I insist on being incarcerated for at least the next twenty years".

In New York's Attica Correctional Facility - the setting of a 1971 Lennon song, 'Attica State' - Chapman served his sentence, spending most of it separated from other prisoners for the sake of his own safety. This was a particular concern because he seemed to become something of a celebrity in his own right, being the subject of a video documentary, television interviews and numerous magazine articles.

However, now eligible for parole, an apparently remorseful and rehabilitated Chapman is, if freed, likely to become as reclusive as his victim was during the 'househusband years'. In jail, he'd blamed 'society' for his crime. He'd also refused written requests for autographs, remarking: "This tells you something is truly sick in our society. I didn't kill John to become famous, and I'm horrified by these people." Take that how you like.

71. George Harrison lived as a recluse throughout the 1980s.

A press-inspired concept of George Harrison as 'the Hermit of Friar Park' began soon after 1981's John Lennon tribute single, 'All Those Years Ago', left the Top Forty. This windfall apart, Harrison had, to all intents and purposes, lost the knack of composing chartbusters. As if in acknowledgement, *Gone Troppo* - an Australian expression suggesting leave of absence - and a 1982 album, was, so he reckoned, to be his last before he retired from pop.

He was not, however, unduly worried because he had found a full life beyond tilting for hit records. It was his HandMade film company - then averaging three or four movies a year - that generated most income these days - and, in front of millions of BBC viewers on 26 January 1986, he received from the Duchess of Kent an award for HandMade's services to British film, and planted a kiss on the royal cheek.

Such Fab Four-ish sauciness was absent on ITV a few months later when *News At Ten* showed George among protesters at an anti-nuclear rally in Trafalgar Square. Next, an appeal from the Cancer Research Fund inspired him 'to try and get something started' in order to publicise the British stretch of Steve Fonyo's marathon 'Journey For Lives' sponsored walk. Fonyo, a Canadian also known as the '$13,000,000 Man', had lost a leg to cancer. *En route* from Scotland to London in March 1987, he was joined along the Thames towpath in olde-worlde Henley-on-Thames by George and son Dhani, posing in mid-stride before press cameras after which all repaired to the Harrisons' Friar Park mansion for afternoon tea.

George continued throughout the 1980s to function as town patrician and patron of Henley events and institutions. Of all his interventions in parochial affairs, none were as intensely public as those concerning the demolition of Bell Street's fifty-year-old Regal Cinema. To a howl of rage from the seven thousand who signed an opposing petition, the art-deco theatre was to be sacrificed to extend the adjacent branch of Waitrose supermarket and create a mall of eighteen shops.

As *eminence grise* behind some of the films shown at the Regal, Harrison had needed little persuasion from borough councillor Tony Lane to join a show of strength outside the cinema on a busy Saturday morning in September 1986. Hemmed in by jotting reporters, he snarled about Waitrose's "Orwellian cynicism". Next up was wife Olivia's attendance at crowded Town Hall meetings, and Dhani joining in the booing as a children's protest march passed Waitrose. Lobbying the constituency's apparently unmoved MP, Michael Heseltine, George's sarcastic suggestion of replacing Henley's antique bridge with a wider concrete construction was met, allegedly, with a look "as if to say, 'Shut your mouth, you Liverpool git'."

Among those supporting George were Dave Edmunds, Alvin Lee, Mick Ralphs (ex-Mott The Hoople), Deep Purple's Jon Lord and other members of the self-styled 'Henley Music Mafia', local pop stars who played together, either in the privacy of their own homes or on stages like Watlington's Carriers Arms or the Crown in Pishill. From these casual, unwindings had come more palpable liaisons. Harrison, for instance, composed 'Flying Hour' with Ralphs, and 'Shelter Of Your Love' with Lee - and Lord had been on keyboards for *Gone Troppo*.

The album was dithering in the lower reaches of the charts when Harrison visited Australia. He was ostensibly house-hunting, but he also took Dhani to Sydney's Sea World, paid respects at the local Hare Krishna Temple, and even joined Elton John and Deep Purple on the boards when their respective world tours happened to reach the city during his stay. When the media got wind of his presence there, he agreed to be interviewed by *Australian Woman's Weekly* and on breakfast TV. He was also snapped arriving at an Everly Brothers concert in Adelaide, spectating at a Grand Prix in Queensland, and back in Sydney to answer questions at two literary luncheons in aid of Derek Taylor's *Fifty Years Adrift* autobiography.

Back in England, he was seen chatting with Peter Sissons, television newsreader and fellow Liverpool Institute Old Boy, at the Chelsea Flower Show, and singing to his own ukelele-plinking at a George Formby Appreciation Society convention in Blackpool. However, he'd gladly shuffled out almost unnoticed after Ringo Starr's wedding at Marylebone Registry Office in May 1981 - though a photograph of him at the reception with the groom and Paul McCartney was syndicated throughout the globe.

Ringo was present too at George's first formal stage appearance in Britain since The Beatles. At the invitation of Dave Edmunds, he was among distinguished guest musicians on *Carl Perkins And Friends: A Rockabilly Special,* a TV special broadcast by Channel Four on New Year's Day 1986 from Limehouse Studios amid London's dockland wharfs. As well as sitting with the others in a devout horseshoe round grey-haired Carl's tapping feet for the finale, Harrison was at the central microphone for three Perkins numbers, hopping from shoe to unbearably excited shoe.

He guaranteed himself a more pronounced stake in the proceedings by booking Perkins as entertainment for 1988's *A Movie Life Of George*, ITV's celebration of HandMade's first decade in business. As he was paying for it, George had no qualms about sharing the limelight with Carl - or beginning his after-dinner speech with, "Thank you all for coming. Now fuck off."

A couple spared this amicable vulgarity were Madonna and her then-husband Sean Penn. Since completing their roles in HandMade's *Shanghai Surprise* in 1986, Harrison "hadn't seen them from that day to this." After sinking ten million pounds into the flick, the company had been "damn lucky to get our money back and not lose our shirts."

He blamed this close shave on "a combination of her thinking she's a star and the way the press was gunning for her." George could sympathise with the plight of Madonna - who'd been a chart fixture for two years -

and said so at a London press conference in March. Later, tabloid stories of the Poison Penns' primadonna hauteur during day-to-day shooting in Kowloon compelled a despairing Harrison to jet out and tidy up the mess. "Sean and Madonna weren't being very nice to the crew. It's hard work, dragging equipment round places where it's freezing cold for hours - and, while she's in a warm trailer, they're trying to drink a cup of tea to keep warm, and a little 'Hello, good morning, how are you?' goes a long way under those circumstances. So when I got there, the crew hated them."

The executive producer's descent into their midst prompted the headline *"GEORGE HARRISON EMERGES AS A MOVIE MOGUL TO TAKE THE PENNS IN HAND!"*, and led Madonna to propose humouring the malcontented underlings with a party. Disgusted, George had already gauged that such tardy sweetness-and-light wouldn't wash, because, "to tell you the truth, no-one would show up". For the second time that year, he submitted himself to another paparazzi ordeal on Madonna's behalf. Clicking shutters froze a thunderous countenance in marked contrast to Mrs. Penn's smirk.

Harrison also rendered unto *Shanghai Surprise* a soundtrack, which embraced a duet with Vicki, Joe Brown's late wife, and a contribution by Jeff Lynne, whose bond with George was to prove considerably more productive in the months to follow. With Jeff at the console, George contradicted his 1982 retirement statement with a new album, *Cloud Nine* and its two hit singles that would enable the so-called Hermit of Friar Park to end the 1980s as the most popular ex-Beatle.

72. John Lennon deserved to be called 'the Howard Hughes of pop'.

By the beginning of 1975, John Lennon's fifteen-month 'lost weekend' had drawn to a close. Moreover, having gone full-cycle artistically with his *Rock 'N' Roll* album of old favourites, and a greatest hits collection entitled *Shaved Fish*, he chose to take a year off to master his inner chaos and take professional and personal stock. At a press conference back in 1964, he'd answered a question about retirement with a rhetorical "Who'd want to be an eighty-year-old Beatle?" Well, he was nearly halfway there now.

Reunited with Yoko, John was finally granted US residential status. His and his wife's happiness was completed by the arrival of their only surviving baby, Sean, on John's thirty-fifth birthday. He judged it an appropriate moment to extend the 'year off' indefinitely as Yoko's 'househusband', chiefly in the family's main home, New York's luxury Dakota Building. His retreat was, he felt, the 'karmic reaction' to the holocaust of pop, summed up by his much-quoted "Don't bother trying to Make It, because when you do there's nothing to Make".

Lennon had chosen not so much to settle cosily into middle age on the consolidated fruits of his success, but to find out what awaited him on the other side of the lost weekend, during which he'd been unable to make long-term plans. Whatever was wrong appeared to be righting itself, and the peaceful life he felt he deserved held potential for domestic stability, and providing Sean with the best of everything, especially more paternal attention than most - certainly far more than John (and Sean's half-brother, Julian) ever had.

It was enough as well to be solvent and in tolerable health after all the physical and mental violations his thirty-five unquiet years had sustained. Every day now was a bonus. In the title track to a 1979 album, *Rust Never Sleeps*, Neil Young, an *apres*-Woodstock bedsit bard, was to blurt lines like "it's better to burn out than to fade away..." that seemed to Lennon to laud the banal live-fast-die-young philosophy involuntarily played out by Jimi Hendrix, Jim Morrison, Janis Joplin, Sid Vicious and others chewed upon and spat out by the pop industry. "For what?", enquired John during one of his last interviews. "So that we might rock? If Neil Young admires that sentiment so much, why doesn't he do it?"

John Lennon had let go, stopped trying to prove himself. However, if he now seemed to have abandoned the world, the world hadn't abandoned him. Not while his work was kept before the public via The Damned's high-velocity overhaul of 'Help!' in 1976, say, or a revival of 'Working Class Hero' by Marianne Faithfull.

A centre-page *New Musical Express* article pleaded for, if not a full-time return, then Lennon's blessing on the burgeoning punk movement, but it elicited no immediate response from one no longer preoccupied with cooking up marketable food of love. Nothing from John Lennon, not even another repackaging, would show its face in the charts, from a belated appearance of 'Imagine' in the UK Top Ten in November 1975 until 1980. Neither would a solitary new melody or lyric be heard commercially from him after 'Cookin'', a self-satisfied donation to *Ringo's Rotogravure* in 1976. What right had anyone to expect more? He said as much in a brief and reluctantly-given press conference in Japan a year later.

Mention of Lennon during his 'househusband' years still brings out strange stories of what alleged 'insiders' claim they heard and saw. What seems to be true is that he attempted to write a third book, "about two hundred pages of *In His Own Write*-ish mad stuff"; that he wouldn't attend a Beatles business meeting, even though it took place in the Dakota; that only the rare postcard filtered from him to former colleagues like George Harrison; and that a visiting Paul McCartney was sent away by a harassed John via an intercom message: "Please call before you come over. It's not 1956, and turning up at the door isn't the same anymore. You know, just give me a ring."

Yet belying a growing legend of Lennon as 'The Howard Hughes of Pop' is that both Mike McCartney - Paul's brother - and Gerry Marsden were able to reach him. "I didn't see John for many years when he was in the States," reminisced Gerry, "or hear much about him other than what I read in the papers. Then once when I was appearing in New York, I called him after a gap of nearly a decade of not communicating - and it was just as if the days of the Seamen's Mission in Hamburg hadn't gone."

There was also a chance encounter with Lennon that caused a *New Musical Express* journalist to report that not only did the myth-shrouded John stand his round, but that his songwriting well was not as arid as many imagined. On the other hand, May Pang, his 'constant companion' during the lost weekend was to assert that most of John's so-called 'new' songs had been composed years before. Nevertheless, in August 1980, he and Ono recorded material sufficient to fill two albums

The first of these, *Double Fantasy* - on which Lennon's contributions could almost be labelled 'Easy Listening' - was issued that autumn when, from Rip Van Winkle-esque vocational slumber, a fit-looking forty-year-old seemed set to enter middle life as a fully integrated mainstay and wanted party guest of 'contemporary' rock's ruling class. He seemed rejuvenated as a songwriter too - as there were enough numbers left after the two albums - including stark demos of 'Free As A Bird' and 'Real Love' - for him to present 'Life Begins At Forty' and three more to Ringo Starr when, that November, the two ex-Beatles spoke for the last time, and parted as good friends.

73. Ringo Starr was absent throughout the Australasian leg of The Beatles' 1964 world tour.

For twelve days of 1964's world tour - i.e. Denmark, the Netherlands, Hong Kong and Australasia - The Beatles weren't quite the full shilling.

Ringo Starr had been spectacularly sick in the toilet during a late-morning sitting for group publicity photographs in a London studio on 3 June. Still off-colour, he'd been examined by a local doctor, who diagnosed tonsillitis and pharyngitis, but it was a high temperature that necessitated Starr's immediate removal to University College Hospital.

With the global trek to commence in Copenhagen the next day, the three functioning Beatles with Brian Epstein and George Martin gathered at Abbey Road to try to resolve the quandary. George Harrison was all for cancellation, as "playing without Ringo is like driving a car on three wheels." Nevertheless, he was persuaded by Epstein that their only choice was a substitute. Who? What was Pete Best doing these days?

"The difficulty," expounded Brian, "was finding someone who looked like a Beatle and not an outcast." Martin mentioned Jimmy Nicol, one of the workmanlike but individually uncredited Ghost Squad on *Beatlemania*, a cheap Pye LP of anonymous Beatles covers. Moreover, he had adopted a moptop, and was drumming presently with Georgie Fame's backing Blue Flames.

On that strange afternoon, twenty-four-year-old Nicol was roused from an after-lunch nap in his suburban living room by a ring from George Martin. Could he be at Studio Two by three o'clock to rehearse with The Beatles? Behind Ringo's famous Ludwig kit, Jimmy ran through the sets with them during two hours of curt tuition, mainly from John Lennon and George Harrison, and "no music script, but that didn't matter. I already knew the numbers from *Beatlemania*."

Reeling with disbelief at this amazing assignment, he telephoned an understanding Georgie Fame and dashed home to pack. On every stage, Lennon "gave me a great build-up", but by the second day, a banner reading 'Ringo Quick Recovery!' [*sic*] was hauled up during The Beatles' quasi-regal procession along the canals of Amsterdam.

The story was much the same in Hong Kong - where The Beatles played two shows - while in Australia, an Adelaide radio station was carrying regular bulletins on the likelihood of Starr rejoining his colleagues for opening night at the Centennial Hall. Across to Sydney, another presenter was whimpering that, rather than Nicol, The Beatles might have given an Aussie musician a chance. There was also alarmist hearsay that Ringo had had enough and was intending to retire.

However, rather than remain huddled under his bedclothes, contemplating a free bus pass, Starr had been touched by a telegram of the 'miss you' variety from the other three and, not wishing to inconvenience them more than was necessary - or miss any of what was still great fun - he rose after not much more than a week in bed, the minimum time allowed by the doctor. Armed with medication, he let Brian bundle him onto a flight to Sydney via San Francisco, where his transfer from Pan-Am to Qantas was accomplished after the usual press conference and fan riot.

A toy koala was thrust into his arms as he disembarked, and the grinning Sydney media let him go after he'd itemised every piece of personal jewellery he was wearing, and knocked back a goodwill glass of Australian lager. When he caught up with The Beatles in their Melbourne hotel on 15 June, a vast police inspector piggy-backed him through a crowd of thousands. Pale and shaking, he ordered a stiff drink even while heading towards the lift to his suite. He may have needed another after the illuminating experience of watching The Beatles perform that evening with Nicol at the city's Festival Hall.

Afterwards, there was a party to thank Jimmy and welcome back Ringo, who was to complete two remaining dates in Melbourne, another in Sydney, three in New Zealand, and two nights back on the mainland in Brisbane from where, on 1 July, The Beatles would fly back to England.

It was from Brisbane too that Jimmy Nicol had returned home on 16 June. By cruel contrast to his twelve days as a Beatle - when "it seemed that the whole population had turned out to meet us" - he'd been greeted by only his wife and infant son when he landed at Heathrow.

74. George Harrison organised the first major pop concert for charity.

Whenever pop charity events are discussed, the ones that trip most easily off the tongue are *Live Aid* - and, thirteen years earlier, *The Concerts For Bangla Desh [sic]*, George Harrison's finest hour.

Nevertheless, George's giant step for Bangladesh was by no means either the most successful - or the first major pop concert of this nature, depending on what you mean by 'major' in terms of both how much of the money it raised reached the unfortunate Bangladeshis, and the size of its audience.

Since the dawn of skiffle, pop musicians, regardless of motive, have given their services to raise money for irrefutably worthy causes. This could be Salisbury's boss groups - and those from other towns in Wiltshire and surrounding counties - appearing for nothing at Durrington Youth Hall on 9 December 1960 for a "Youngsters 'Rock' and Help Refugees" concert; or Belgian *chansonier* Jacques Brel taking part in Helsinki's international festival of *L'Humanité* for world youth charities in 1965. At the very start of his career, Roy Orbison sang *gratis* at huge Lions Club rallies, while, since declaring himself a born-again Christian in 1964, Cliff Richard has appeared at numerous gospel concerts in aid of the Evangelical Alliance Tear Fund to help the needy in the Third World.

Like Jacques, Cliff and most other occidentals, George Harrison was "not interested in the politics of the situation," which had emerged from the division of East and West Pakistan by both geography and worsening antagonism. In March 1971, four months after East Pakistan - now Bangladesh - had been devastated by a cyclone, General Yahya Khan amassed a Moslem army mighty enough to eradicate the Hindu minority that opposed his military dictatorship in both regions. Prostrated by the tempest's aftermath of homelessness, lack of sanitation, cholera and starvation, the East Bengalis were further traumatised by this reign of terror. Carrying their pathetic bundles, millions of refugees stumbled towards the safety of India, which had received hardly a tenth of the foreign aid required to cope with the disaster.

Ravi Shankar's own family and friends were among the ceaseless fatalities and exiles. In California during these distracted months, Ravi conceived the notion of a modest fund-raising show. When George arrived in Los Angeles in late June, a better answer clicked in Shankar's mind like a key sliding into a lock. "He wanted to do something which would make a little more money than he normally made," explained Harrison. "He gave me all this information and articles about what was going on in Bangladesh, and I slowly got pulled into it. I started getting carried away with the whole idea of doing something good, maybe making ten million dollars."

He instructed Allen Klein to book no less a venue than New York's twenty thousand-capacity Madison Square Garden, where no Beatle had gone before. The most convenient date was Sunday, 1 August 1971, which left George just sufficient time to recruit whatever musicians he could muster to support him - and Ravi, who was to open proceedings. The coup of the decade would have been the regrouping of The Beatles. Paul declined as the legal turmoil over the break-up was still a sore point, but John seemed keen until it was made clear by George that there'd be no place for Yoko on stage that day.

Ringo Starr, however, was a punctual attender at a rehearsal studio near Carnegie Hall, beating the skins alongside Jim Keltner behind the rest of the ex-Delaney and Bonnie minions - 'supersidemen' - that Harrison now gathered around him. A sort of bloated 1970s equivalent of a 'scream circuit' package, this combo, as well as a small choir and three members of Badfinger, adapted itself to a cache of 'featured popular vocalists' such as Bob Dylan, Eric Clapton, Billy Preston and George and Ringo themselves, as well as Eric Clapton, conspicuously breaking sweat over his fretboard on 'While My Guitar Gently Weeps'.

With two sold-out houses to entertain, as well as consumers of the extravaganza's movie and triple-album spin-offs, Harrison knocked together a disciplined presentation embracing hardly anything that hadn't been a smash hit for someone in the band or wasn't well-known enough for a spatter of clapping to swell and subside over its unannounced introduction. "The whole vibe on the concert was that it was something bigger than the lot of us," believed George. The customers would agree that they'd taken part, however passively, in the proverbial "something to tell your grandchildren about".

CBS was to broadcast highlights on North American television, but the rest of the world would have to wait until the following spring when the flick went on general release via Twentieth Century Fox. Out in time for Christmas, the disc package earned a Grammy and spent most of 1972 in the US *Hot 100* - though George's 'Bangla Desh' [*sic*] spin-off single was only a middling hit.

Mentioned on the LP's picture sleeve was the Bangladesh Disaster Fund organised by UNICEF, the intended destination for the $243,418.50 generated by the show plus the greater amounts accrued by disc, movie and other by-products such as George's Material World Charitable Foundation. This last was created to "encourage refugees to start growing their own food and thereby make the cash go further than it would in outright purchases." However, though record companies might have waived royalties, Harrison discovered that "the law and tax people do not help. They make it so that it is not worthwhile doing anything decent."

With no axe to grind, cells within the general public had taken George's challenge: "There were a lot of people who gave a lot of money. I suppose I inspired them - though I didn't really want the task in the first place."

The concerts might have been over, but "just that one decision to help Ravi, it took two years solid of my life". He was contemplating riding roughshod over official interference by travelling personally to India to ensure delivery of what he'd describe in a 1973 B-side, 'Miss O' Dell', as "the rice that keeps going astray on its way to Bombay." Composed the day after 1 August, another number, 'The Day The World Gets Round' had smouldered with the angry question of why a mere pop star (rather than a head of state) was obliged to pinpoint iniquities.

Headlines like *Rolling Stone*'s "Did Allen Klein Take The Bangladesh Money?" were not reassuring. More insidiously, turgid bureaucracy on both sides of the Atlantic dissected the Bangladesh millions with unhelpful slowness. George hadn't registered the event as a charity, so computer run-offs and frozen ledgers supertaxed the starving, the diseased and the huddled masses fleeing from the terror. Only a fraction of the net takings was received by Hugh Downs, an executive on the US committee for UNICEF.

With *The Concerts For Bangladesh*'s shipwrecks as his sea marks, Bob Geldof - who sought Harrison's advice beforehand - would be knighted for *Live Aid* in 1985, but further back on rock's road to respectability, George Harrison's efforts would be rewarded by an elevation to *Playboy*'s 'Musicians' Hall Of Fame'. He'd been awarded the MBE for less.

75. *Ringo was an unremarkable drummer at best.*

Among Paul McCartney's many musical skills are the hand-and-foot co-ordination and accurate time-keeping that are the basic requirements of a good drummer. Recognised as such, he has been heard on releases such as Paul Jones's 'And The Sun Will Shine' and Jackie Lomax's 'Thumbin' A Ride'. Even before The Beatles enlisted a permanent drummer in Pete Best and then Ringo Starr, Paul would be obliged sometimes to beat the skins on stage. He would be behind the kit too when Best was required to sing and demonstrate the Peppermint Twist.

Although it was never implemented, there was debate about a Ringo Starr dancing display too - 'But only for certain audiences,' mused McCartney, 'We all mess around on the drums a bit, and we could take his place now and then.'

On disc, they were to do so when, during Ringo's absence for a fortnight during sessions for 'the White Album', McCartney, John Lennon and George Harrison managed between them a composite drum part for 'Back In The USSR', and were about to minister likewise to 'Dear Prudence' when he returned (though some sources attribute the drumming on both to McCartney alone). Some of the stick-thwacking on the second side of *Abbey Road* was entirely McCartney's doing - as was all of it on 'The Ballad Of John And Yoko'.

In every case, it had nothing to do with Lennon's joking "Ringo wasn't even the best drummer in The Beatles". Instead, corner-cutting pragmatism had ruled as it had when a session drummer was on hand to ghost the drumming on one of the released versions of 'Love Me Do'. This was standard practice and no conscious slight on Starr's - or Pete Best's - ability as an instrumentalist. Nevertheless, when asked in 1992 if he ever felt sorry for Pete, Starr insisted, "No. Why should I? I was a better player than him. That's how I got the job. It wasn't on personality." In parenthesis, John was to qualify this later with "Pete Best's a great drummer, but Ringo's a great Beatle."

As one of Rory Storm's Hurricanes, Starr had been bullied into commanding the stage alone under his own voodoo spell for minutes on end, but solos were tedious to him and, if ever he had a pet hate amongst their perpetrators, it was bandleader Buddy Rich. Rich was every smart-alec's notion of percussive splendour because "he does things with one hand that I can't do with nine". In mitigation, however - and to Starr's reported delight - Rich was to tell one of the authors [SL], that he considered the Beatle's drumming "adequate". Yet Ringo would lay himself open to misinterpretations and derogatory *bon mots* with "I like to make mistakes" with regard to his chosen instrument.

Yet praise indeed had been George Martin's acknowledgement that, in *Sgt. Pepper*'s fragmented finale, 'A Day In The Life', the distinctive scuffed drum section was entirely Ringo's idea. With Martin, Starr had been responsible too for swathing loose-skinned tom-toms with dishcloths and even blankets. "It makes me, like, thuddy," he elucidated. As the corrupted snare sound on David Bowie's *Low* LP would be in 1977, so Starr's "pudding effect", as it was jargonised - as well as his non-resonant snare - were much copied.

Within professional circles, however, he was deemed less worthy of respect than lapsed jazzmen like Bobby Elliott of The Hollies, The Rolling Stones' Charlie Watts and Pete York from The Spencer Davis Group. He was, however, in a *different* rather than *lower* league to them. Like Watts, Ringo's style was outstanding for the frugality whereby "I try and not move at all throughout a whole song, not embellish or decorate at all, keep it really, really simple." This is exemplified on 1968's 'Birthday', paradoxically one of only two instances of a Starr drum solo on disc (the other was on *Abbey Road*'s 'The End'). Although his new Drum City kit had two hanging tom-toms, neither were hit for eight petulant 'Birthday' bars of kick-bass, snare and hi-hat being bashed simultaneously on every beat - just like Mick Wilson had throughout Dave Dee, Dozy, Beaky, Mick and Tich's 1966 hit, 'Hold Tight!'.

More technically proficient sticksmen noticed too that Starr - like Pete Best - hit solidly and defiantly behind the beat by a fraction to both invest material with stronger definition and increase tension. A strategy that dated from having to *mach schau* for hours on end in Hamburg, it would not be too presumptuous to say that this - and other subtleties - were to alter pop drumming procedures forever.

"Drumming's simple," may remain yet as Ringo Starr's most enduring testament. "I've always believed the drummer is not there to interrupt the song. I am the foundation, and then I put in a bit of glow here and there. I know I'm no good on the technical things, but I'm good with all the motions, swinging my head, like. That's because I love to dance, but you can't do that on the drums."

76. 'Sgt. Pepper's Lonely Hearts Club Band' was the first pop 'concept album'.

EMI's liaison with The Beatles heralded a new attitude towards the long-playing pop record, a product that was often a testament to commercial pragmatism rather than quality, and targeted - especially in the USA - at fans so beglamoured by an artist's looks and personality to be rendered uncritical of frankly sub-standard, haphazardly programmed output, excused as an exhibition of 'versatility', but of no cultural value. Brian Wilson of The Beach Boys was to say of *Rubber Soul* that "it was the first time in my life I remember hearing a rock album on which every song was really good."

The Beatles first LP was padded with a brace of singles, but each that followed was a conscious musical progression, with an increasing proportion of tracks that were at least as good as the A-sides of the singles. Moreover, by the close of the decade, it had become common procedure to issue a 45 from an already successful album – such as 'Something'/'Come Together' from *Abbey Road*.

Nevertheless, the absence of the usual Christmas single in 1966 had made it necessary for the next 45 rpm release to consist of two tracks, 'Penny Lane' and 'Strawberry Fields Forever', intended initially for the forthcoming *Sgt. Pepper's Lonely Hearts Club Band*. This was regrettable, but not disastrous - for, with Paul McCartney and George Martin as prime movers, *Sgt. Pepper's Lonely Hearts Club Band* was being conceived not so much as a regular LP with about a dozen separate tracks, more a continuous work, with no spaces between songs.

George Harrison was to admit, "There are some good songs on it, but it's not our best album." However, with its expensive and all-encompassing precedent, record companies found themselves underwriting albums of like persuasion (e.g. *Days Of Future Passed* by The Moody Blues, John Mayall's *Bare Wires*); 'rock operas' (The Pretty Things' *SF Sorrow*, *Arthur* by The Kinks, and The Who's *Tommy* - all, technically, song-cycles) and other *magna opi* (The Small Faces' *Ogden's Nut Gone Flake)*.

George Harrison described *Sgt. Pepper* as both "a milestone and a millstone". Even if it does have epochal status, it's possible to argue - albeit with with a certain logical blindness and retiming of the truth – that it wasn't the first time such an idea had been attempted in pop. Perhaps all albums are concept albums in the sense that all pop songs expose a point of view. Is being thematic the same as having a concept?

Do soundtrack and cast recording LPs count? Before *Sgt. Pepper*, there had been any number of instances of tributes paid to a particular artist or genre over an entire album: *I Remember Hank Williams* by Jack Scott; Elvis Presley's devotional *His Hand In Mine*; *Sounds Of Christmas* by Johnny Mathis; Marty Robbins' *Gunfighter Ballads*; *Twist With Danny Peppermint*; the *Big Big Hits Of '62* medleys by Brian Poole and the Tremeloes; *Sinatra Sings Great Songs From Great Britain*; *Beatlemania* by The Ghost Squad; *Roy Orbison Sings Don Gibson*; 1966's budget-priced *A Tribute To The Rolling Stones* by The Pupils; and 1965's *The Silkie Sing The Songs Of Bob Dylan*. These are less than the tip of a boundless iceberg. What about 1963's *Little Deuce Coupe* on which The Beach Boys string together a bunch of songs about hot-rod cars, whether lauding the record-breaking 'Spirit Of America' or weeping over 'Old Betsy', maybe one oil-change away from the breaker's yard? After Brian Wilson heard *Rubber Soul*, "It flipped me out so much I said, 'I'm going to try that, where a whole album becomes a gas.'" Certainly, the consequent *Pet Sounds* - if more subtly than *Little Deuce Coupe* - created more of a specific and recurring mood than *Sgt. Pepper*.

The same is true of *I Hear A New World Part One*, a narrowly circulated 1960 EP of mood music to help audio dealers demonstrate these new-fangled 'stereo' gramophones, and its cancelled *Volume 2 sic*) follow-up. As you might gather from titles like 'Orbit Round The Moon', 'Magnetic Field', 'Love Dance Of The Saroos' and 'Dribcots' Space Boat' - not to mention the wordless 'little green men' vocals and overall electronic aetheria - it was a sound painting concerned entirely with Joe Meek's almost child-like fascination with outer space. Part of Meek's reputation as a record producer had rested for decades on *I Hear A New World* - as the officially unissued *Smile* still does for Brian Wilson - when all thirty minutes of the two *I Hear A New World* EPs was made available as a CD album in 1991, courtesy of RPM Records.

Until then, not a note from Joe's project had reached the ears of Joe Average - who, to this day, has heard nothing of an LP that was knocked together by Paul McCartney late in 1965. As reported in the *Disc And Music Echo* gossip column, a few copies were pressed as Christmas presents for just the other Beatles and his then-girlfriend, Jane Asher. It was said to be an in-joking send-up of a radio variety show with the irrepressible Paul as a one-man compere, singer, instrumentalist, comedian and all-purpose entertainer. If it ever existed, the roots of *Sgt. Pepper* may lie in this *ultima thule*, this unobtainable prize for collectors of Beatles artefacts.

If a copy ever turned up in a memorabilia auction, it would fuel McCartney's assertion that it was he who came up with the basic notion of Sgt. Pepper's Lonely Hearts Club Band, "giving The Beatles *alter-egos* simply to get a different approach", on a return flight from a holiday in Kenya in November 1966. However, he was to agree that "only later in the recording did Neil Aspinall have the idea of repeating the 'Sgt. Pepper' song, and The Beatles and George Martin began to use linking tracks and seques to pull it together, making it more into a concept album."

Whether it was 'more' or 'completely' into a concept album remains open to debate. While it did contain various segues and links plus the reprise of the title theme, it wasn't 'about' anything in the way that *SF Sorrow* or *Days Of Future Passed* were. Only at the beginning and near the end was the listener reminded of what was supposed to be Sgt. Pepper's show. "It was as if we did a few tracks," said Ringo Starr, "and suddenly there was a fire, and everyone ran out of the building, but we carried on playing." Yet, regardless of its diverted intention, *Sgt. Pepper's Lonely Hearts Club Band* is tied forever to psychedelic times past - and perhaps that's the lasting 'concept'.

77. Paul McCartney is dead.

The above statement is worthy of an entire book, but we can only scratch the surface here.

A habit of reading hidden meanings in record grooves left the runway when the music of certain pop stars was elevated from ephemera to Holy Writ. This was, of course during the time that Roy Orbison called "the crazy late sixties when it got real weird - politics, music, fashion. Everything went crazy, sort of." A classic example was the man who was so obsessed with analysing Bob Dylan's lyrics that, in order to prove one pet theory (about how his man's stimulant intake affected his muse), he placed a 'wanted' advertisement in a New York underground magazine for a Dylan urine sample.

Likewise, Beatle fans - especially in North America - began listening to their records in the dark, at the wrong speeds, backwards. Every inch of the sleeves and labels was scrutinized for veiled but oracular messages that would turn listeners into more aware, more creative human beings, truly at one with The Beatles.

The most widespread so-called *communiqué* from The Beatles was based on evidence, traceable to *Sgt. Pepper's Lonely Hearts Band,* that supported a rumour that Paul McCartney had been beheaded in a road accident on 9 November 1966 and replaced by a *doppleganger*. All that actually happened was that he cut his lip that day in a mishap whilst riding a moped. But surely you can hear John say 'I buried Paul' in a daft voice in the last seconds of 'Strawberry Fields Forever' - and at the end of 'I'm So Tired', he mumbles "Paul is dead. Bless him, bless him, bless him..." Morbid Beatle-ologists would see too the front cover of *Abbey Road* as a funeral march, with John as the Priest, the new 'Paul' the Deceased, denim-clad George as the Gravedigger and Ringo as the Sexton. There's also a car number plate with '28 IF' on it. Like, Paul would've been twenty-eight *if* he hadn't been killed (in fact, he was twenty-seven).

None of them were hits, but there was an impressive array of 'Paul Is Dead' singles behind shop counters by the close of 1969. Penetrating the crowded airwaves then were the likes of 'Brother Paul' by Billy Shears and the All-Americans, 'Saint Paul' from Terry Knight - future manager of Grand Funk Railroad - and Zacharias and his Tree People's 'We're All Paul Bearers (Parts One And Two)'. As an ex-Beatle, Lennon's snigger was almost audible when, not content with airing grievances against McCartney in the press, he sniped at him on disc in 1971 with 'How Do You Sleep' from *Imagine*, confirming that Billy, Terry, Zacharias *et al* were "right when they said that you were dead".

Ghoulish Beatlemania had reared up to an infinitely more sinister end when Charles Manson and his 'Family' had had 1968's *The Beatles* on automatic replay as they'd prepared for the Sharon Tate bloodbath, having heard revolutionary directives in Lennon and McCartney's 'Helter Skelter' and a George Harrison composition, 'Piggies'. Manson had translated the throwaway line "What they need's a damn good whacking," as an especially strident call to arms, not realising that it was originally suggested by George's mother to rhyme with "There's something lacking".

The list goes on and on, and still provides hours of enjoyable time-wasting for Beatle freaks, old and new - despite, say, a lyrical error ("two foot small" instead of "two foot tall") on 'You've Got To Hide Your Love Away' that Lennon insisted should be uncorrected because "The pseuds'll love it." More pointedly, his 'Glass Onion' on *The Beatles* denied that there were ever any secret subtexts to be found in the first place, while inserting false clues - like "the Walrus was Paul" (not Ringo) - and misleading self-quotations, "just to confuse everybody a bit more".

78. Accusations that The Maharishi was a charlatan were completely justified.

There remains bitter division over His Divine Grace, the Maharishi Mahesh Yogi. Was he a well-meaning sage sucked into a vortex of circumstances he could not resist - or was he, indeed, a complete charlatan? Born Mahesh Prasad Varma in 1918, he graduated from the University of Allahabad with a physics degree before spending the next thirteen years studying Sanskrit and the scriptures. Styling himself 'Maharishi' ('great soul'), he travelled to London in 1959 to set up a branch of his International Meditation Society, which had garnered a British membership of some ten thousand.

As implied in the titles of some of his seminars - 'Spiritual Regeneration', 'Philosophy In Action' - the overall aim was - via short, daily meditation sessions - to eradicate piecemeal all human vices and ego until a pure state of bliss was achieved. Furthermore, such washing of spiritual laundry was feasible without forsaking material possessions (bar the Society's membership fee) and, within reason, worldly pleasures. This seemed an excellent creed to a millionaire Beatle.

Practising what he preached, Varma commissioned the most up-market press campaigns, and stayed at the best hotels. While he luxuriated in New York's Plaza prior to speaking at a sold-out Madison Square Garden, handbills distributed by a one-man picket line outside railed against "capitalistic little devils within the holy man's robes". Cross-legged on a Louis XV *chaise longue*, His Divine Grace toyed with his silvery beard or a flower from the cut bouquets surrounding him whilst dealing with the North American media. "I deal in wisdom, not money," he replied when some tried to bully him into talking finance. Yet, for all the disarming public attitudes - the tee-hee-hee chuckle, the gentle voice - there was no mistaking the steel underneath.

The media uproar that The Beatles' involvement with him engendered, brought home to Varma what a catch he'd made. Previously, he'd been unaware of the group's stature, but, armed with the relevant records, he underwent a crash-course in their music, and began inserting quotes from their lyrics into his talks about karma, the transmigration of souls and the world of illusion. The band members were flattered, although a cynical comment from Ringo's uncle - 'He's after your money, lad'- reinforced certain misgivings . But this wasn't as bad as the press conference that Varma's public relations agent had set up in the main hall when The Beatles attended his initiation course at the the University College of North Wales, in Bangor. Because they hadn't exactly said no, he assured US investors that the four would be co-starring in a documentary about him. "He is not a modern man," explained George Harrison as much to himself as anyone else, "He just doesn't understand such things."

The mere mortal that *Private Eye* was to dub 'Veririchi Lotsamoney Yogi Bear' also treasured hopes of a successful recording career, having already negotiated the release of an eponymous LP - *Maharishi Mahesh Yogi* - on Liberty Records in 1967. The following year, he would also receive credit as nominal 'producer' - with pride of place on its cover - of *Cosmic Consciousness*, an album by flautist Paul Horn, one of his earlier disciples.

Horn was among the sixty seekers of nirvana - including The Beatles - at the Maharishi's *yoga-ashram* (theological college) in the Himalayas in February 1968. This visit ended on a sour note when Alex Mardas - 'Magic Alex', director of Apple Electronics - accumulated enough tittle-tattle to speak to Lennon and Harrison about Varma's alleged claudestine and earthly scheming for the downfall of a female student's knickers. The Maharishi had allegedly propositioned her with the forbidden meal of chicken as other cads would with a box of chocolates. With Alex urging him on, John confronted the Great Soul with his infamy. Deaf to protestations of apparently genuine innocence, Lennon announced his immediate departure.

Not knowing what to think then, George chose to wash his hands of the Maharishi too - though, in 1977, Harrison was to find it in himself to vindicate the guru: "I can see much more clearly now what happened," he told *Crawdaddy* magazine. "There was a lot of ignorance that went down. Maharishi was fantastic, and I admire him for being able, in spite of the ridicule, to keep on going."

Fifteen years later at London's Royal Albert Hall, George Harrison undertook what amounted to his first full-scale UK concert as an ex-Beatle. It took place on 1 April in the run-up to the 1992 General Election. His intention was to raise funds for the Natural Law Party (NLP), a political organization whose manifesto promises - for "a disease-free, crime-free, pollution-free society" - were traceable to the Maharishi. The guru was by then in his seventies and still in favour with George, if not his former colleagues.

79. Brian Epstein committed suicide.

Brian Epstein's painful commitment and often severely-tested loyalty to his principal charges was profound. He even offered, in vain, his personal fortune to compensate promoters for agreeing to cancel the final US tour in the light of real fear of an assassination attempt on John Lennon after his "We're more popular than Christ" remark. Yet as the expiry date - October 1967 - of Epstein's five-year contract with The Beatles crept closer, once-merry rumours darkened to a certainty that, perturbed by the unresolvable bungles he'd made whilst learning the job, the group were to reduce their manager's cut, and his say in their affairs.

In an interview given to *Melody Maker* in August 1967, however, he'd been "certain that they would not agree to be managed by anyone else". Television chat-show appearances - frequent by then - also assured fans that he was as much The Beatles' clear-headed mentor as he'd ever been. Indeed, he was in the midst of setting the wheels in motion for the *Yellow Submarine* cartoon film on their behalf.

To David Frost on ITV, however, he'd spoken less of the Fab Four than London's Saville Theatre in which he'd had a controlling interest since 1965. The current 'Sundays At The Saville' pop presentations, which sometimes mitigated the poor takings for the drama and dance productions during the week, had been Brian's brainwave. However, his preoccupation with this and other projects were but analgesics, alleviations to the pangs of general depression - brought on by a combination of overwork and a bout of glandular fever the previous summer - and a lonely and essentially guilt-ridden homosexuality. These had been symptomized by Brian's interrelated and increasing apathy towards the needs of his clients, even Cilla Black, his main concern after The Beatles. She was so disenchanted that she'd been on the point of leaving him until moved by both a tearful plea for her to reconsider, and a consequent swift negotiation of a weekly TV series for her.

Cilla's feelings about Brian as a businessman were not indicative of any loss of personal affection. She was among the few to whom he confessed his private anxieties. Another was Pattie Harrison, who urged George to warn Brian of the dangers inherent in the over-prescribed tablets that he took to sleep, to stay awake, to calm his nerves, to lift his melancholia.

Pattie's concern was justified, because, Westminster Coroner's Court would conclude, Brian Epstein was killed by 'incautious self-overdoses' on Sunday, 27 August 1967. The capacity of bromide in his blood was significant, reckoned the consultant pathologist. It had built up over weeks rather than hours. Too much of it makes a person forgetful about, for example, how many tablets he'd taken already. Epstein's bromide was in a drug called Carbitol, and he'd taken just enough - certainly not a massive amount - to tip him over the edge.

The previous afternoon, his secretary, Joanne Newfield, had noted that he seemed relaxed when smiling and waving to her as he drove away from his Belgravia flat for a dinner party at Kingsley Hill, his country home in Surrey. He seemed in good spirits too when he stopped at an antique shop in Uckfield. Nothing suggested that he was in anything but an agreeable mood. He also telephoned his mother, telling her that he was planning to visit her in Liverpool next week.

"We had a normal dinner, and he seemed in complete control of himself," confirmed Epstein's personal assistant, Peter Brown, at the inquest, "He showed no sense of being disturbed in any way, and the meeting was a happy and friendly one."

Brown mentioned too that, during coffee, Brian made a telephone call after which he said some other guests might be along later. When they didn't turn up within the hour, Brian - though full of bonhomie and a quantity of alcohol - announced his intention at around 10.30 p.m. to return to London. "It was not unusual for him to go off on a whim," thought Brown.

Evening was approaching the following day when Brian - still in bed - called Brown. "He said he'd taken quite a number of sleeping pills, and he still felt drowsy." Nevertheless, his butler, Antonio Garcia, was about to serve him a meal. Then he fell asleep again - or, at least, failed to answer the ringing of his bedside telephone that evening.

By mid-afternoon on the Sunday, Epstein had not yet risen, and a worried Antonio got no response on banging loudly on the bedroom door - which he found to be locked as it sometimes was. Garcia summoned Joanne Newfield. She arrived with a doctor, who advised forcing open the door. Inside, Brian Epstein had been lifeless for hours.

Though the police reported no suspicious circumstances, ridiculous conspiracy theories flew up and down before the autopsy was finished - notably that Brian had been bumped off by a hitman connected to a New York syndicate who'd offered him millions for The Beatles three years earlier. Nevertheless, though no written gathering of final thoughts rested on his bedside cabinet either, the most commonly-held notion was that he'd committed suicide. There'd been a purported attempt late in 1966, followed by a spell - not the only one - in a London clinic to combat stress and exhaustion. Next, Brian's sixty-three-year-old father had died of a heart attack, but, as a responsible and attentive elder son, it was unthinkable for him to have added to his beloved and newly widowed mother's grief by killing himself.

Moreover, in keeping with the *Melody Maker* interview, a letter he sent on 24 August 1967 to Nat Weiss, The Beatles' US attorney, was quite upbeat, ending "be happy and look forward to the future." As in the 'happy ending' in a Victorian novel, with all the villains bested and the inheritance claimed, he could spend the rest of a life rich in material comforts, enjoying the fruits of his success. Money, however, can't buy you love - at least, not the love that Brian thought he might lose since the armoured car had whisked his Beatles away from Candlestick Park.

80. Magical Mystery Tour was a total disaster.

Nearly two years after *Help!*, The Beatles were discussing the third flick they'd been contracted to deliver to United Artists. After they'd turned their noses up at suggestions ranging from a western to an adaptation of *Lord Of The Rings*, Paul McCartney came up with a plan to make something up as they went along.

He'd heard of The Merry Band of Pranksters, an itinerant multi-media troupe based in the flower-power capital of San Francisco. Their press releases promised, advisedly, "a drugless psychedelic experience". Why not, said Paul, hire a coach and some cameras and, like the Pranksters, just drive off somewhere - anywhere - and see what happens. Who needed a screenplay?

Like many Beatle ideas - particularly after Brian Epstein's death - it was more intriguing conceptually than in ill-conceived practice. Less than a fortnight after the funeral, journalists were pursuing a charabanc with 'Magical Mystery Tour' emblazoned on the sides was trundling through the West Country containing, reportedly, The Beatles and a supporting cast as variegated as a disaster movie's.

Among those described later by one critic as "a motley collection of uncouth and unlikeable trippers" were a midget, a fat lady (as Ringo's badgering aunt), a funnyman in a bow-tie, a courier, a little girl, an actress playing Paul's girlfriend, and Paul himself, who needed only the knotted handkerchief on his head to complete his parody of a holiday-maker coping with the meteorological whims of a British September. Picked up *en route* were minor characters of such diversity as Spencer Davis, Scottish humorist Ivor Cutler and bikini-clad truant Judith Rogers, who was roped in by McCartney because "I decided to use some glamour in the film on the spur of the moment."

Judith had been but one of hundreds who'd discovered the hotels where The Beatles had been provisionally booked. As well as the chaos that their very presence summoned, the forty-seater bus - now divested of its too-distinctive trappings - failed to negotiate Devon's twisty country lanes, thus ruling out such potentially stimulating locations as Berry Pomeroy Castle and Widecombe Fair.

Though the bulk of *Magical Mystery Tour* was drawn from this troubled excursion, many interior sequences were shot elsewhere, mainly back in London where The Beatles began six weeks in a darkened cutting room, wading through the formless celluloid miles of improvised dialogue and scenes that had seemed a good notion at the time. As Paul was less uncertain about the finished picture, John and George - both uneasy about it from the start - and Ringo left him to it. Unless called to give opinions, they whiled away hours in an adjacent office with such diversions as inviting in and clowning around with 'Rosie', a Soho vagrant who'd been immortalised in a recent hit by street busker Don Partridge. More pragmatically, Harrison, Lennon and Starr attempted to quell media forebodings with phrases like "aimed at the widest possible audience," "children, their grandparents, Beatle people, the lot" and "interesting things to look at, interesting things to hear".

A completed *Magical Mystery Tour* was premiered on BBC 1 on Boxing Day for the majority of Britons still with black-and-white TVs, and repeated on BBC2 on 5 January prior to general big screen release across the Atlantic. Other than predictable plaudits from the underground press and the *New Musical Express* - and a less foreseeable one in *The Guardian* - *Magical Mystery Tour* was almost universally panned. "Blatant rubbish" sneered the *Daily Express*. On its very front page too, the *Los Angeles Times* howled "Beatles Bomb With Yule Film". As expressive as the most vitriolic review was the discerning Scott Walker's rise from his armchair to switch it off after twenty minutes.

"It just freaked everybody out," groaned Ringo years later, "which was a pity. If it came out today, it would be more accepted."

Looking at *Magical Mystery Tour* now, most viewers agree it wasn't the most suitable viewing - especially in black-and-white - for a nation sleeping off its Yuletide revels. You can't help wondering too how many would have watched it to the bitter end if it had starred, say, The Tremeloes or Amen Corner.

Nevertheless, while it isn't *Citizen Kane*, thirty-five years of celluloid extremity later, *Magical Mystery Tour* is less the hybrid of turn-off and cultural duty it used to be than an oddly fascinating curate's egg. Witness The Bonzo Dog Doo-Dah Band accompanying the cavortings of a stripper, and the visuals for The Beatles' own songs - that were, according to Paul McCartney's biographer, Barry Miles, 'the vehicle for a number of prototype rock videos, some of which, like "Fool On The Hill", could be shown on MTV and look as if they were freshly made.' Finally, when divorced from the film, the soundtrack - 'I Am The Walrus', 'Flying' and the rest of the double EP that all but topped the UK singles chart - is still a winner.

81. *None of John Lennon's early collaborations with Yoko Ono contain any artistic merit.*

By the end of 1968, John Lennon was regarded by the man in the street as being as nutty as a fruitcake, owing to his behaviour after he left his wife and infant son to move in with Yoko Ono, a Japanese American who had been a mainstay of Fluxus, a New York art collective that had connections with Andy Warhol. A sort of Screaming Lord Sutch of the art world, Yoko's activities in the mid to late 60's included wrapping Trafalgar Square statues in brown paper and *Bottoms*, a film of myriad naked human buttocks in tight close-up.

Yoko had also found a niche in free jazz, and was esteemed by genre legend Ornette Coleman for using her voice like a front-line horn - as she did at a performance on a Sunday in March 1969 at the University of Cambridge. Her accompanists included Lennon at her feet, back to the audience, either holding an electric guitar against a speaker - causing ear-splitting spasms of feedback - or causing some electronic device to create bleeps, flurries, woofings and tweetings. These complemented the peep-parps from Danish saxophonist John Tchikai, the clatterings of drummer John Stevens and Yoko's evocative screeches, wails and nanny-goat jabberings.

After clapping politely when the recital ceased, the highlight of the night for the audience seemed to be the opportunity afterwards to talk about how 'interesting' it all was, this 'spontaneous music' that was an avenue to drop names like 'Ornette', 'Stockhausen' and 'Berio'.

Many were intrigued by Lennon and Ono's debut album together for perhaps 'the wrong reasons' too. *Unfinished Music No. 1: Two Virgins* was, its makers explained, an Art Statement. Joe Average was, however, too nonplussed to give an Art Reply. The challenging aural content might have been anticipated, even tolerated, but the ordinary Beatle fan's reaction to the macabre sleeve photographs of the pair naked, back and front, was best articulated in the topical disc, 'John You Went Too Far This Time' by Rainbo, alias Sissy Spacek, then a struggling starlet.

Lennon, however, wasn't bothered. He seemed so bound up in himself - and Yoko - that every occurrence and emotion was worth broadcasting to as wide an audience as possible just as it happened. He ordered the issue on Zapple, Apple's short-lived subsidiary record label, of his second LP with Yoko. *Unfinished Music No. 2: Life With The Lions*, was concerned principally with Yoko's first miscarriage - and included the dying foetus's heartbeat, which was offered to and rejected by Richard Branson's *Student* magazine as a giveaway flexidisc.

Most self-obsessed of all was autumn 1969's *Wedding Album*; one side of this feast of entertainment was the two's repeated utterances of each other's name suspended over pounding heartbeats.

There was a shadowy link between the three albums and Marcel Duchamp's 'ready-made' Art and the provocation of Dada just after the Great War. If that was the case, then *Self-Portrait* paralleled Duchamp's *Fountain*, a urinal with 'R Mutt 1917' painted on it. This forty-two minute movie starring Lennon's penis - and some fluid that dribbled from it - was screened at London's Institute of Contemporary Arts in September 1969 as one of several British premieres of Warhol-esque films of similar non-events made by John and the more seasoned movie director, Yoko. Liké other of Ono and Lennon's artistic collaborations during this period, most of them were laboured, inconsequential and generally misconstrued comedy.

The chief exception was *Rape*, a disturbing hour or so of an obtrusive cameraman following an increasingly more alarmed foreign student around London. *Rape* aside, however, some viewers convinced themselves that Yoko and John's celluloid ventures were quite absorbing in parts, even as others fidgeted in their seats. *Rape*, however, was broadcast to some critical acclaim on Austrian television on 31 March 1969, just as Yoko and John, on a very public honeymoon at the Amsterdam Hilton, were completing their first 'Bed-In for Peace'.

To say things most people didn't want to hear or understand, John and Yoko had made their headline-hogging lives an open and ludicrous book with further eye-stretching pranks such as as press conferences from inside kingsize white sacks; sending acorns to world leaders; his scrawly lithographs of themselves having sex; and ordering the plastering of billboards proclaiming 'War Is Over!' all over eleven city centres. The Ancient Greeks had a word for such conduct: 'hubris', which defies adequate translation, but alludes to a heroically foolish defiance rooted in a feeling that one is beyond the reaches of authority and convention.

This was reciprocated when a lot of the 'War Is Over!' signs were defaced within a day of their appearing. Yet something those who did so could comprehend more readily, if not sympathize with, had emerged from another crowded 'Bed-In' - this time in Toronto - where Lennon's 'Give Peace A Chance' was taped - and attributed to the ad hoc 'Plastic Ono Band'. The subsequent full-page advertisement in the music papers assured readers "*You* are The Plastic Ono Band!". Yet, over thirty years later, we still haven't received any royalties for 'Give Peace A Chance'. Have you?

Never mind, it was a catchy effort, even if the verses were just syllables strung together to fill enough two-four bars to separate each instantly familiar *omnes fortissimo* chorus - which if nothing else carried the message of the title across.

'Give Peace A Chance' was heard too on *Live Peace In Toronto 1969*, an album chronicling John, Yoko and some hastily-rehearsed Plastic Ono Bandsmen - Eric Clapton, drummer Alan White (from The Alan Price Set) and, on bass, Klaus Voorman - at an open air pop festival in Canada, delivering a ragged set otherwise consisting mainly of 1950s classic rock, a nascent arrangement of 'Cold Turkey' - a forthcoming new Plastic Ono Band single - and Yoko's screech-singing.

The album sold less than a million, while 'Cold Turkey' - once put forward by Lennon as a possibility for a Beatles A-side - touched a high between 10 and 30 in most charts by Christmas. Its B-side was Yoko's 'Don't Worry Kyoko (Mummy's Only Looking For Her Hand In The Snow)' - which could have been about anything - or nothing.

John found 'Don't Worry Kyoko' as potent as his adolescent self had Little Richard's 'Tutti Frutti'. Work-outs of 'Don't Worry Kyoko' and 'Cold Turkey' filled his last stage appearance in Britain - with a 'Plastic Ono *Supergroup* at a charity knees-up at London's Lyceum ballroom in December 1969. However, when 'Don't Worry Kyoko' plunged into its twentieth minute, he and the other renowned musicians - even The Who's madcap drummer, Keith Moon - exchanged nervous glances.

82. Apple was a ruinous business venture.

Apple Corps was to be an umbrella term for artistic, scientific and merchandising ventures under The Beatles' self-managed aegis when the company was launched in April 1968 - the beginning of the tax year. "We saw Apple housing all our ideas, and we believed it would go well," sighed Ringo Starr in 1969 when it didn't, "But we weren't businessmen, and we aren't now."

Some of their pop peers had also diversified for fun and profit, random examples being Chris Farlowe's military memorabilia shop in Islington; Merseybeat Tony Crane's stake in a Spanish night club; Monkee Davy Jones's New York boutique, and Trogg Reg Presley's patenting of his fog-dispersal device. The far wealthier Beatles could be more altruistic. According to eye-catching newspaper advertisements, actively encouraging people to send in tapes, a kindly welcome awaited not just those who'd nurtured a connection withn the group's inner circle, but any old riff-raff who wished to solicit Apple for finance for pet projects.

When 3 Savile Row was established as Apple's permanent address, sackfuls of mail would overload its postman; pleading voices, who'd winkled out Apple's ex-directory number, would bother its switchboard, and supplicatory feet would ascend its steps from morning 'til night, until a narrow-eyed doorman was appointed to shoo most of them away. "We had every freak in the world coming in there," groaned George Harrison. Yet to loitering pavement fixture Alex Millen - an 'Apple Scruff' - his fallible idols "did strengthen the belief that Joe Soap was important and, yes, you too could have something to say."

So it was that impetuous cash was flung at such as 'Magic Alex', a so-called 'electronics wizard' whose wondrous inventions progressed little further than him talking about them; two unprofitable boutiques that closed within three months; a troupe of grasping Dutch designers, trading misleadingly as 'The Fool'; film-makers who wouldn't make films; poets who didn't write poems, and, remembered Ringo, "a tent for a guy to do a Punch and Judy show on a beach. They'd take the money and say, 'Well, maybe next week'."

While Apple Films was to produce worthy if rather specialist efforts that just about broke even - like *Messenger Out Of The East*, a documentary of Ravi Shankar and the land that bore him - Apple Records was the only department that, said Starr, "didn't let us down." It was subject to a leasing deal - and Parlophone catalogue numbers - with parent company EMI - who were to refuse to release *Two Virgins* and one-man-band Brute Force's 'The King Of Fuh' (containing a chorus that ran, "I'm the king of Fuh/I'm the Fuh king.") Nevertheless, the founding of an ostensibly independent label reduced the number of middlemen and increased The Beatles' own quality control of product. With guinea pigs like ex-Undertaker Jackie Lomax, Welsh soprano Mary Hopkin, Billy Preston, Badfinger, Ronnie Spector and former James Brown *protegée* Doris Troy, George Harrison and Paul McCartney developed their skills as record producers, calling on famous friends like Eric Clapton and Steve Stills to help on the sessions.

None of the - sometimes critically-praised - records Lomax, Spector and Troy made for Apple would make them rich, but Hopkin began a three-year chart run when her 'Those Were The Days' debut knocked inaugural Apple single, The Beatles' 'Hey Jude', from the top of the British charts - and both Billy Preston and Badfinger had lesser hits, but hits all the same. The Modern Jazz Quartet and classical composer John Tavener also reached a wider public through Apple Records.

Crosby, Stills and Nash were approached to sign with Apple too, but as none in the trio could extricate himself from existing contracts, the deal fell through - as did Apple's negotiations with another promising group, Fleetwood Mac. A lesser star in embryo, James Taylor, was taken on, but Paul McCartney remembered an encounter with a then struggling performer called David Bowie. Freddie Garrity also slipped through the Beatles' fingers after being interviewed, incongruously, by Yoko Ono. While a one-shot Apple single by Hot Chocolate was issued in 1969, did The Beatles miss something too by auditioning and then rejecting Bamboo, a Swedish outfit that would connect genealogically with what was to become Abba? This was via Swedish vocalist Michael Rickfors of whom The Hollies thought high enough to Shanghai from Bamboo in 1971, when Allan Clarke briefly flew the nest.

A preponderance of North American literary figures - including Allen Ginsberg, Richard Brautigan and Ken Kesey, mainstay of The Merry Pranksters - were lined up to record for subsidiary label, Zapple, intended as a platform for the spoken word and experimental music. "It seized up before it really got going," shrugged George Harrison, "as with so many things at Apple." Among Zapple projects that foundered were an LP of children's stories related by film actress Hermione Gingold; another of extant recordings by US night-club raconteur Lord Buckley, and a twenty-four album retrospective of comedian Lenny Bruce. With commendable honesty, Harrison confessed that "both of the Zapple albums that did come out were a load of rubbish" - namely John Lennon and Yoko Ono's *Unfinished Music No. 2: Life With The Lions* and George's own self-indulgence, *Electronic Sounds*.

John and George's Beatle status guaranteed that these sold enough to make them worthwhile marketing exercises, and Lennon's first three singles with his Plastic Ono Band all reached the Top 30 in both Britain and the States. Nevertheless, even Apple Records, the enterprise's only money-spinner, was to be subject to inevitable cuts as unviable releases were cancelled, contracts unrenewed, and Jackie Lomax's small retainer stopped now that it had become clear that he couldn't get a hit to save his life. After Mary Hopkin, Billy Preston and Badfinger's well of chart strikes dried up, all that remained were The Beatles, together and apart, whose Apple discs continued to sell by the mega-ton - and the profits were more than adequate to mitigate the money wasted on Magic Alex, The Fool, the Punch and Judy Show and all the other follies.

83. *Rubber Soul inspired Brian Wilson to compose 'Pet Sounds'.*

Three years before a friend arrived at Brian Wilson's Laurel Canyon home with a copy of - as we shall see - not **the** *Rubber Soul* but **a** *Rubber Soul*, the pop airwaves in North America had been dominated by Californian surf music. Ruling the genre were The Beach Boys, who celebrated surfing, and its companion sport, hot-rod racing with chugging rock 'n' roll backing overlaid with a chorale more breathtaking than that of The Beatles. Beach Boys albums, however, were hasty and catchpenny affairs hinged on a hit single, with often as little as six weeks gap between releases.

To the chagrin of the Boys and others on Capitol - The Beatles' US label - John, Paul, George and Ringo were launched with one of the most far-reaching publicity blitzes hitherto known in the record industry. While the intruders swamped the *Hot 100*, The Beach Boys' resident genius, Brian Wilson, felt both threatened and inspired artistically too. "I knew immediately that everything had changed, and that if The Beach Boys were going to survive, we would really have to stay on our toes," Wilson wrote in 2001, "After seeing The Beatles perform, I felt there wasn't much we could do to compete onstage. What we could try to do was make better records than them. My father had always instilled a competitive spirit in me, and I guess The Beatles aroused it."

"I do my best work when I am trying to top other songwriters and music makers," he'd remarked to a journalist in 1964. "That's probably my most compelling motive for writing new songs: the urge to overcome an inferiority feeling."

"When 'Fun Fun Fun' came out," added Phil Spector, "he wasn't interested in the money, but how the song would do against The Beatles."

Though Wilson studied the opposition's output assiduously, he had caught individual tracks on the radio but did not listen to *Rubber Soul* in its entirety until early 1966 - several weeks after its release in December 1965. "I was sitting at a table, smoking a joint, when I heard it for the first time," recalled Wilson, "and the album blew my mind because it was all good stuff. I was so blown out, I couldn't sleep for two nights." He was particularly impressed with 'Girl' and 'Michelle', and overall aspects that he was to perceive as "religious, a white spiritual sound".

After *Rubber Soul* had spun its little life away four times, Brian told his wife, Marilyn, "I'm going to make the greatest rock 'n' roll album ever made." Almost straightaway, he started work on what was to become *Pet Sounds* - though its first spin-off single, 'Sloop John B', had been recorded during sessions for the previous Beach Boys LP, *Summer Days (And Summer Nights)*.

Party!, The Beach Boys album before that, had included three Beatles covers, 'I Should Have Known Better', 'Tell Me Why' and 'You've Got To Hide Your Love Away'. The latter song was from the *Help!* album, which, like all Beatles US albums thus far, had had a different selection from that issued by Parlophone - mainly because Capitol tended to include fewer tracks on its LPs than its UK counterpart. *Help!*, for example, was short of 'I've Just Seen A Face' and 'It's Only Love'. These appeared on the US *Rubber Soul* in place of 'Drive My Car', 'Nowhere Man', 'What Goes On' and 'If I Needed Someone'. Incidentally, a guitar introduction to 'I'm Looking Through You' was edited from the British version.

While 'Drive My Car' and 'Nowhere Man' - a US Top 10 strike as a single - were highlights of the UK *Rubber Soul*, the two remaindered from *Help!* were on a par with 'If I Needed Someone' (with which The Hollies reached a relatively lowly Number 20 in Britain), though superior to 'What Goes On', perhaps The Beatles' most nondescript original.

Brian Wilson's *Rubber Soul* was, therefore, not as hard a yardstick as it might have been, even as - so Brian commented in a 1995 television documentary – "We prayed for an album that would be a rival to *Rubber Soul*. It was a prayer, but there was no ego involved - and it worked. *Pet*

Sounds happened immediately." It wasn't up to *Rubber Soul*'s fighting weight commercially, but *Pet Sounds* was The Beach Boys' most critically-acclaimed LP, causing The Beatles' nervous backwards glances - with Paul McCartney citing Wilson as "the real contender" rather than The Rolling Stones.

Exacerbating the indignity of coming third to the Stones in the *New Musical Express*'s yearly chart points table, the paper's 1966 popularity poll had The Beatles second to The Beach Boys as World Vocal Group. "Good luck to them," smiled Ringo Starr. "We haven't been doing much lately, and it was run at a time when they had something good out."

Starr was referring not only to *Pet Sounds*, but also 'Good Vibrations', Brian's chart-topping 'pocket symphony'. This was part of *Smile*, a masterwork that he reckoned would surpass both *Rubber Soul* and *Pet Sounds*, but the release of *Sgt. Pepper's Lonely Hearts Club Band* was among factors that caused the abandonment of *Smile*. "When I heard it," recalled Brian, "I knew that The Beatles had found a way to really take rock in a new direction. It scared the heck out of me."

84. It was a mistake for The Beatles to involve Allen Klein in their business affairs.

Allen Klein was an entertainment business go-getter from New York – "like the archetypal villain in a film", according to Ray Davies of The Kinks. Since Brian Epstein's death, Klein had hovered over John, Paul, George and Ringo like a hawk over a partridge nest. His reputation as the 'Robin Hood of pop' stood on his recouping of disregarded millions for his clients from seemingly irrefutable recording company percentages.

His administrative caress had come already to encompass The Dave Clark Five, The Kinks and the uncut rubies - including The Animals, Herman's Hermits and Donovan - that had been processed for the charts by freelance producer Mickie Most. The Rolling Stones had also bitten, grinned Most, after "they'd seen me driving around in a Rolls and owning a yacht, and started wondering where their money was going." Klein bet Most's wife that he'd be superintending The Beatles too by Christmas 1967, having heard that Paul McCartney had been particularly impressed by his wheedling of an unprecedently high advance from Decca for the Stones two years earlier.

"Allen tried to come in when Brian was there, just as a business manager, and not run our lives," Ringo Starr would recall, "and Brian would have nothing to do with him." Klein wasn't popular amongst other moguls as he wasted no time with small-talk while driving hard and unrelenting bargains on the telephone and in the boardroom. Nevertheless, though no love was lost between them, EMI chairman Sir Joseph Lockwood said, "In fairness to Klein, I ended up doing deals that I have never regretted."

To Lockwood and the rest of EMI's executive body, Klein was everything that Brian Epstein wasn't. An observer of a routine ruled by the clock, he was an impassive, reflective type at home, who liked to distance himself from the office, and from his clients because "otherwise you can really get on each other's nerves." Yet, though to him, pop was simply a commodity to be bought, sold and replaced when worn out, he wasn't self-depreciating about his knowledge and love of it, and when his wooing of The Beatles moved into top gear, Klein - like a certain Indian mystic they'd encountered - underwent a crash-course in their music to better butter them up. By 1969, his prophecy that he'd one day represent the group seemed to be fulfilling itself.

One of many Goldwyn-esque homilies attributed to Klein was, "What's the point of Utopia if it don't make a profit?" and Apple was living proof. In its white-walled, green-carpeted headquarters in Savile Row, it had been a boom time for certain members of staff after they'd assimilated the heedlessness of their paymasters' expenditure. A dam burst for a river of wastefulness to carry off gluttonous restaurant lunches; bottle after bottle of liquor; illicit trunk calls to other continents, and wanton purchases of trendy caprices to lie swiftly forgotten in desk drawers. Not far from the truth would be a scene from 1978's spoof Beatles bio-pic, *The Rutles* (*All You Need Is Cash* in the US), in which a thinly-disguised Apple Corps is pillaged by its employees, while in the foreground, its press agent chats to a television news commentator (played, incidentally, by George Harrison).

Out of his depth, a Beatle might commandeer a room at Savile Row, stick to conventional office hours and play company director until the novelty wore off. Initially, he'd look away from the disgusting realities of the half-eaten steak sandwich in a litter bin; the employee rolling a spliff of best Afghan hash; the typist who span out a single letter (in the house style, with no exclamation marks!) all morning before 'popping out' and not returning until the next day. A great light dawned. "We had, like, a thousand people that weren't needed," snarled Ringo, "but they all enjoyed it. They were all getting paid for sitting around. We had a guy there just to read the tarot cards, the *I Ching*. It was craziness."

As no individual Beatle felt responsible for straightening out a venture that had taken mere weeks to snowball into chaos, the task had fallen to Allen Klein. To Ringo, however, he'd come across as "a powerful man, and also, no matter what anyone says, he's fair." Yet, though Starr, Lennon, and Harrison yielded to Allen's contractual seduction, McCartney, once his champion, preferred to believe his lawyer brother-in-law's tales of Klein's sharp practices, high-handedness and low cunning.

Yet even Paul had to applaud the purge that pruned staff, installed a clocking-on system, curbed the embezzlememts and fiddles, and discontinued sinecures. Overnight, glib lack of concern deferred to pointed questions. Which typist rings Canberra every afternoon? Why has so-and-so given himself a rise of £60 a week? Why is he seen only on pay-day? Suddenly, lunch meant beans-on-toast in the office kitchen instead of Beluga caviar from Fortnum & Mason.

Paul, like the other three, was saddened that the ruthlessness also meant the casting adrift of old retainers. "We used to keep everyone on," concurred Ringo, "until our new business manager came along and showed us the real facts of what they were all doing. A lot of them got sacked because they weren't doing their jobs, and that's fair." Now something of a pop personality in his own right too - as Epstein had been - Klein confirmed in a *Melody Maker* interview his intention "to make Apple financially successful and tailored to The Beatles' own specifications, but when you get a lot of energy wasted, it doesn't make for an efficient organisation."

He also proved his worth via his re-negotiation of a royalty rate with Capitol that amassed millions for The Beatles - albeit a Beatles soon to disband - within months. Among reasons for the split would be the lines drawn over Allen Klein, who was to oversee the solo careers of Lennon, Harrison and Starr until 1973. This came to an end when the ex-Beatles finally began to credit provocative stories - not all of them true - from their friends, and various of Klein's incensed former colleagues, about shifty manoeuvres regardless of whether or not any of it had any creedeence. This was the apparent behaviour later shrugged off by Rolling Stone Keith Richards as "the price of an education".

85. *Phil Spector made a 'pig's ear' of the Let It Be album.*

Of all The Beatles, John Lennon and George Harrison had been the keenest on the record productions of a self-important young New Yorker named Phil Spector. He was hot property in the early 1960s for his spatial 'wall of sound' technique, whereby he'd multi-track an apocalyptic *melange* - replete with everything, bar the proverbial kitchen sink - behind artists who'd submitted to his masterplan. Styled 'the Svengali of Sound', Spector was known mainly for hits with beehive-and-net-petticoat vocal groups, The Crystals and The Ronettes. George in particular swore by him: "He's brilliant. There's nobody who's come close to some of his productions for excitement."

In the wake of the British Invasion, Spector was among many top US record-business folk who crossed the Atlantic to stake claims in the musical diggings. He said he wanted to work with The Beatles - and several years later, he - rather than a disinclined George Martin - was drafted in to edit, spruce up and mix what was to be described as a "new-phase Beatles" album' and eventually titled *Let It Be*.

As heard on numerous bootlegs - and a forthcoming official release - the raw material had resulted from the disintegrating Beatles' harrowing weeks of loose jamming, musical ambles down memory lane and hitting trouble whenever they came up against each other's new compositions - as well as the bickering, discord and intrigues that make pop groups what they are. The idea had been to tape nothing that couldn't be reproduced on stage. "It would be honest," so George Martin had understood, "no overdubbing, no editing, truly live, almost amateurish."

In keeping with this unvarnished production choice - as well as a flagrant spirit of self-interest - anything that needed too much thought got a thumbs-down. The strained atmosphere was alleviated slightly with the recruitment of keyboard player Billy Preston, who joined in the famous afternoon performance - The Beatles' last ever - on the flat roof of Apple's central London storm centre.

Afterwards, the participants decided that their musical appetites had been ruined by sessions that, overall, had resulted in music that was lacklustre, raucous or just plain terrible, depending on the mood of the hour. They were tempted to jettison the frayed miles of *Let It Be* tapes, but, at the urging of both Allen Klein - Spector's manager - and John Lennon, chose instead to let Phil Spector apply his skills to salvaging whatever he could from it.

George Martin was to comment that Let It Be was "produced by George Martin and over-produced by Phil Spector". Spector countered this with "George Martin had left it in deplorable condition and it was not satisfactory to any of them. They did not want it out as it was. So John said, 'Let Phil do it,' and I said, 'Fine. Would anybody like to work on it with me?' 'No.' They didn't care."

It was a dirty job, but someone had to do it. In the first instance, the New Yorker's doctoring satisfied Paul McCartney who, over the phone to Ringo, "didn't put it down, and then suddenly he didn't want it to go out. It was two weeks after that he wanted to cancel it."

"The record came with a note from Allen Klein saying he thought the changes were necessary," McCartney told the London *Evening Standard*. His riposte was a written plea to *bête noire* Klein - to little effect - that the *Let It Be* album be stripped of Phil Spector's superimposed orchestral and choral grandiloquence that he regarded as gratuitous frills, and contradicted George Martin's original uncluttered production criterion. In the pungent words of engineer Glyn Johns, Spector "overdubbed a lot of bullshit all over it, strings and choirs and yuck".

Johns - and McCartney - may have considered this the case with 'Let It Be' itself but Spector had chosen a comparatively unvarnished approach on several tracks - notably 'Get Back', the first spin-off single. Moreover, he made pragmatic use of his 'wall of sound' trademark to smother Lennon's poor bass playing on 'The Long And Winding Road'. Furthermore, on 'Across The Universe', "I was singing out of tune," confessed John, "and instead of getting a decent choir, we got fans from outside - Apple Scruffs or whatever you call them. Phil slowed the tape down, added the strings. He did a really special job." He certainly made the best of a bad one.

Actually present at other of the overdubbing sessions, George Harrison was impressed too - so much so that he, like Lennon, continued working with Spector after The Beatles disbanded.

Furthermore, given that even a mediocre offering by The Beatles would have sold well, *Let It Be* was successful in a statistically commercial sense in that it outsold several previous Beatles LPs - despite a then-forbidding UK retail price of £3 (albeit with a glossy book thrown in) - topped the US *Hot 100*, and won a Grammy award - which was collected, incidentally, by Paul McCartney.

86. Paul McCartney was the first to leave The Beatles.

Ringo Starr would not look back on the making of 'The White Album' with much affection, although there'd been no discernable animosity at first. However, to engineer Ken Scott, under Paul McCartney's instructions during brass overdubs to 'Mother Nature's Son', "Everything was going really well, and then John and Ringo walked in - and, for the half-hour they were there, you could have cut the atmosphere with a knife." Since the advent of Yoko Ono, and John's co-related and growing indifference to Beatle activities, McCartney's attempts to motivate the group had backfired, his boisterous determination translated as barely tolerable bossiness.

An irksome lecture from Paul about a fluffed tom-tom fill had been the delayed-action spark that had propelled Ringo to stalk out of Abbey Road mid-session. Sooner than any Beatle imagined, he'd testify in court: "Paul is very determined. He goes on and on to see if he can get his own way." While that may be a virtue, it did mean that musical disagreements inevitably arose from time to time. Starr added that such discord had stimulated the group's creative resources. Nonetheless, he'd had a surfeit of Paul's schoolmasterly perseverance - and the withdrawn John letting him get away with it.

Treated as but a tool for Lennon and McCartney's ebbing collective genius, "things were getting a bit rough" for Ringo. After motoring from faraway Elstead - where Surrey bleeds into Hampshire - his hackles would rise further when it became usual for the studio receptionist to see him facing her and "reading a newspaper. He used to sit there for hours, waiting for the others to turn up." When a quorum of Beatles finally got to work, he'd be on the edge of agitated debates that would scale such a height of vexation and cross-purposes that console assistants would slope off for embarrassed tea breaks until the flare-up subsided to a simmering huff. Then, in his isolated drum booth, Starr's ears in the headphones would tingle after thumping out take after rejected take, his concentration split through straining to decipher the drone of murmured intrigue. Crowned by Paul's questioning his very competence as a musician, "I couldn't take any more."

That their weary drummer's resignation was more than a registered protest or one of his infrequent fits of pique became clear with his verbal notice to John and then Paul. Yet neither they nor George dared credit this extreme strategy by the recognised standard bearer of group stability.

During a fortnight in the Mediterranean on Peter Sellers' yacht, the stress of the preceeding weeks had evaporated, and, for all that had driven him from the group, it made abrupt sense to ring up and report for duty again. Half expecting a row, the returned prodigal was greeted at Abbey Road with a drum-kit festooned with remorseful flowers and 'welcome back' banners.

A second departure that aggravated the absolute one took place - for much the same reasons - when The Beatles were in the throes of *Let It Be*. Now self-appointed leader of the four since Lennon's tacit abdication, McCartney was so purposefully confident that, glowered Harrison, "when he succumbed to playing one of your tunes, he'd always do good, but you'd have to do fifty-nine [*sic*] of his before he'd even listen to one of yours." George's progress as a composer was among factors that had led to the present discord - and a connected bone of contention was that whereas John could get away with 'Revolution 9' and Paul with 'granny music', a gradually more irritated Harrison, like a travelling salesman with a foot in the door, had to make a pitch with his most enticing samples: "The numbers I think are the easiest to get across, and will take the shortest time to make an impact."

McCartney was to inform his solicitor that Harrison had actually quarrelled with everybody during *Let It Be*. Nevertheless, it was still the Beatle that Harrison had known the longest that drove him over the brink. George had breezed into the draughty film set-cum-rehearsal studio, fully adjusted to Greenwich Mean Time after a pleasant interlude in the USA where he'd observed the easy professionism of a Frank Sinatra record date, and where a few days at Bob Dylan's home in upstate New York had spawned a Harrison-Dylan opus, 'I'd Have You Anytime'.

If George was full of himself as a result, Paul was there to take him down a peg or two: "The very first day, Paul went into this 'you do this, you do that, don't do this, don't do that', and I thought, 'Christ, I thought he'd woken up by now.'" Frustrated to the point of retaliation, Harrison was no longer prepared to studiously avoid confrontation or continue to be McCartney's artistic pawn.

The *Let It Be* movie was to contain "a scene where Paul and I are having an argument and we're trying to cover it up. Then in the next scene, I'm not there." Not knowing why this was, the reviewer for *The Morning Star* had still been aware of "George Harrison's shut-in expressions". Up until his temporary disappearance, Harrison's huff at McCartney's subtle harangues had welled to overflowing. "You're so full of crap, man," was his rejoinder to Paul's proposal to play a show amid desert ruins in Tunisia.

The final straw was when it transpired that McCartney had already ordered an aeroplane to be put on stand-by to carry The Beatles to Tunis. The assumption that they'd bend to his will was but one aspect of - as George's court statement would attest - Paul's "superior attitude". Of course, if it hadn't been Paul, he might have focused his resentment on the early starts, Yoko's screech-singing or a film technician who hummed all the bloody time. It took a week for George to up and quit the chilling encampment with mains leads fanning out in all directions across the echoing chamber: "I didn't care if it was The Beatles. I was getting out."

Yet none of the others thought to remonstrate or plead with Harrison to return, although Ringo called with a reminder of the following week's boardroom meeting at Apple. This, however, was not conducted as though nothing had happened. John and Paul looked at the youngest Beatle with new respect. Who'd have thought it: George with an unprecedented glint in his eye; George making a stand; George without a metaphorical thumb in his mouth?

Another outcome of the incident was that McCartney could believe no more that he held the group in the hollow of his hand. Soon, with his maiden solo album underway, he'd be preparing a press release that almost-but-not-quite proclaimed his departure from The Beatles. He'd also be setting wheels in motion for the formal dissolution of Messrs Harrison, Lennon, McCartney and Starkey as a business enterprise. Yet months before the writs were served, the group had, to all intents and purposes, broken up. John had slipped a teasing "when I was a Beatle" into an interview with *Disc*, and, feeling as little regret, had announced privately his own resignation well before Paul - though this had been hushed up mainly for fear of it cramping Allen Klein's bullying of Capitol for a higher royalty rate.

As if in prophecy, John wasn't around for what seemed to be The Beatles' final recording session on 3 January 1970, causing George to indulge in a little taped tomfoolery at his expense: "You all will have read that Dave Dee is no longer with us, but Micky, Tich and I would like to carry on the good work that's always gone down at [Studio] Number Two."

Long before, Lennon had been flunking out of more and more group commitments as his collaborations with Yoko took priority. Nonetheless, the atmosphere throughout *Abbey Road* had been more co-operative than it had been during *The Beatles* and *Let It Be*. The sub-text was that *Abbey Road* was to be the last LP, and they might as well go out under a flag of truce.

87. George Harrison's 'My Sweet Lord' was the first hit single by a solo ex-Beatle.

Long before their partnership was dissolved formally in the Chancery Division of the London High Court on 12 March, 1971, all four Beatles were - however reluctantly or unknowingly - well into solo recording careers. As early as 1966, Paul McCartney had written the soundtrack to the film, *The Family Way*. George Harrison too ventured into composing for the movies with 1968's *Wonderwall*.

Other pre-1971 disc projects that indicated that The Beatles were growing apart included John Lennon's three singles with his Plastic Ono Band splinter group. Of each Beatle's preparations for the end, John's were the most lucrative - on vinyl anyway - as 'Give Peace A Chance' (with a generous composing credit to 'Lennon-McCartney'), 'Cold Turkey' and 'Instant Karma' all scored in the Top 30 on both sides of the Atlantic. Yet, even as *Let It Be* lorded it over the likes of *Led Zeppelin II*, Andy Williams' *Greatest Hits* and the latest from The Who, Crosby, Stills, Nash and Young and Simon and Garfunkel in May 1970's album lists, Paul's eponymous solo debut and Ringo's *Sentimental Journey* were inching up too - though neither spawned a spin-off 45.

Nonetheless, McCartney's first non-album single, 'Another Day', penetrated the UK chart on 27 February 1971, and the US *Hot 100* a week later. Just over a month earlier, the first and biggest-selling single from George's *All Things Must Pass* triple-LP, 'My Sweet Lord', eased Clive Dunn's 'Grandad' off the top in Britain within a fortnight of its release on 23 January. By February, it was Number One virtually everywhere else too - and its US B-side, 'Isn't It A Pity' registered in the domestic Top 40 too.

Both 'My Sweet Lord' and 'Another Day' were still in the charts after the 12 March cut-off point. Otherwise, the first hit by an official ex-Beatle was 'Power To The People' which penetrated the UK Top 40 on 20 March, and that in the States on 10 April. However, if you're a pedant who accepts the argument that, as the artist credit on the record label read 'John Lennon and the Plastic Ono Band', it wasn't strictly-speaking a solo effort, then the honour goes to Ringo's 'It Don't Come Easy' which, issued on 17 April, climbed swiftly to Number 4 in both Britain and the USA.

88. The phrase 'A Hard Day's Night' was originated by Ringo Starr.

Immediately on joining The Beatles in 1962, Ringo Starr shaved off his scrappy beard, and had his hair restyled into a moptop at Horne Brothers, *the* place to get trimmed in central Liverpool. Neil Aspinall dropped off the result at 10, Admiral Grove where Ringo still lived with mother Elsie. Her surprise at her son's new look was parried with, "It's no different change really," registered by Aspinall as the first Beatle 'Ringoism.'

Verbally, he was comparable to Dr. William Spooner, in that he didn't have to try to be funny. Rather than conscious narrative jokes, his attempts to nutshell oral discussions were often inadvertently hilarious because, although his wits would creak, quiver and jolt into life, his thoughts would emerge from his lips almost as mangled as a monologue by British music hall comedian Stanley Unwin. When he was a schoolboy, fellow pupils amused themselves by getting him to talk.

Among the most pivotal examples of his Ringoisms as a Beatle was a chance remark that caused Lennon and McCartney to change the title of *Revolver*'s eerie omega, 'The Void', to 'Tomorrow Never Knows'. Another was the title of the group's first movie.

Nevertheless, 'A Hard Day's Night' was not original. The expression was coined obliquely by US singing actress Eartha Kitt in her self-composed 'I Had A Hard Day Last Night', B-side of 1963's 'Lola Lola' (EMI Columbia BD 7170).

Ringo may have heard - or at least been made aware of - this track via George Harrison, who listed Eartha Kitt as one of his two favourite singers (the other was Little Richard) in 'Lifelines of The Beatles' in the *New Musical Express* on 15 February 1963. Less than a year later, Ringo and George were sharing an apartment below Brian Epstein's in Whaddon House, William Mews, Knightsbridge, London, a target for graffiti and marathon vigils by fans.

89. After 1971, John Lennon never again
trod British soil.

When he departed from London's Heathrow Airport for the United States on Tuesday, 31 August, 1971, how could John Lennon have known that he'd never return to his country of birth again? The closest he came, domestically if not geographically, was during his so-called 'househusband' years when, encouraged by his wife, he began spending holidays outside North America.

These included a stay in Hong Kong - before its secession from the British Empire - where, because it was one of the last places you'd expect to find an ex-Beatle, he discovered how pleasurable it was to be a nobody again, unphotographed when stepping from a lift, unstared at in a restaurant, unaccosted for autographs in the street.

It was the same in summer 1980 when he spent several weeks in what was still the British Crown Colony of Bermuda. Among his activities there was visiting a botanical garden that contained a freesia called 'Double Fantasy', composing some of the songs for the album of the same name, and attending the Queen's birthday parade in Hamilton, the island's capital.

There was also a chance encounter in a night club with a journalist for a local newspaper, who was able to report later that Lennon stood his round and promised an exclusive interview when next he was in Bermuda. It was hardly John's fault that he was unable to keep that promise.

90. *John Lennon, Paul McCartney and George Harrison were indifferent instrumentalists.*

"You really play that harmonica, don't you," remarked John Lennon to Brian Jones in 1963, "I can't really play. I just blow and suck."

John wasn't a virtuoso mouth-organist, true enough. He wasn't a Manitas de Plata as a guitarist either - and neither were George and Paul, though McCartney came to be regarded by other musicians as an agile bass player. Nevertheless, each functioned fully - most of the time - according to his capacity within the context of the group.

Yet while they exemplified on stage the rhythm-lead-bass guitars plus drums archetype of the British beat explosion, the demarcation line was often crossed in the studio, mainly when the named composers of given songs needed to cut corners. John, for instance, played tough lead guitar on 'Get Back' as Paul had on 'Another Girl' from the *Help!* album - on which he also plucked 'Yesterday' on acoustic six-string very prettily.

Moreover, while Paul was to admit "George was far ahead of the rest of us as a guitarist", the concept of Lennon cementing Harrison's runs with rudimentary chord-slashing had become rather misleading even before The Beatles' first Abbey Road session in 1962. Lead and rhythm guitar merged frequently in interlocking harmony, evolved over hundreds of hours on the boards. As John elucidated, "I'd find it a drag to play rhythm all the time, so I always work out something interesting to play, [although] I never play anything George couldn't do better - but I like playing lead sometimes."

The interaction of Lennon's good-bad rawness and Harrison's hard-won expertise were compulsively exquisite, even to more proficient guitarists, like Colin Manley of The Remo Four and Mike Hart of The Roadrunners, who could hear what was techically wrong. "George was good," disclosed Bill Harry, "but he didn't rank with Colin Manley and, later, Brian Griffiths [of The Big Three]. People like that were rated and talked about."

Throughout the mid-1960s, nonetheless, Harrison would win polls as the kingdom's top guitarist on the strength of The Beatles doing the same in the 'Best Vocal Group' category, even as a *Sunday Times* critic in 1966 shrugged him off as "a passable player (say, among the best thousand in the country)". Of no less import was an opinion by a stranger during a concert by The Jimi Hendrix Experience. He sidled up to Paul McCartney and, pointing towards Hendrix, muttered, "You ought to get a bloke like that in your band, mate".

Such implied slights on Harrison were unfair - and ludicrous - as The Beatles' stylistic determination left little space for improvisations of the kind popularized by Hendrix - although, judging by bootlegs of the four jamming to tedious effect at Abbey Road, this was probably just as well. Like those of The Dave Clark Five's Lenny Davidson, Tony Hicks of The Hollies and other mainsteam pop guitarists, George's solos and riffs were constructed to integrate with the melodic and lyrical intent of a given number - as exemplified by the superimposing of two backwards - and tuneful - parts to create the apt 'yawning' feel on 'I'm Only Sleeping'. Depending on your perspective, this and George's few bars on, say, the play-out of 'I Don't Want To Spoil The Party' seemed either bland if unobtrusive, or appealingly unfussed.

Harrison also mastered sitar and, as The Beatles' disbandment loomed, took the first steps towards becoming what the Electric Light Orchestra's Jeff Lynne would call "king of rock 'n' roll slide guitar" when holding his own amongst the rank-and-file of Delaney And Bonnie And Friends during a winter tour of Europe. The group was built around musicians with first refusal of virtually all studio sessions in Los Angeles.

Into the bargain, Harrison, Lennon and McCartney weren't slouches as keyboard players - though John "only learnt to play to back myself". He was hunched over a Vox Continental organ when necessary during

The Beatles' final tour, while George played harmonium - as well as guitar and percussion - on The Radha Krishna Temple's 'Hare Krishna Mantra'. Paul, however, was the most versatile. Indeed, his non-attendance at Brian Epstein's housewarming party in May 1967 dismayed the host, who was anticipating McCartney pounding the ivories for a communal sing-song.

91. The Beatles smoked marijuana when they went to Buckingham Palace to receive their MBEs.

Soberly attired, The Beatles were driven in a black Rolls-Royce through cheering masses to Buckingham Palace for their investiture as Members of the British Empire on 26 October 1965.

In the run-up to the post-Profumo general election, a *Daily Express* cartoon had the two main political leaders, Alec Douglas-Home and Harold Wilson, soliciting the Fab Four for their support, thus lending credence to the homily, "I care not who makes a nation's laws as long as I can compose its songs".

Camouflaging vote-catching as acknowledgement of John, Paul, George and Ringo's contributions to the export drive, and that British pop in general generated vast financial power, Wilson's new Labour Government had, seemingly, taken to heart a March headline in *Melody Maker* that ran, "Honour The Beatles!". No honours list, before or since has ever been as controversial. "I didn't think you got that sort of thing," exclaimed George, "just for playing rock 'n' roll music."

Neither did the disgusted civil servants and retired admiral who returned their medals to Her Majesty - or the writer of a letter to the *Express*, suggesting that, if The Beatles had to be so honoured, they ought to subject themselves to a 'decent' short-back-and-sides haircut prior to setting off for the Palace.

How many in this trickle of protesters would have held their peace had they known how unwillingly the chief Beatle had been to go through with the ceremony. A delighted McCartney had cut short his holiday to attend the press conference necessary to flesh out the newsflash on 12 June of the forthcoming decoration, while Lennon sauntered in over an hour late after Brian Epstein had had to send a car to fetch him. "Taking the MBE was a sell-out for me," he snarled later, "One of the biggest jokes in the history of these islands."

That the whole business was anathema to John was reflected further when he insisted that, to unwind tense coils within while waiting to be presented to the Queen at 11.10 am, The Beatles had passed round one of several reefers he'd had about his person in a Buckingham Palace washroom. Yet Lennon's recollections may have been an attempt to beef up an image of himself as a rebel rocker - and his story was to be shrugged off by Harrison, who maintained that nothing more narcotic than ordinary cigarettes were smoked. In any case, it's unlikely that the washroom was for The Beatles' exclusive use. Other gentlemen using it would, therefore, have noticed by the smell and further signs if John, Paul, George and Ringo hadn't been inhaling mere tobacco - and wondered why these millionaire pop stars were sharing one cigarette between four.

Certainly, none of The Beatles seemed under the influence of marijuana's admittedly short-lived magic when either talking to the sovereign or discussing the morning's events with the media at London's Saville Theatre.

Nonetheless, we must add the raw information that The Beatles had giggled through the shooting of *Help!* in a marijuana haze that spring, and were using the drug more and more as a herbal handmaiden to creativity as they began thinking of themselves as more than mere entertainers. Furthermore, two years later, they were to affix 'MBE' after their signatures to lend respectability to a full-page petition in *The Times*, calling for the legalization of marijuana. The only other uses any of them made of the decoration was Lennon's renunciation of it as a political gesture in 1969, and the printing of "Featuring The Dancing Feet Of Richard Starkey MBE" for a laugh in the credits for 'Step Lightly' on 1973's *Ringo* album.

92. Cynthia Lennon was a shrinking violet, lost in John's shadow.

After it cottoned on to The Beatles in 1964, *Confidential*, Hollywood's most scurrilous showbiz gossip magazine, assured readers that Cynthia Lennon had once been considered as the group's lead singer. Such deathless claptrap was disregarded, however, because it was received wisdom that Cynthia was the shrinking violet of the Beatles clique.

Yet the speed of events after take-off with 1962's 'Love Me Do' had not seemed to overwhelm the first Mrs Lennon as she coped with Beatlemania - marathon fan vigils outside the home, stifled giggles from those who'd winkled out the ex-directory number and even an attempted kidnap of her only child, Julian, the future 1980s chart contender. Disguises, decoy tactics and secret destinations were as essential as spare underwear whenever the Lennons went on holiday. On one occasion, Cynthia had to be smuggled out of a hotel in a laundry basket.

She was also the only Beatle spouse to be accorded a fan club of her own. "They wrote about about what I wore to film premieres," Cynthia told one of the authors [AC] in 1995, "and what I said. They were really sweet. I was only a housewife, but a very special housewife to them until divorce divorced me from the Beatles."

While it did not reactivate the Cynthia Lennon Fan Club, that year's release of a debut single, a revival of Mary Hopkin's chart-topping 'Those Were The Days', precipitated a reassessment of one previously lost in John's shadow. Produced by Isle of Man neighbour Chris Norman, once of Smokie, for his own Dice Music label, Cynthia's is not in the same novelty league as, say, Freddie Lennon's unmelodious 'That's My Life' in 1965.

Bereft of Hopkin's incongruous maidenly innocence, 55-year-old Cynthia turned in a surprisingly appealing vocal - though perhaps not so surprising considering that "from the age of ten until I was fourteen, I was in the Hoylake Parish Girls Choir, and I ended up as soloist.

"As an adult, I had no aspirations to be a singer. I didn't even sing around the house or in the bath, but a fax came through from a German record company who wanted to get in touch with Julian. So Jim, my then-partner, phoned back and said sarcastically, "Julian's not here, but you can have his mother' - a throwaway comment that they answered in all seriousness, 'We can't do anything unless we know whether she can sing.' My voice had dropped about two octaves - probably because of all the cigarettes I smoke - but I'm game for anything nowadays, so I taped a selection of songs *a capella*. Chris asked to hear it out of curiosity, and said, 'Let's give it a whirl.'"

"Chris thought 'Those Were The Days' would be a good song for a person of my age, and very pertinent, looking back. For weeks after the session, I was on cloud nine. I was so pleased with it - and it was so creative for me. Six months earlier, if somebody had told me a record of mine was going to be on the radio, I'd have fallen about on the floor in hysterics, but – what's John's expression on *Double Fantasy*? – 'Life is what happens when you're busy making other plans.'"

Though Cynthia had gained a lucrative design contract in 1984 through her own merits, her memoir of life with the first of three husbands, *A Twist Of Lennon*, did brisk business when published in 1978. A revised account may follow "because so much has happened since then. It would be very easy to get in a ghost writer, but, because the first one was all my own work, it'd have to be in the same vein, in the way that I saw it - not the way other people want to see it. In the film *Backbeat*, I was portrayed as a simple girl who wore tweed coats and head scarves, and that all I ever wanted in life was marriage, babies and a house - which was totally untrue. I was training to be an Art teacher for four years, and it was only when I became pregnant that marriage followed, and The Beatles followed after that.

"People think of the Beatles in terms of millions of dollars. I don't see those dollars. What dollars I see are from my own damned hard work since I was out on my own after the divorce. From being so, so protected by millions that I never saw, and having a secure family, it was desperate really.

"At nearly every interview I've done, I've got one of the same two questions: 'Don't you think you're jumping on the bandwagon?' 'Won't people think you're cashing in?' I've tried for intelligent answers that don't sound aggressive, but no-one other than me will ever understand. 'Cashing in' is earning a living as far as I'm concerned. Why should you feel guilty for working?

Who could begrudge Cynthia for doing so with unprecedented abundance? As well as 'Those Were The Days', appearances as guest speaker at Beatles conventions, and a 1999 exhibition of her paintings at the KDK Gallery down London's Portobello Road was only part of it. Three years earlier, Cynthia had been headliner of *With A Little Help From Their Friends*, a round-Britain revue sub-titled "a celebration of the Beatles by those who were part of the story". Other 'insiders' on the bill were more battle-hardened to both poor turn-outs and general stage exposure than Cynthia - notably Denny Laine - once of The Moody Blues and then Wings - and The Merseybeats, who appeared with her ex-husband's group more times than anyone else. Yet *With A Little Help From Their Friends* was not a convention-like evening of selective reminiscences, but a musical spectacular in which outlines often dissolved between acts linked by scripted patter.

At every theatre, the customers - typically British - loved Cynthia Lennon for being a survivor - and for reaching her half-century in such great shape too. Thus, a palpable wave of goodwill washed over her the second she walked centre-stage before a backdrop mock-up of the graffiti-covered Cavern wall. From being a softly-spoken outcast after the world and his wife were confronted with a John they'd never known before in 1968, Cynthia, if no Ken Dodd, proved a self-assured, personable MC. Moreover, the former chorister also dropped sufficient reserve to open the second half with 'Those Were The Days' - and who could not forgive her for singing as she did "Once upon a time, there was a *Cavern*"?

93. The Rolling Stones copied The Beatles.

In spring 1963, The Rolling Stones were resident at the Crawdaddy, a blues club that convened in the back room of a Surrey pub. As they offered both stylistic credibility and teen appeal - in, for example, Mick Jagger's grotesque beauty and the blond moptop of Brian Jones - club promoter Giorgio Gomelsky - who knew Brian Epstein - arranged for The Beatles to visit the Crawdaddy one April evening. It would be a fillip for the Stones if they impressed an act who were then bigger than Frank Ifield.

As Giorgio had foreseen, The Beatles took a shine to the Stones, and the cordiality between the two groups afterwards led to Jagger *et al* receiving complimentary tickets to a Beatles show at the Royal Albert Hall on the 18th. Less incidental to the Stones' future was George Harrison's judging of a 'Battle of the Bands' tournament at Liverpool's Philharmonic Hall a month later. On the panel too were Bill Harry - and Dick Rowe, the Decca recording manager who'd turned The Beatles down in 1962. Because Rowe had been honest in not over-justifying this mistake, George decided to help him out by recommending this southern group he'd seen recently, who were "almost as good as The Roadrunners" [noted Liverpool outfit], and were having the same effect on their audience in a provincial club as The Beatles had had on theirs at the Cavern. "Dick caught the next train back to sign The Rolling Stones," observed Bill Harry.

The Beatles' largesse extended to a gift of a Lennon-McCartney song, 'I Wanna Be Your Man', as a stabilising second single, bestowed prior to its appearance on *With The Beatles*. Stirred when John and Paul completed the number virtually to order while looking in at a Stones rehearsal, Jagger and Keith Richards had a go at songwriting too. Formidable though Lennon and McCartney's head start was, a year after their first self-penned A-side - 1965's 'The Last Time' - Mick and Keith penned all fourteen tracks on their *Aftermath* LP - which solicited a shoal of cover versions just as *With The Beatles* had done.

As it had been with 'Yesterday' - both when issued on *Help!* in August 1965, and as a UK hit for Matt Monro in October - orchestral stringed instruments either fairy-dusted or gnawed at various Jagger-Richards items by other artists - notably Chris Farlowe's chart-topping 'Out Of Time' - as well as the Stones own arrangement of 'As Tears Go By' in 1966. Just as The Beatles had invested 'Norwegian Wood' with sitar, and added 'harpsichord' (i.e. speeded-up piano) to 'In My Life', so Brian Jones wove quaint instrumentation into the fabric of *Aftermath*, such as the dulcimer on 'Lady Jane', and provided a masterful sitar *obligato* for the Stones' third Number One, 'Paint It, Black'. After a horn section drove *Revolver*'s 'Got To Get You Into My Life', trumpets did likewise on the 'Paint It, Black' follow-up, 'Have You Seen Your Mother Baby Standing In The Shadow?'.

Then, following the precedent set by *Sgt. Pepper's Lonely Hearts Club Band*, a Stones album in a similar conceptual vein, *Their Satanic Majesties Request*, appeared in the shops, complete with tracks of psychedelic hue, linked by segues, and a fold-out sleeve with an elaborate and expensive front cover as freighted with symbolism as *Sgt. Pepper*'s. Next up was a double A-side of 'We Love You', a month after 'All You Need Is Love' - and 'Dandelion', with a similar pixified scenario to that in 'Lucy In The Sky With Diamonds'.

Yet it cut both ways. Although The Beatles sniped at the Stones in the press (the Stones rarely retaliated), fuzz-box was heard on on *Rubber Soul*'s 'Think For Yourself' a few months after it had powered '(I Can't Get No) Satisfaction', and it was reported that, during the *Revolver* sessions, The Beatles had commanded an underling to go out and buy their competitors' *Aftermath*. The Stones *were* competitors. 'A Hard Day's Night' and 'It's All Over Now' had monopolized the first two positions in Britain's hit parade for weeks in summer 1964, necessitating the avoidance of such revenue-draining clashes in future. In North America, the Stones were, arguably if briefly, ahead of their chief UK rivals - albeit as the wilder, fouler and more peculiar opposite side of the same coin, an image propagated by manager Andrew Loog Oldham, once hired briefly by Brian Epstein as a freelance publicist for NEMS artists other than The Beatles.

Crucially, most of the Stones' raw material was strong enough to withstand accusations of borrowing conveniently trendy gimmicks from The Beatles. 'Paint It, Black' worked just as well as a 1967 A-side by Chris Farlowe, produced by Jagger, who traded Brian's sitar for an eastern European setting, complete with gypsy violins and a syncopated *bolero* passage. Moreover, if reduced to the acid test of just voice and piano or guitar, 'Have You Seen Your Mother' isn't much of a song in retrospect - and neither is 'The Ballad Of John And Yoko' - but 'Jumpin' Jack Flash' surfaces more frequently than 'Yesterday', for all its syndications, as a pop evergreen on nostalgia radio, and as frequently in 'Sounds Of The Sixties' nights as 'Yesterday' does in 'quality' cabaret.

And in the end, the Stones won the game in the sense that they outlasted The Beatles by more than three decades, continuing to break box-office records and sustain chart-making interest - just - with their latest output. Meanwhile, Ringo Starr follows the nostalgia trail, and Paul McCartney continues to overpaint his artistic canvas.

94. The Beatles were always Germany's most popular British group.

In his best-selling novel, 1993's *Fatherland*, Robert Harris mentions "a piece by a music critic attacking the 'pernicious Negroid wailings' of a group of young Englishmen from Liverpool, playing to packed audiences of German youth in Hamburg".

Between 1960 and 1962, The Beatles had, indeed, graduated from trying to entertain a handful of customers at the tiny, back-street Indra to thrilling fire regulation-breaking crowds at the plush and capacious Star-Club, the most famous landmark on the Reeperbahn. There, they warmed up for visiting US idols like Ray Charles, Little Richard and Gene Vincent after Peter Eckhorn, proprietor of the second-best Top Ten had flown to Liverpool in April 1962 to be disappointed by the price that Brian Epstein had now put on them.

Adding insult to injury, a promise of an engagement at the Star-Club was used as bait by agents who wanted Dave Dee and the Bostons, an outfit based in Salisbury, Wiltshire, to work at the Top Ten and a newer Eckhorn club a hundred miles away in Hanover. They frequently required the band to perform at each club twice, between the dusk and dawn of a single night.

Unlike The Beatles, Dave and his Bostons didn't arrive in Hamburg as provincial clodhoppers, having undertaken their first cache of far afield professional engagements early in 1959. In the process, Dee had become an outstanding showman, possessed of that indefinable something else - the 'common touch' maybe - that enabled him, via a wink and a grin diffused to the general populace, to make any watching individual feel - for a split second anyway - like the only person that mattered to him and his Bostons in the whole of Hamburg.

In this atmosphere of frenetic gaiety too, informal clowning evolved into quasi-vaudeville routines, and it quickly became apparent how much

English-speaking servicemen appreciated Dee's rich fund of dirty jokes. More importantly, the group - like The Beatles before them - became the most celebrated exponents of *mach schau*, a backbeat that a half-wit couldn't lose.

Soon, each Top Ten set by the Wiltshire lads was ending with a thunderous hurrah. A few fans remained near the lip of the stage to better gawk at the group after the break. "On my life, they used to dance to the tuning-up," exclaimed guitarist Trevor 'Dozy' Davies.

So it was that Dave Dee and the Bostons evolved into Hamburg's most adored musical attraction while, as 'Love Me Do' lost its tenuous grasp on the British charts, The Beatles were second-billed to Johnny and the Hurricanes, a saxophone-dominated combo from Ohio, whose hits had dried up in 1961.

Nevertheless, when it seemed that The Beatles were going to stay lucky: "We learnt all the songs off *With The Beatles*," said Dave Dee, "and all President Kennedy's fleet were coming into the Top Ten - it was the year he went to Germany and did his *Ich bin ein Berliner* line - and they said to us, 'What is this music you are playing?' We told them it was Beatle music, and they said, 'Gee, why don't you play it in America?'. I guess they were the first Americans that ever heard of The Beatles and Beatle-type music."

The Beatles in-person absence from Germany between that final Star-Club season in 1962 and their performance on 26 June 1966 at Hamburg's Ernst Merke Halle meant that they were never booked for *Beat Club*, one of the most atmospheric pop series on television in the 1960s. Transmitted from Hamburg, it was as important in its way as *Top Of The Pops* or *Ready Steay Go* as a crucial inclusion on the European itineraries of chartbusting foreign outfits. Chief among those who came across as well on screen as they did on the boards was the entity formerly known as Dave Dee and the Bostons.

After thus renaming themselves by using each member's nickname, Dave Dee, Dozy, Beaky, Mick and Tich were bigger in Germany than anywhere else. As well as higher chart positions for 'You Make It Move', 'Hold Tight!' and subsequent UK smashes, there were entries for album tracks issued as German A-sides, and the irritation and flattery of attempted pre-emptions by domestic hopefuls such as The Sean Buckley Set on Polydor with 'Hold Tight!', and - sounding even less like she understood what she was singing - Deutsche Vogue's Pat Simon with the same song. Mispronounced lyrics also marred (or brightened) The Image's 'Hideaway', 'Hard To Love You' by Dave Gordon *und der* Rebel Guys and, in late 1966, The Four Kings' 'Nose For Trouble'. When they made a triumphant debut that year at the Star-Club - where they'd never appeared before they had hits - Dave Dee, Dozy, Beaky, Mick and Tich had become big enough to lord it over Cream and The Jimi Hendrix Experience in Stadhalles all over the federal republic.

During the following year, 1967, Dave and his boys - perhaps via the mobilization of their German fan base - racked up their heftiest achievement in overseas climes when – as The Dave Clark Five were fleetingly ahead of The Beatles in January 1964, the Wiltshire quartet beat John, Paul, George and Ringo by over three thousand votes to win the Fatherland's pop magazine *Bravo*'s Golden Otto award. This was the equivalent of being Top Vocal Group in the *New Musical Express* readers' poll (where they would always be outside a leading ten headed by The Beatles).

A year later The Beatles would be back on top in the Bravo tabulation, but just for a moment , Dave Dee, Dozy, Beaky, Mick and Tich had ruled German pop.

95. *The Beatles were the first group to use feedback on disc.*

Feedback results from the sound of an electric instrument - most commonly a guitar - being absorbed by the instrument's pick-ups again, after it has come through its loudspeaker. This produces distortion ranging from floorboard-shuddering bass boom to a shriek almost beyond the highest pitch of human hearing. If used as a deliberate contrivance, the effect is not unlike that of the ring modulators and other devices known since the 1940s to Edgard Varese, John Cage and other pioneers of modern classical circles.

Before replacing Eric Clapton in The Yardbirds, Jeff Beck had actively pursued feedback when mainstay of an also-ran R&B outfit, The Tridents. During a brief stint backing singer Craig Douglas in 1963, the group were prompted to approach Craig's record label, Fontana, with an acetate of Little Eva's 'Keep Your Hands Off My Baby' and the blues standard, 'Trouble In Mind'. This was, however, rejected by letter because 'the guitar sounds distorted' - as well it might with Beck overdriving his new Stratocaster through one of the early Marshall amplifiers to purposely create an effect similar to those he'd heard guitarists create on old urban blues records.

Within his archive of party tricks too was leaving the guitar squealing against the speaker as he prowled the stage. Beck was, therefore, a master of feedback by the time he joined The Yardbirds two years later. In other groups - including The Beatles - it might have been an irritating occupational hazard, but, like Beck, Dave Davies of The Kinks and The Who's Pete Townshend did not dismiss feedback as such, recognizing it instead as a method of sustaining notes, reinforcing harmonics and, when necessary, creating severe dissonance.

By mid-1964, The Yardbirds, The Kinks and The Who were all featuring feedback on the boards, a strategy logged by The Beatles when, for example, The Kinks were low on the bill to them at Bournemouth's Gaumont Cinema on 2 August. In the teeth of audience chants of "We want The Beatles", Dave Davies began 'You Really Got Me', their recent chart breakthrough, by turning up his amplifier to feedback level, "and the high-pitched frequency cut right through the screams of The Beatles' fans," wrote brother Ray in his *X-Ray* autobiography (Viking 1994). Ray Davies noticed too that John Lennon was watching from the wings.

Come December, and Lennon had composed 'I Feel Fine'. "That's me completely," he was to insist, "The record with the first feedback anywhere. I defy anyone to find a record - unless it's some old blues record in 1922 - that uses feedback that way. So I claim it for The Beatles before Hendrix, before The Who, before anyone - the first feedback on any record."

Straight in at Number One in Britain, 'I Feel Fine' began with a dentist's drill whine - mid-range feedback. Rendering the circle unbroken, The Kinks would approximate this at the start of 'I Need You', B-side to 'Set Me Free' the following summer. At the same time, The Who were enjoying their second hit, 'Anyway Anyhow Anywhere' - and, lubricated with feedback too would be The Yardbirds' 'Shapes Of Things' and its flip-side 'You're A Better Man Than I' in 1966. Each made a most effective melodrama of what was merely implicit in the mild gimmick that kicked off 'I Feel Fine' - a rival group's idea that The Beatles had appropriated so fast that - as was often the case - the general public assumed that they'd thought of it first.

96. As the most 'spiritual' of the four, George Harrison was always less concerned than the others about the material benefits of being a Beatle.

"We'd be idiots to say that it isn't a constant inspiration to be making a lot of money," said Paul McCartney in 1964. Nevertheless, even as they continued to prosper while other beat groups came and went, The Beatles still expected the axe to fall at any second. "It's been fun, but it won't last," thought John Lennon. Neither was Ringo so dazzled by his sudden fame to imagine that pop stars were immortal, or that he'd never have to consider a 'proper' job again: "A couple of Number Ones and then out eighteen months later won't make you rich. You'll be back on the buses."

Contingency plans had been afoot for The Beatles to ensure that they'd recoup more than golden memories if or when their time was up. Like Starr's, George Harrison's main source of income before 1966 was a quarter share in Beatles Ltd., a budgetary receptacle for all net income from concerts. "Ringo and I are constantly reminded that John and Paul make so much more money than us," snarled George, who didn't need reminding that the two main songwriters each owned twenty times as many shares as he in Northern Songs, The Beatles' publishing company.

Although his eyes would glaze over during the four's quarterly meetings with accountants ("confusing and boring and just like being back at school"), it would be George - nicknamed 'the Money Beatle' then - who prodded most about where this percentage had come from or why so-and-so had been granted that franchise. His vocabulary filling with phrases like "tax concession" and "convertible debentures", Harrison's attitude was: "It's easy to get blase and think we're making plenty, and somebody's taking care of it, but I like to know how much is coming in, where it's being put, how much can I spend... I've no more money mad than the others. I've just persevered and found out."

As the others made ready to go, George would stay put for a discussion about his private investments, the most interesting of which was a stake in Sybilla's, a London night club. With Lennon and ex-Quarry Man Pete Shotton, he would also be co-director of a supermarket in Hayling Island, Hampshire, until he resigned in 1969.

With most group earnings likewise tied up, George's wallet held little real capital, obliging him to borrow small amounts from Beatle menials, usually the road management. Larger bills were settled through the NEMS office. Like any backstreet lad abruptly rich, his consumption was more conspicuous than those - like Mr. Epstein - for whom wealth was second nature. Though he'd later rein in his extravagance, purchasing a succession of fast cars was beyond rapture for a youth who for too long had had his nose glued to showroom windows.

For all the dicta he absorbed from the Maharishi and the Krishna Consciousness Society in the later 1960s, enough of the Money Beatle of old remained for George to compose 'Taxman' - containing a libretto dark with dry fuming at the ravages of the Inland Revenue - and to worry - with sound reason - about Beatle finances that Joe Average assumed were beyond calculation. If Harrison ever believed that his means were infinite, a letter from the group's accountants in 1969 disabused him of this. Yet his overdraft on the corporate account of £35,850 was light against Paul's £66,988 and John's £64,988 - partly because George had sold his comparatively small number of shares in Northern Songs to form a separate and more personally lucrative publishing division, Singsong Ltd. He was, therefore, well out of it when ATV - amid howls of impotent rage from Lennon and McCartney - had managed to buy a major shareholding of Northern Songs that spring.

By the time his official career as an ex-Beatle was up and running, George's wealth was secure enough for him to resist embarking on a world tour in the aftermath of the 'My Sweet Lord', *All Things Must Pass* and the Bangladesh spectacular. No time was ever to be better for Harrison to cash in. Dollars danced before his eyes, but the former Money Beatle told *Record Mirror* in 1972 that he "wouldn't really care if no-one ever heard of me again."

No more would it be taken for granted that George Harrison existed only to vend entertainment with a side-serving of cheap insight. The world wouldn't let him stroll unmolested in a public park, so he'd had to buy a private one. Unobserved, he'd stride forth on a clear morning across the stepping stones of Friar Park's lake, and into the woods and pastures of his acres. At one with nature, all the intolerable adulation his life contained - the Number Ones, the money down the drain - could be transformed to matters of minor importance.

97. After The Beatles' disbandment, John Lennon and Paul McCartney never recorded together again.

Before the 'Free As A Bird' single in 1995, the closest The Beatles came to an artistic reunion was 1973's *Ringo* album, embracing as it did compositions and active assistance by all four, albeit not at the same time. Lennon's contribution, 'I'm The Greatest', came close as it featured himself, Starr and Harrison at Los Angeles' Sunset Sound Studio. McCartney had been amenable to pitching in too, but was refused a US visa owing to a recent fine for possessing narcotics, which had been seized during a European tour with Wings, his new outfit - in which his wife, Linda, played keyboards.

Ringo, nonetheless, was coloured as a bastardised Beatles collection, supplemented as it was by Klaus Voorman's *Sgt. Pepper*-ish lithograph and Starr's teasing insertion of the odd-Lennon-McCartney song title into its lyrics. Whether they conjured up magic or mere music wasn't the issue; that the Fab Four were theoretically together on the same piece of plastic was sufficient to feed fans' hopes that soon everything would be OK again, and The Beatles would regroup officially to tour and record the chart-toppers that John and Paul - all friends now - would be churning out once more.

Yet, when Lennon's insulting 'How Do You Sleep' was in the air in 1971, he and McCartney, its target, had still been on speaking terms; John ringing Paul when the track was on point of release. Three years later, Lennon was saying how wrong it had been for The Beatles to have split so decisively, and McCartney mentioned in interview that he wouldn't mind working with John again on a casual basis.

With hormones raging in a premature male menopause, Lennon had then left his wife in New York to live with a girlfriend, May Pang, in a well-appointed beach villa in Santa Monica beneath the cedared sweep of the Hollywood hills. The place was open house for his circle of friends and friends of friends as well as callers like Alice Cooper, ex-Monkee

Mickey Dolenz and - fanning dull embers for Beatle watchers - Paul McCartney.

The leader of Wings' most significant visit took place when John was in the throes of producing Harry Nilsson's *Pussycats* album at Los Angeles' suburban Burbank Studios, whilst taping demos back at Santa Monica. 'We picked songs off the top of our heads and just did them,' he explained.

This strategy was very much in force when McCartney, staying at the Beverley Hilton Hotel, looked in - with Linda - at what were becoming shambolic sessions at Burbank on Thursday 28 March 1974. Paul helped out on an arrangement of 'Midnight Special', once in The Quarry Men's skiffle repertoire, and was invited to a musical evening the following Sunday at Lennon's place.

Present too would be Nilsson, guitarist Jesse Ed Davis - Eric Clapton's understudy at *The Concerts For Bangla Desh* - 'supersideman' saxophonist Bobby Keyes - and blind singing multi-instrumentalist Stevie Wonder, Tamla Motown's cosseted former child-star, who'd notched up his first US hit, 'Fingertips', in 1963. He'd been on the bill with Lennon of two benefit concerts - for jailed White Panther John Sinclair in December 1971, and for a children's charity the following August - and was to score a British Number One with McCartney, 'Ebony And Ivory', in 1982.

As there were so many distinguished participants, it was decided to tape the results for posterity - and the inevitable bootlegs - on equipment borrowed from Burbank. With McCartney choosing to beat the drums, the lads cranked out an interminable quasi-reggae version of Ben E King's much-covered 'Stand By Me' - which Lennon was to revive for inclusion on 1975's *Rock 'N' Roll* LP - a slow and raucous 'Lucille' and, with Wonder to the fore, a medley of Sam Cooke's 'Cupid' and 'Chain Gang'.

These were punctuated by various meanderings in which were heard the vague strains of 'Little Bitty Pretty One' and, beneath Paul's improvised vocal, Santo and Johnny's 'Sleepwalk' as well as blues-derived chord cycles over which Lennon - who complained throughout about the low volume of his voice in the headphones - kicked off an extrapolation that, amongst other subjects, touched on his frustrated efforts to settle in the States.

None of the sung or spoken dialogue was anywhere as entertaining as that on the celebrated 'Troggs Tape' - an illicit recording of a cross-purposes studio discussion riddled with swearing - and, musically, the clouds parting on the gods at play revealed nothing more remarkable than an idle session crew's ramblings not intended for public ears.

Regardless of quality, however, the tapes - and 'Midnight Special' at Burbank - encapsulated a Lennon and McCartney reunion of sorts, though it wasn't the harbinger of any permanent amalgamation. "You can't reheat soufflé," concluded Paul.

98. *After conquering Britain and North America, The Beatles were treated like visiting royalty in every other country they played.*

In the last weeks of their moptop period, The Beatles followed three nights in Japan - where there'd been frenzied protest demonstrations about these *ketos* polluting the Budokan Hall, Tokyo's temple of martial arts - with two performances on 4 July, 1966 at the Rizal Memorial Football Stadium in Manila, capital of the Philippines.

After a fashion, these appearances were totally successful in that thirty thousand turned up in the afternoon, and fifty thousand in the evening for what were more tribal gatherings than concerts. The group dished out a routine thirty minutes-worth of unheard music through an inadequate sound system into the teeth of the usual screaming pandemonium. Shortly before the matinee, there was a press conference, where the band fielded the stock questions about haircuts and when Paul was going to marry Jane Asher. Certain representatives of the local media took umbrage that the Fab Four seemed vague about what country they were actually visiting, having long ceased to care about the glimpses they caught of the places where their blinkered lives had taken them. A luxury hotel in Barcelona was just like one in Sydney. The Coca-Cola tasted just the same. Everywhere was the same. If it's Monday, it must be Manila.

Manila, however, would always be remembered. At the hotel, Brian Epstein received an invitation for his Beatles to be guests of honour at a party to be thrown by Imelda, wife of the Philippines' autocratic President Ferdinand Marcos, at Malacanang Palace on the morning after the Rizal shows. Not appreciating that it was less an invitation than a directive, Epstein let the weary entourage slept through the arrival and ireful departure of presidential lackeys who had been commanded to bring them to the waiting Imelda and her three hundred other guests, exclusively the families of the totalitarian government and military junta. George Harrison would recall his bafflement when, over a late breakfast, "someone turned on the television and there it was, this big palace with lines of people, and this guy saying, 'Well, they're not here yet,' and we watched ourselves not arrive at the party."

The following day, the expected crowd of teenage well-wishers at Manila International Airport were puzzled that no security measures had been laid on. Close enough to be touched, their agitated idols lugged their baggage up static escalators a few steps ahead of a jeering mob of adults, apparently assured of official leniency and even connivance, no matter how they behaved.

Open-mouthed, the fans watched as naked malevolence stopped just short of open assault when their prey threaded slowly and in a cold sweat through a customs area resounding with pushing, shoving unpleasantness and every fibre of red tape that Philippine bureaucracy could gather.

"It was the roughest reception we've ever had," gasped Ringo Starr, who, reportedly, bore the brunt of the aggression. "They really had it in for us."

Out on the tarmac, the British party scuttled for the aeroplane and escape - which was delayed when Mal Evans and Tony Barrow were summoned back to the terminal to be interrogated over some freshly unearthed paperwork.

The exultant oppression had started the previous night when incessant inteference contrived by studio engineers had wiped out every word of Brian Epstein's televised apology for his clients' unwitting insult to the hallowed person of Imelda Marcos. The First Family's honour was further assuaged by vast tax deductions from box-office receipts still in the grasp of accountants at the stadium. Nobody was ready to jeopardise his prospects and possibly his freedom, by not co-operating with the President's harassment of these long-haired foreigners.

Sent on their way by the boos and catcalls of the tyrant's creatures, never had arguments against The Beatles' continuation of touring made more sense.

99. George Harrison was present at the famous Rolling Stones drugs bust.

LSD - lysergic acid diethylamide 25 - had been 'turning on' factions within London's in-crowd for about a year before it was outlawed for recreational purposes in 1966. Members of The Yardbirds and The Small Faces knew it well. So did The Pretty Things, if the worst was thought of song titles like 'Trippin'' and just plain 'LSD'. It had become so widespread that Dave Dee insisted to *Melody Maker* that, as far as the clean-minded lads in his group were concerned, LSD still stood for pounds, shillings and pence.

George Harrison apparently felt less of a need to exonerate himself entirely. He admitted to taking it unknowingly when a mischievous dentist with whom he was friendly – "a middle class swinger", reckoned John Lennon - had concluded an otherwise pleasant evening by slipping into his guests' coffee a lysergic mickey finn. "From the moment I had it," confessed George, "I wanted to have it all the time… It was important that people you were close to took it too."

At a party at Brian Epstein's country house, Derek Taylor was to succumb to George's urgings to try acid - and, earlier in Hollywood in August 1965, Neil Aspinall and Ringo had also 'turned on' when George and John underwent a second 'trip'. Joining them at the rented nerve-centre of this particular US tour were members of The Byrds. As The Beatles' dabbling in drugs was not yet public knowledge, Aspinall was instructed to usher another visitor - a *Daily Mirror* reporter - from the place.

By 1967, Harrison and the other Beatles were talking openly about their psychedelic escapades, acknowledging no difference now between the 'straight' press - such as the *Sunday Times*, in which Paul was the first to admit taking LSD - and underground journals like the fortnightly *International Times* - in which a gaga George mentioned the 'magic eyes' in the beads of his necklace, and a grasshopper that only he could see jumping into a speaker cabinet. LSD was being imbibed by John and, to a lesser degree, George as carelessly as alcohol. It was passing as common currency among others who'd viewed the world from the Olympus of pop stardom since 1963.

Rolling Stones Keith Richards and Brian Jones had been initiated in Los Angeles during a 1965 US tour too, but Mick Jagger remained wary of LSD until he and girlfriend Marianne Faithfull spent the weekend of 19 February 1967 at 'Redlands', Keith's lodge in West Wittering, Sussex. Among the other nine guests were George and Pattie Harrison - and a moneyed young Californian known as 'Acid King David', glad to breathe the groovy air round the Stones as an unpaid and unrecompensed minion.

He ingratiated himself with his host by producing tabs of 'Sunshine', a particularly refined type of LSD, for the party's use on an unusually mild Sunday morning - so mild that, after brunch, everyone climbed into a convoy of cars to search for a suitable starting point for a ramble round the surrounding countryside.

Back at Keith's by the early evening, George and Pattie decided to return to 'Kinfauns', their home in Esher, Surrey. An erroneous story did the rounds later that the Harrisons were still present, but were shooed away when, two hours later, 'Redlands' was invaded by the West Sussex Constabulary, armed with a search warrant. Thanks to a tip-off from *The News Of The World* - then recipients of a libel writ from Jagger for alleging that he consumed controlled drugs - the force had reason to believe that the premises were being used for the consumption of controlled drugs, contrary to the provisions of the 1966 Dangerous Drugs Act, section 42.

Richards and Jagger were to be acquitted of consequent convictions in July, but Keith believes to this day that they'd have been immune from arrest if George - a national treasure with an MBE - had stayed another night. However, just over two years later - on 12 March 1969 - a squad of Scotland Yard officers, under the direction of plain-clothes Sergeant

Norman Pilcher, raided 'Kinfauns' as they had John Lennon and Yoko Ono's London flat the previous October.

This time, the police uncovered a quantity of cannabis, and charged the householders with possession of same. In the dock at Walton-on-Thames Magistrates Court on the last day of the month, George and Pattie pleaded guilty and were fined. National treasures or not, The Beatles were no longer above the law.

100. Mark Chapman's was the first attempt to kill a Beatle.

In unconscious anticipation, 'To Kill A Beatle', a single by a Johnny Guarnier, was issued sixteen years before the slaying of John Lennon in 1980. Its lyric was from the perspective of a US teenager insanely jealous because every other girl at high school had lost her marbles over the new sensations from England.

Yet, even as Johnny's record was making its journey to the bargain bin, two death threats directed at The Beatles were received during the group's very first tour of North America in the late summer of 1964. On 20 August, an anonymous telephone caller informed the management of the Convention Center in Las Vegas that a bomb had been planted somewhere in the building after the group's matinee performance at 4 p.m., but this was not taken seriously enough for the second show at 9 p.m. to be nixed.

Eighteen days later, the switchboard operator at The Beatles' hotel in Montreal put through a call to Brian Epstein from someone who said that a bullet would have Ringo Starr's name on it when he perched behind his kit that evening at the city's Forum auditorium. Better safe than sorry, Epstein arranged for a detective to hunch beside the drum rostrum - to catch the slug, maybe - as Starr 'played low' like Pete Best, with cymbals positioned straight up *a la* Buddy Rich. Nobody minded that his posture impaired the performance. Who could hear it - or gunfire - anyway against the bedlam?

The danger was to be less specific, but more omnipresent during the final trek round the continent in 1966 in the light of John Lennon's "We're more popular than Jesus" comment. As the ripples of the 'holy war' spread, so did fears of an assassination attempt on Lennon and perhaps the others too. For most promoters, however, the possible in-concert slaughter of the artists was insufficient reason for cancellations.

Engagements in the north, however, passed without unanticipated incident, other than picketing by Ku Klux Klansmen outside Washington's DC Stadium. Below the Mason-Dixon line, the anti-Beatles ferment was counterbalanced by "I love John" lapel badges outselling all associated merchandise. Nonetheless, a promise was made to Epstein from a pay 'phone that one or more of them would die on the boards at the Mid-South Coliseum in Memphis. Yet, though a firework that exploded on stage gave all four a horrified start, the show was delivered. The next morning, The Beatles slipped smoothly away into a temporary airborne respite from what was becoming an uneasy existence.

101. The Beatles pioneered the use of
Indian sounds on pop records.

Over a year before George Harrison's sitar lessons with Ravi Shankar, one of India's leading musical ambassadors, The Yardbirds and The Kinks had each invested respective chartbusters, 'Heart Full Of Soul' and 'See My Friend' - both issued in summer 1965 - with a suggestion of somewhere in India. A sitarist and tabla-player had been present at the Yardbirds session, but the group preferred the twang of lead guitarist Jeff Beck, who was given to tossing in Eastern-sounding *leitmotifs* during his stage solos, even with his pre-Yardbirds outfit, The Tridents.

If Beck was more like the real thing than the real thing, The Kinks' 45 exhaled a more pungent breath of the Orient. Overlooking the pibroch-liked thrum of Scottish combo, The Poets' 'Now We're Thru'' - a UK Top Forty strike in 1964 - 'See My Friend', penned by Ray Davies, was, estimated The Who's Pete Townshend, "The first reasonable use of the drone - far, far better than anything The Beatles did, and far, far earlier." Davies's art school friend Barry Fantoni would recall being "with The Beatles the evening that they sat around listening to ['See My Friend'], saying, 'You know this guitar thing sounds like a sitar. We must get one of those.' Everything Ray did, they copied."

An alternative story has been told by Giorgio Gomelsky, The Yardbirds' manager: "Jimmy Page was visiting the 'Heart Full Of Soul' session, and when he heard the sitar, he freaked out. He decided that he wanted to buy the sitar from these two Indian guys we'd hired - which, after some negotiation, he did for twenty-five pounds, which was a lot of money then. I remember him walking down the street with the sitar wrapped in an old Indian carpet. The next day, he showed it to Big Jim Sullivan, another well-known session guitarist, who, a few days later, told George Harrison about it."

Maybe - as Philip Norman suggests - George first came across a sitar on the set of *Help!*, but the plain fact is that he played one on 'Norwegian

Wood' from December 1965's *Rubber Soul*. It was then just one of many funny noises on discs by The Beatles - and, next, The Rolling Stones, as heard on both *Aftermath*'s 'Mother's Little Helper' and their 1966 chart-topper, 'Paint It, Black' - while Mick Jagger's production of Chris Farlowe's version of the jazz standard, 'Moanin'', had sitar where a busking sax might have been.

With a seal of approval from both the Stones and Beatles, this wiry-sounding nine-stringed instrument with bulging gourds, moveable quarter-tone frets and 'sympathetic' under-strings became as essential an accessory as a fuzz-box or volume pedal during pop's fleeting 'classical' period. Roy Wood of The Move invented the 'banjar', which combined properties of sitar and banjo, and both Dave Mason (of the then-half-formed Traffic) and Donovan acquired sitars after an exploratory hour or so on George Harrison's imported model.

It was treated by most like some fancy guitar. Session guitarist Chris Spedding was to confirm that: "It's a sound effect. Every time I use it, I charge £10 on top of my usual fee." By 1968, an electric sitar was to be the selling point of The Box Tops' 'Cry Like A Baby' - and one was featured too on Alan Randall's inspired revival of George Formby's 'Hindu Meditating Man'.

However, beyond mere gimmickry, Eastern musical theories had long been a trace element in folk and modern jazz, becoming more pronounced in the mid-1960s through the work of British acoustic guitarist John Renbourn, John Mayer's Indo-Jazz Fusions and the 'trance-jazz' of Gabor Szabo, as implied in titles such as 'Search For Nirvana', 'Krishna', 'Raga Doll' - and 'Ravi'...

The last was a nod towards Ravi Shankar, a name unknown to the European man-in-the-street until he came into the lives of The Beatles. His 1965 LP, *Portrait Of Genius*, had been recommended to George Harrison by David Crosby of The Byrds. To George, it was immediately transfixing - for the chasm between Shankar and rock 'n' roll was not unbreachable. The Duane Eddy instrumentals that had captivated the teenage Quarry Man were also based on folk tunes and repeated *ostinati*. Years later, under Harrison's supervision, Eddy would add a bridge to a Shankar melody, making the composing credit 'R Shankar-D Eddy', one of the strangest to be printed on a record label.

The Beatle and the middle-aged Indian virtuoso were first introduced at a mutual friend's London home in the late spring of 1966. For several months, George had been rending the air in the main living room of his Surrey home, trying to extend his ability as a sitarist beyond the few notes that had lacquered 'Norwegian Wood'. Ravi put him right about the folly of trying to teach yourself sitar. Ideally, it was best to be accepted as a *shishya* - a cross between a student and a disciple - for extensive training in India under a master like himself - but as George's Beatle duties beckoned until the following March, he would have to get by with Ravi's tape-recorded correspondence course.

Thus began a lifelong amity akin to that of a liberal-minded teacher and a waywardly earnest pupil. Ravi's association with Harrison and, by implication, the other Beatles was to do him a lot of good. Tickets sales for his recitals were guaranteed to pick up if there was a hint that George might be attending. He even tilted for a hit single with 'Song Of The Hills' from *Portrait Of Genius*. "There was a sitar explosion," he explained. "All of a sudden, I become superstar (*sic*)."

This was splendid news for stockists of Indian goods in the West. In provincial Britain, for instance, a certain sort of teenager might loiter for hours outside a record shop debating whether to blow three weeks' paper-round savings on, say, *Portrait Of Genius* or Ustad Ali Akbar Khan's *Young Master Of The Sarod* (for which George had provided sleeve notes). Youths whose short hair broke their hearts would board trains to London to buy joss-sticks. One hipper-than-thou Hampshire schoolboy, known to one of the authors, even came home with a sitar.

Even if they hadn't originated Indian sounds in pop, The Beatles were chiefly responsible for furthering the cause of the sub-continent's music to Western consumers. In the short-term, they'd instigated what could be construed as a trend. Half-a-world away in San Francisco, 'raga rock' was an ingredient in the psychedelic brew being concocted by Jefferson Airplane, The Grateful Dead and others in a city soon to be as vital a pop Mecca as Liverpool had been. A few miles down the coast at the Monterey International Pop Festival in June 1967, Ravi Shankar played an afternoon set, thus confirming a wider world's acceptance of him and his chosen instrument.

Eventually, the sitar and Indian music in general was to hold less allure because of the fine line between its ear-catching extraneousness and the real danger of it seeming like a parody of Indian-inspired Beatles, not to mention George Harrison's *Wonderwall* soundtrack; his chart-climbing productions of 'Hare Krishna Mantra' and 'Govinda' for The Radha Krishna Temple, and creations like the startling 'It Is He (Jai Sri Krishna)' from 1974's solo *Dark Horse*. The point was driven home in the coda of George's 'When We Was Fab' hit in 1988.

Starting too late in life and with his pop career precluding hours of daily practice, George himself had effectively ceased to be an active student of the sitar by 1968. Moreover, John Peel, BBC Radio One's hippest presenter, was no longer inserting twenty-minute ragas between the 'progressive' rock fare on his *Night Ride* programme. Instead, he bowed to frequent requests for obscurities exhumed from Broadcasting House's sound archives. A national pop station filling the ether with nose-flutes, Romanian *cobzas*, Zulu step-dancing and further outlandish examples from what would be termed later as 'world music' had been unthinkable three years earlier, when George Harrison had double-tracked the sitar on 'Norwegian Wood'.

In this respect, George and The Beatles' entries in the *Guinness Book Of Hit Singles* count for less than their inspiration to occidental pop musicians to burgle the treasury of world music. Malcolm McLaren,

Adam and the Ants and Peter Gabriel were among post-punk artistes who helped themselves - while, in 1982, a British act called Monsoon had made the Top Fifty with 'Shakti (The Meaning Of Within)' and other Indian-flavoured excursions.

Further examples were to be heard as blatently in the grooves of Kula Shaker, that most exotic of all the Britpop newcomers in the mid 1990s, with items like 'Acintya Bhedabheda Tattva', 'Sleeping Jiva' and 'Temple Of Everlasting Light'. Furthermore, this London unit's fourth single was a revival of 'Govinda'. More than the stimulus of the Radha Krishna Temple smash on the A-side, the flip, 'Gokula', lived so obviously in a *Wonderwall* guitar riff (from 'Skiing') that permission had to be sought by Kula Shaker from Northern Songs via a direct appeal to the composer himself.

Afterword : Just Like Starting Over

Most musicians don't give up. Even if they stop playing professionally, they still entertain their families or their friends down the pub.

In Liverpool, the Merseycats charity has been successful in finding musicians of the 1960s and coaxing them back on stage to strut their stuff through 'Roll Over Beethoven', 'What'd I Say' and 'Some Other Guy'. The Undertakers, The Fourmost, Ian and the Zodiacs, The Remo Four and Denny Seyton and the Sabres: the list is endless. Almost.

Few musicians have resisted the call to appear at a Merseycats reunion, but John Lennon has always said no.

John Lennon, you may remember, was a leading figure in The Beatles - maybe even the leader - until that fateful date on August 16, 1962 when he was sacked by Brian Epstein. The Beatles were on the verge of a national breakthrough - and Paul, George and Pete with a new vocalist, the effervescent Gerry Marsden, achieved worldwide success with 'How Do You Do It' and then 'I Like It'. Paul's melodic flar was brought out in the million-selling 'Yesterdays', although if John were around, Paul would never have rhymed 'yesterdays' with 'sequesterdays' in what was thought to be the most inspired couplet of the 60s.

John and Eppy never got on. John hated him saying that The Beatles would be bigger than Elvis. 'Come on, Eppy, he would shout, 'even Cliff could make a better film than *G.I. Blues*.'

He rebelled when Epstein wanted to replace the raucous, American rhythm and blues from their act ('Twsit And Shout', 'Money') with cheerful, Tin Pan Alley, three-chord pop. John was adamant; 'If you want The Beatles to sing 'How Do You Do It', Eppy,' he said, throwing him his Rickenbacker, 'you can take my place - but have some singing lessons first.'

Then there was Cynthia. Brian had wanted to market four desirable, unattached young men…and here was John with a pregnant girlfriend. He told John that a married Beatle would be disastrous for their following but John, even though a noncomformist, did not want his child born out of wedlock.

Many recall the outburst at the Cavern on 15 August. Eppy was redfaced about John sabotaging his plans, and John chided him, 'You're the mistake, Eppy. We should have stayed with Allan Williams.'

Albert Goldman's infamous hatchet job on Paul McCartney states that Paul, forever ambitious for The Beatles, shared Epstein's thoughts that night and agreed that John should go. Epstein asked John to call into his Whitechapel office the following morning. No one has ever repeated that conversation, but John went into The Grapes and announced, 'I'm not a Beatle anymore.'

At first, John with typical Merseyside arrogance announced, 'I'm going to do it on my own.' He'd heard the new American folksinger, Bob Dylan, and he decided on a similar approach. Too similar unfortunately as the melody of his first and only single, 'Working Class Hero', lent heavily on Dylan's own 'Masters Of War' and he was sued for plagiarism. 'Of course I pinched the bloody tune,' said Lennon in court, 'Folk songs are for the people: there shouldn't be such a thing as copyright.' His record company lost and after Lennon had had 'a visit from the boys', he decided that he wanted nothing further to do with 'capitalist record companies'.

There was nothing to report: he never played his guitar, never wrote songs, never jammed with another band. In fact, he never did anything: long before the term was fashionable, he was a househusband, looking after his son while his wife worked as a designer.

Although the only tracks on record by John Lennon are 'Working Class Hero', its Utopian B-side 'Imagine', and some rock'n'roll that The Beatles cut with Tony Sheridan in Hamburg, a cult now surrounds him. Beatlefans long to meet the group's original lead singer and rhythm guitarist. 'I love looking at photos of George, Paul, Gerry and Pete,' says Lee Mavers from The Beatles Fan Club, 'but look at this photo of The Beatles from 1962 and it is John's face that you are drawn to first. I can't understand why he gave it all up.'

Eventually, after calls to the *Liverpool Echo*, John Lennon was found, living off his Giro in Birkenhead: his marriage had ended, following his affair with a Japanese artist. 'That was just an excuse,' says John., 'The truth is, there is no call for househusbands once your kid has left home.'

After all this time, John Lennon has been persuaded to perform again. Tonight, after 40 years, John is going to be playing at The Cavern in a band which includes Ringo Starr from The Hurricanes on drums, his son Julian and a few former Quarry Men. 'I have nothing to prove,' he insists, 'It's just a way of spending some time. I know I was the best. The Beatles are the nowhere men, not me. They're the ones on the fucking Flying Music tour.'

No one knows how good John Lennon will be. The Grapes is across the road. He might drink too much. He might curse at the audience. No one will mind. Everyone is waiting for the moment when Paul's former partner steps on to the stage. Paul has sent a goodwill message to The Cavern. 'Well, he would, wouldn't he?' is John Lennon's savage rejoinder.

BIBLIOGRAPHY

There are thousands of books on The Beatles and the authors of this book have contributed to the total.

Alan Clayson has written *The Quiet One - A Life Of George Harrison* (Sidgwick & Jackson, 1990), *Ringo Starr - Straight Man Or Joker* (Sidgwick & Jackson, 1991), and *Backbeat - The Real Life Story Behind Stuart Sutcliffe* (with Pauline Sutcliffe, Pan in association with Sidgwick & Jackson, 1994), as well as the general histories, *Call Up The Groups - The Golden Age Of British Beat 1962-7* (Blandford, 1985), *Beat Merchants - The Origins, History, Impact And Rock Legacy Of The 1960s British Pop Groups* (Blandford, 1995) and *Hamburg - The Cradle Of British Rock* (Sanctuary, 1997).

Spencer Leigh has written *Speaking Words Of Wisdom - Reflections On The Beatles* (Cavern City Tours, 1991), *Drummed Out - The Sacking Of Pete Best* (Northdown, 1998), and *The Best Of Fellas - The Story Of Bob Wooler, Liverpool's First DJ* (Drivegreen, 2002), and the general history, *Let's Go Down The Cavern* (with Pete Frame, Vermilion, 1984).

Many sources have been used to check the details in this book. The individual newspaper and magazine articles are not listed but the most useful books were,

Babiuk, Andy: *Beatles Gear* (Backbeat, 2001)

Yes, The Beatles were gear, but this very detailed book concentrates on their instruments. Very well written and researched with superb illustrations on quality paper. As good as it gets.

Badman, Keith: *The Beatles, After The Break-Up* (Omnibus, 1999)

It's a busy life being an ex-Beatle and this book contains 600 pages of densely-packed information in chronological order. The trivia is alongside the serious but it is close to impossible to read straight through. Its main advantage is as an archive, so why isn't there an index?

Beatles, The: *Anthology* (Cassell, 2000)

With its weight on a par with a paving slab, this 'Beatles story told for the first time in their own words and pictures' is a likeable and sometimes courageous account, albeit aimed at fans who prefer not to know too much about what kind of people their idols were like in private. Otherwise, there are not so much new twists in the plot as further samples of detail for those who know the story backwards.

Coleman, Ray: *John Winston Lennon, 1940-1966* and *John Ono Lennon, 1967-1980* (Sidgwick & Jackson, 1984)

Albert Goldman said that Coleman was after 'the fan's buck', which tells you something about both of them. This two-volume work, combined for a fall-apart paperback, has been very well researched, and Coleman is on Lennon's side throughout.

Coleman, Ray: *Brian Epstein - The Man Who Made The Beatles* (Viking, 1989)

Because so much has been written about John Lennon, Ray Coleman's biography of Brian Epstein is probably the more valuable. Superb research on his business dealings. The more recent biography, *The Brian Epstein Story*, based on the BBC *Arena* specials, added nothing extra.

Davies, Hunter: *The Beatles - The Authorised Biography* (Heinemann, 1968)

'Authorised' may mean 'whitewashed' but, hey, The Beatles were still a working group and they didn't want to reveal too much. Very easy to read but Hunter admitted its shortcomings in his excellent biography, *The Quarrymen* (Omnibus, 2001).

Epstein, Brian: *A Cellarful Of Noise* (Souvenir, 1964)

Epstein and his ghost writer, Derek Taylor, put this together too hurriedly. Taylor wrote the draft and he wasn't privy to Epstein's thoughts or insights in any depth. Epstein didn't want to elaborate and, in a few instances, wanted to change history. A candid autobiography would have been a first in 1964, but being there first is what The Beatles were all about.

Gentle, Johnny with Ian Forsyth: *Johnny Gentle And The Beatles* (Merseyrock, 1998)

Very little has been documented about the Scottish tour, and here's why - nothing happened. Gentle's memoir is hampered by appalling proofreading.

Goldman, Albert: *The Lives Of John Lennon* (Bantam, 1988)

John Lennon's second assassination. Goldman had the funds to carry out major research, but he twisted everything to fit his own salacious theories. Quite a different John Lennon book could have been written with the same research. Await Ron Ellis's account of working with Goldman.

Gottfridsson, Hans Olof: *The Beatles - From Cavern To Star-Club* (Premium, 1997)

Too much detail for the casual fan and possibly even too much for the devoted follower. Every nuance and variation of their Hamburg recordings is discussed lovingly by Gottfridsson. Great illustrations too, but Gottfridsson does enjoy telling you the same thing again and again.

Harrison, George: *I Me Mine* (Genesis, 1980)

Unlike James Taylor who had his lyrics stolen from his hotel room, George Harrison kept all the scraps of paper on which he wrote his thoughts, very often on hotel stationery. The long introduction to his songs has been written by Derek Taylor and it is evident that George is distancing himself from The Beatles.

Harrower, David: *Presence* (Faber & Faber, 2001)

Well-researched play about The Beatles in Hamburg. Considering John Lennon's fondness for one-liners, it is curious that Presence should keep him off-stage. However, the Paul McCartney character assumes much of his abrasiveness. It may be fiction but it is very entertaining - which also applies to a few, supposedly factual Beatle books.

Harry, Bill: *Mersey Beat: The Beginnings Of The Beatles* (Omnibus, 1977)

Bill Harry's book of reprints from his *Mersey Beat* newspaper should be permanently in print, but it isn't so. This collection comprises 80 key pages with a long introduction from Harry. The musicians often wrote their own copy and there are classic examples of John Lennon's wit. The original ads surrounding the text give a feeling of time and place.

Leach, Sam: *The Rocking City* (Pharaoh, 1999)

The Liverpool impresario Sam Leach occupies centre-stage and accepts no criticisms in a fast-moving and often very funny account of The Beatles' years in Merseyside clubs. The facts should have been better checked and Leach, who used to call himself 'The Man That Mersey Beat Forgot', now claims credit for everything.

Lewisohn, Mark: *The Complete Beatles Chronicle* (Octopus, 1992)

A marvellous book bringing together Lewisohn's previous works, *The Beatles Live!* (Pavilion, 1986) and *The Complete Beatles Recording Sessions* (EMI / Hamlyn, 1988). Barry Miles's *The Beatles - A Diary* (Omnibus, 1998) follows similar ground and, unsurprisingly, he cites Lewisohn as a primary source. Lewisohn's book has been remaindered at the time of writing (January 2003) and it is easy to pick up a hardback copy for under £10 - a wonderful bargain.

MacDonald, Ian: *Revolution In The Head* (Fourth Estate, 1994)

A thought-provoking song by song analysis of all The Beatles' official releases. Don't overlook the 50 page table combining The Beatles' history with other chart music, cultural events and world news.

Miles, Barry with Paul McCartney: *Many Years From Now* (Secker & Warburg, 1997)

An authorised biography with many first-hand quotes from McCartney. Although Paul wants to show himself in the best light, things occasionally slip as in his childhood story about killing frogs.

Norman, Philip: *Shout! The True Story Of The Beatles* (Elm Tree, 1981)

There is a feeling throughout this book that Norman would like to have the courage to do a Goldman, but he pulls back. Well-researched and definitely on Lennon's side, but you would expect that in the wake of the assassination.

Peebles, Andy: *The Lennon Tapes* (BBC, 1981)

Like the long and rambling *Rolling Stone* and *Playboy* interviews, this book desperately needs an index. Lots of fond memories of home, but John hadn't been back to Liverpool since he showed Yoko around in 1969.

Pritchard, David and Alan Lysaght: *The Beatles - Inside The One And Only Lonely Hearts Club Band* (Allen & Unwin, 1998)

Pritchard and Lysaght have an impressive list of guests for their US radio series and here their interviews are presented verbatim. Some unlikely subjects include George's sister, Louise, and Murray The K, but when one of them is Brian Epstein, you begin to doubt the veracity of their claims. Did Brian Epstein really offer Little Richard 50 per cent of The Beatles? Why on earth would he do that? And why didn't Richard take it?

Sheff, David: *The Playboy Interviews With John Lennon* (Playboy, 1981)

Yoko has her opinions but she doesn't get a chance to say much while John's around. He'd not mellowed as much as some thought.

Taylor, Alistair: *A Secret History* (John Blake, 2001)

The first memoir of The Beatles' Mr. Fix-It, *Yesterday - The Beatles Remembered* (Sidgwick & Jackson, 1988) was irritatingly written as letters to an imaginary fan. A Secret History is far better but neither book has an index, perhaps because there are few references to anyone other than Alistair, Brian Epstein and The Beatles.

Thomson, Elizabeth and David Gutman: *The Lennon Companion* (Macmillan, 1987)

Many excellent newspaper and magazines features are gathered here including contributions from Martin Amis, Bernard Levin, William Mann, Kenneth Tynan and Tom Wolfe. The correspondence in *The Times* over the MBEs is hilarious and Noël Coward describes them as 'bad-mannered little shits'.

Wenner, Jann: *Lennon Remembers* (Straight Arrow, 1971)

Wonderfully barbed quotes from John and occasionally Yoko. Is this what therapy does for you? Best to read with *John Lennon / Plastic Ono Band* in the CD player.

Williams, Allan with William Marshall: *The Man Who Gave The Beatles Away* (Elm Tree, 1975)

Allan Williams doesn't want to make anyone look good, least of all himself, and even if some stories are fictional, the book does contatin the spirit of Liverpool and Hamburg around 1960. Allan is working on a second volume of memoirs with *Liverpool Daily Post* writer, Lew Baxter, and Lew is also writing Beryl Adams' memoirs, a lady who worked for Brian Epstein and Ray McFall, married Bob Wooler and is Allan Williams' significant other.

A NOTE ABOUT THE AUTHORS

Alan Clayson

A description of Alan Clayson by the Western Morning News as the "AJP Taylor of pop" is supported by Q Magazine's "his knowledge of the period is unparalleled and he's always unerringly accurate". He is the author of many books about music - including the best-selling *Backbeat*, subject of a major film; *The Yardbirds*; *Call Up The Groups – The Golden Age Of British Beat 1962 – 1967; The Quiet One – A Life Of George Harrison; Ringo Starr – Straight Man Or Joker; The Troggs Files; Beart Merchants – The Origins, History, Impact and Legacy Of British Pop Groups Of The 1960's* as well as biographies on Serge Gainsbourg and Jaques Brel.

He has written for journals as diverse as The Guardian, Record Collector, Mojo, Mediaeval World, Folk Roots, Guitar, Hello!, The Independent and The Times. He has also performed and lectured on both sides of the Atlantic, and broadcast on national TV and radio.

From 1975 to 1985, he led the legendary Clayson and the Argonauts - though his latest solo album, *Soiree*, may stand as an artistic apotheosis were it not for the promise of surprises yet to come.

Alan lives near Henley on Thames with his wife and two sons.

Further information is available from www.alanclayson.com

Spencer Leigh

Spencer Leigh was born in Liverpool in 1945. His 'On The Beat', programme has been broadcast on BBC Radio Merseyside for 20 years and he writes for numerous magazines including 'Country Music People', 'Goldmine', 'MOJO', 'Now Dig This' and 'Radio Times'. He writes obituaries for 'The Independent' so he is often tempted to offer musicians a complete package of radio interview, magazine article and forthcoming obituary. Through extensive first-hand interviews, his books always include new facts, his 'Drummed Out - The Sacking Of Pete Best' (1998) being particularly enlightening.

His other books include *Paul Simon – Now and Then; Presley Nation; Stars In My Eyes; Let's Go Down The Cavern* [with Pete Frame]; *Speaking Words Of Wisdom – Reflections Of The Beatles; Aspects Of Elvis* [with Alan Clayson]; *Memories Of Buddy Holly* [with Jim Dawson]; *Halfway To Paradise – Britpop 1955-1962* [with John Firminger]; *Behind The Song* [with Michael Heatley]; *Brother Can You Spare A Dime – 100 Years Of Hit Songwriting; Baby That Is Rock and Roll - American Pop 1954-1963* [with John Firminger]; *Sweeping The Blues Away – A Celebration Of The Merseysippi Jazz Band* and *The Best Of Fellas – The Story Of Bob Wooler.*

Spencer still lives in Liverpool with his wife.

Further information is available from www.spencerleigh.demon.co.uk

The Beatles: As It Happened

CIS2001
ISBN 1 84240 096 7

A 4-CD collection featuring spoken word recordings from each of the
Beatles: John Lennon, Paul McCartney, George Harrison, Ringo Starr,
as well as George Martin, Brian Epstein, Derek Taylor, Yoko Ono.
These recordings were made between 1963 and 1992, largely at press
conferences or from one-to-one interviews with reporters and journalists.
Throughout the recordings the individual Beatles and their entourage
talk on a variety of subjects, both directly relating to themselves, their
music and a host of other issues. With the inclusion of a 32-page colour
booklet illustrated throughout with rare photographs and memorabilia,
this set provides a fascinating picture of the Beatles' personalities, views,
hopes and fears.

Maximum Beatles

ABCD127
ISBN 1 84240 200 5

Written by renowned Beatles expert Alan Clayson, this newly researched
audio-biography CD contains an overview of the story of this legendary
band. From their rise to fame, countless years at the top and the various
directions the fab four took after the dissolution of the band, interspersed
by interviews with the Beatles themselves. Packaged within a deluxe
card slipcase with 8 page illustrated booklet and free fold out poster
'Maximum Beatles' is ideal for fans both old and new.

Maximum Lennon

ABCD070
ISBN 1 84240 108 4

Possibly the most influential figure since the inception of rock music, John Lennon was a man whose songs touched people the world over. However his personal life was just as intriguing as his music was, and indeed is, inspirational. On 'Maximum Lennon' the full story is told using newly researched information to compile the first ever spoken word recording about this icon of our age. Covering his early life, the Beatles years and his solo career, this is the perfect collectors item for fans both old and new and comes packaged in deluxe card slipcase with 8 page illustrated booklet and free fold out poster.

Maximum George Harrison

ABCD107
ISBN 1 84240 177 7

One of the Worlds greatest guitarists and most creative songwriting talents, George Harrison's untimely death in late 2001 was marked with a blaze of media publicity and candle lit vigils, proving the enduring popularity of both the man and his music. Now Chrome Dreams presents a unique audio-biography of this highly revered artist complete with comments from the man himself. Written by renowned Harrison biographer Alan Clayson, it not only gives the story of his Beatles days and solo career, but also the real truth behind his private life, ill health and final days. This CD comes packaged within a deluxe card slipcase with 8 page illustrated booklet and free fold out poster.

PHOTO CREDITS

Front and back cover photos courtesy of
REX

Inside photos courtesy of
REX
REDFENS
CAMERA PRESS
Spencer Leigh